THE DESERT AND AIR SERVICES

Other National Historical Society Publications:

THE IMAGE OF WAR: 1861-1865

TOUCHED BY FIRE: A PHOTOGRAPHIC PORTRAIT OF THE CIVIL WAR

WAR OF THE REBELLION: OFFICIAL RECORDS
  OF THE UNION AND CONFEDERATE ARMIES

OFFICIAL RECORDS OF THE UNION AND CONFEDERATE NAVIES
  IN THE WAR OF THE REBELLION

HISTORICAL TIMES ILLUSTRATED ENCYCLOPEDIA OF THE CIVIL WAR

CONFEDERATE VETERAN

THE WEST POINT MILITARY HISTORY SERIES

IMPACT: THE ARMY AIR FORCES' CONFIDENTIAL HISTORY
  OF WORLD WAR II

HISTORY OF UNITED STATES NAVAL OPERATIONS IN WORLD WAR II
  by Samuel Eliot Morison

HISTORY OF THE ARMED FORCES IN WORLD WAR II
  by Janusz Piekalkiewicz

A TRAVELLER'S GUIDE TO GREAT BRITAIN SERIES

MAKING OF BRITAIN SERIES

THE ARCHITECTURAL TREASURES OF EARLY AMERICA

For information about National Historical Society Publications, write:

The National Historical Society, 2245 Kohn Road, Box 8200,
Harrisburg, Pa 17105

THE DESERT AND AIR SERVICES

Ashley Brown, Editor

Jonathan Reed, Editor

Editorial Board

Lisa Mullins, Managing Editor, NHS edition

A Publication of
THE NATIONAL HISTORICAL SOCIETY

Published in Great Britain in 1986 by Orbis Publishing

Special contents of this edition copyright © 1990 by the
National Historical Society

Library of Congress Cataloging-in-Publication Data
The Desert and air services / Ashley Brown, editor, Jonathan Reed,
    editor.—NHS ed.
      p.   cm.—(The Elite)
    ISBN 0-918678-53-6
    1. Great Britain. Army. Special Air Service—History.   2. Great
Britain. Army. Long Range Desert Group—History.   3. Military
history. Modern—20th century.   4. Great Britain—History.
Military—20th century.   5. World War. 1939–1945—Campaigns.
I. Brown, Ashley.   II. Reed, Jonathan.   III. Series: Elite
(Harrisburg, Pa.)
UA659.S67D47   1990
358.4′135′0941—dc20   89-13866
                                                          CIP

CONTENTS

INTRODUCTION

There is an old religious axiom that "many are called, but few are chosen." It could as well apply to the kinds of men and units that have always composed THE ELITE. Nowhere can this be seen more starkly than in the Long Range Desert Groups (LRDG's), the air fighters, the SAS, and the rest of the specialists who made war on the deserts and in the skies, yesterday and today.

In Sicily and Italy in 1943 the men of 1 SAS and other allied special units carried out four successful amphibious assaults behind Italian lines in just three months. In August 1944 more men of C Squadron, 1 SAS, dropped behind German lines to disrupt communications while Patton's Third Army punched eastward. Two years earlier, LRDG patrols secreted themselves in the burning deserts of North Africa to gather intelligence on Rommel's movements for the Allies. Other LRDG's went to the Dodecanese Islands in the Aegean to hold them against Luftwaffe air attacks. Perhaps most riveting of all are the exploits of the LRDG's who operated behind German lines in the Libyan desert, racing in machine-gun equipped jeeps and trucks, to make lightning attacks on the foe and then escape into the desert.

In later years these elite units continued to stand out—in Yemen, in Vietnam with the Australian SAS, in Malaya with the Jungle Patrols, and in Zambia. And they have been active in supposedly peaceful climates, attacking terrorists and rescuing hostages.

Wherever these outstanding units have been called upon to practice their special skills, they have done so with the daring, dedication, and precision, that have always marked those who are truly "chosen" to stand among THE ELITE.

ROAD WATCH

In 1942, LRDG patrols carried out long road watches behind Axis lines to supply invaluable intelligence of Rommel's convoys in the Desert

IN FEBRUARY 1942 the Long Range Desert Group (LRDG), already earning an enviable reputation for reconnaissance in the Western Desert, finally secured the vehicles and logistical support it needed for the sustained deep-penetration operations envisaged by its founder, Major Ralph Bagnold. One month earlier, Rommel's Afrika Korps had broken

Below: Men of Y Patrol, several of them wearing goggles to protect their eyes against the harsh desert wind, are photographed by their commanding officer, Captain David Lloyd Owen, on the way back to Kufra following a successful mission. Displayed in the foreground is their patrol flag, a Jolly Roger that was run up by a seamstress in Kufra.

out of El Agheila on the Gulf of Sirte in Libya and the Allies were desperately in need of reliable intelligence for their intended counter-offensive in Cyrenaica. Although the Allied plans were pre-empted by Rommel's continued attacks, they nevertheless formed the background of the LRDG's activities for the following six months.

The pattern for LRDG operations in early 1942 had been set in September and October of the previous year. Operating old 30cwt Fords, the LRDG's S (Southern Rhodesian) Patrol, under John Olivey with Tony Browne as his navigator and intelligence officer, had carried out two 168-hour surveillances of

Above: Every Long Range Desert Group patrol was equipped with a radio and all operational signals were encoded before transmission. Above right: Captain Jake Easonsmith, destined to become commanding officer of the LRDG in October 1943, cleans his Thompson sub-machine gun. Below right: Trucks of an LRDG patrol line up under Marble Arch.

the coast road lying 28 miles west of El Agheila. The patrol had established itself on a 100ft hill about two and a half miles from the road and had maintained a constant surveillance through powerful binoculars. In addition, a forward observation post had been manned during daylight hours by two patrol members lying in a shallow sand pit about 300yds south of the route. Radio silence was broken only on the homeward journey in order to ensure patrol security.

The September reconnaissance was able to supply details of the redeployment of the Italian 101st Trieste Motorised Division during the 21st Panzer Division's 'El Hamra Scurry'. In the light of this and other successes, Eighth Army Intelligence requested Lieutenant-Colonel Guy Prendergast, commanding officer of the LRDG, to make arrangements for further reconnaissances of the coast road on an indefinite basis. Prendergast chose the two Southern Rhodesia Patrols (S1 and S2) to begin the job as they already had experience of collecting intelligence in the area. On 25 February 1942 both patrols departed the LRDG base at Siwa: S1, commanded by Gus Holliman, set out to monitor traffic from Barce, while S2, under John Olivey, returned to its previous observation point near Marble Arch.

In March there was a new development in the career of the LRDG. Battle HQ Eighth Army issued instructions concerning sabotage operations to be conducted behind the enemy lines. The collective codename for these was 'Green Room'. The operations planned to take place in the enemy forward area were allocated to units under the command of XIII Corps; those in the Matuba-Mechili-Benghazi area were allocated to A and C Squadrons of the

ON FORWARD WATCH

In order to begin a road watch in March 1942, Jake Easonsmith's R1 Patrol set up camp in a wadi lying about three and a half miles from an important Axis supply route. Every night a picket of two men would leave the camp and walk down to the road to fulfil a period of duty on forward watch. Mick Shepherd, one of several New Zealander brothers who served with T and R Patrols, described the procedure:

'Each one jogged to right and left to find a small bank. It didn't have to be much – just enough to stop a driver from running off the road for a comfort stop, and I never had any trouble with this. We met at a marker point and then went straight to the bank, whence we simply walked back towards the wadi and dropped into the first suitable depression we came to. One took the east-west, the other the west-east traffic. The closest I ever was to the road was about 30m and the most distant about 100m.'

The observers were most at risk from gangs of road workers, who tended to wander about during their breaks, and from convoys pulling in for meals or repairs. (This actually happened on 21 March, when a convoy pulled in 150yds away, forcing the men to lie silent and motionless for the rest of the day.) As darkness came, the picket would move up to some 20 or 30yds from the road, but soon it became impossible to distinguish the details of passing vehicles. The men would return to camp at daybreak, after a period on duty of about 26 hours.

Middle East Commando; the area south and west of Benghazi was given to the Special Air Service (SAS) Brigade. The LRDG was to act as co-ordinator, primarily carrying out reconnaissance but also guiding or collecting sabotage parties and participating in offensive action when necessary. In this way it was ensured not only that direct action was properly implemented, but also that it interfered as little as possible with the LRDG's own all-important intelligence-gathering missions.

Between the departure of the 'road watch' patrols in February and preparations in August for large-scale raids in September, the LRDG mounted six combat operations in support of the Middle East Commando, 12 in conjunction with the SAS, and eight direct-action missions on their own. The Group also carried out 17 intelligence-related operations in addition to their standing commitment to maintaining road watches on a number of major supply lines behind the enemy front. The new 30cwt Chevrolets came into their own during this period, for each patrol required four trucks, operated by one officer and 12 other ranks, and the road watches alone put heavy demands on the LRDG's vehicles.

Patrols would initiate night 'beat-ups' in the Sirte area, attacking Italian road-houses and transport

The remarkable achievement of the LRDG in its road watch programme of 1942 may be illustrated by examining a single case. At midnight on 1/2 March, S2 Patrol completed the camouflage of an observation post in the Wadi el Turchi, some 35 miles west of El Agheila and five miles east of Marble Arch. The patrol was to observe and report all movement on the main Axis supply route to Cyrenaica. This position was manned 24 hours a day until T2 Patrol was ordered to abandon it on 21 July, by which time the enemy logistical chain had shifted to supply the Alamein position. During the long watch, which was maintained behind enemy lines without serious compromise, loss of personnel or major interruption, patrols gleaned a wealth of intelligence for the Eighth Army. Involving all four of the LRDG's New Zealand Patrols, the two Rhodesian and two

Yeomanry Patrols, and G2 drawn from the Guards, the watch was a fine example of this unique Commonwealth unit's skill and professionalism.

In this period preceding the major raids of September 1942, the LRDG patrols had 31 contacts with the enemy. Patrols would initiate night 'beat-ups' on the coast road in the Sirte area, attacking Italian road-houses and transport. Their machine guns, including 0.303in Vickers, double and single Brownings, 0.303in Lewis guns and Italian 12.7mm Bredas, wrought terrible execution, not to mention the mines they laid on the road to discourage pursuit. Contacts also included enemy counter-measures, however. Mines laid in old LRDG tracks near Marada caught one of S1's trucks, and another belonging to T1 near the airstrips off the Matruh-Quarah road, though neither explosion resulted in personnel casualties. Patrols were also subjected to air attack three times during this period, the most serious being in July when three Macchis dived on G2 as it carried members of the Free French SAS to make an attack on an enemy airfield. The patrol commander, Robin Gurdon, died of his wounds despite all efforts by the patrol to save him, while two other men were hit but survived.

Patrols at this time also took 16 prisoners of war, many of whom proved useful to Intelligence because they came from far behind the Axis lines. A minimum of 28 enemy troops, mostly Italians, were killed, for the loss of one guardsman killed.

The intelligence operations of the British and Commonwealth forces in the Middle East, including those of the LRDG, initially suffered from a lack of up-to-date information concerning enemy uniforms and equipment. Those publications that did exist could not offer the reliable details needed by the reconnaissance patrols, and so sketches of unfamiliar equipment were produced on the spot. GHQ Eighth Army helped solve the problem by enlisting a university professor equipped with a constantly updated photograph album, a man who was soon nicknamed 'Grey Matter', whose job was to pass on to the observers every new detail gleaned by Eighth Army Intelligence. The early patrols of 1941, of course, had only their own observations to guide them, and as late as March 1942 Jake Easonsmith,

Located some miles from the road selected for surveillance, the main party of an LRDG road watch patrol ran little risk of discovery once it was in position. The greater danger lay in the detection of the two forward observers who were carrying out the exacting and often nerve-racking job of spying on the road and documenting its traffic. Bottom left: There was seldom sufficient cover to allow any method other than crouching in a shallow hollow with binoculars. Bottom: An Axis convoy takes supplies up to the front in the open desert. Bottom right: His watch over, the observer (left) dozes with two others at the patrol base. Behind him is a truck, well camouflaged by netting threaded with camel scrub to avoid unwelcome attention from the air. Bottom far right: Captain 'Wimpey' Henry, whose S Patrol was the unit that began the road watch near Marble Arch in February 1942.

then commander of R1 Patrol, acknowledged in his patrol report that:

'Too high a standard of accuracy should not be anticipated as, although all ranks are extremely keen, they have had no previous training in this type of work, and had no special knowledge of guns or armoured vehicles.'

They sighted the captured British armoured command vehicles that were being used by Rommel

A remarkable aspect of R1's March patrol was that it was accompanied by a cameraman of the Army Film and Photographic Unit who was preparing a story on the LRDG. His still photographs, which survive today as a unique record of a New Zealand patrol on road watch, interested GHQ Eighth Army in the possibility of observers photographing some of their sightings. However, they regretfully concluded that it simply would not be practical to implement the idea. Observers would need to move close to the road to take photographs of sufficient clarity, and this would have risked not only the forward observation picket but also their entire road watch operation. Another idea that was suggested, that of tapping the telephone lines that ran alongside the Libyan roadsides, was also found to be impracticable.

The quality of the LRDG's road watch reports improved greatly during the summer of 1942, often running to over 20 pages of typed foolscap and containing a wealth of accurate detail. Eighth Army Intelligence was quick to turn the unprecedented volume of indications of enemy intentions to good use. Certain elements of the reports, such as the daily 'nose counts' of armoured vehicles and estimated logistical tonnages, were extracted and signalled from Cairo to London. A sighting by T2 Patrol on 14 March also helped to resolve an argument between the War Office and GHQ Eighth Army, who had taken increasingly divergent views over the interpretation of Enigma messages concerning the enemy's armoured strength. Middle East Forces (MEF) Intelligence was also informed of many interesting technical developments observed by LRDG patrols. For example, they reported the appearance of increased barrel length on PzKpfw III tanks, presaging the arrival of the PzKpfw IIIJ L/60, and it is probable that on two occasions they sighted the captured British armoured command vehicles that were being used by Rommel. The patrols had been instructed to report everything, and that is exactly what GHQ Eighth Army got, down to one report from T2 Patrol on 31 March 1942 of a possible mobile brothel. No assessment of this item appears to have survived!

In order to carry out road watch missions, the LRDG patrols crossed some of the hottest, roughest, least trafficable terrain in the Western Desert. The apparent ease with which they accomplished this has obscured the fact that the missions would have been impossible without the exceptional steadiness, toughness and reliability of the men, and a logistics

Green Room Operations
Long Range Desert Group, 1942

Derna
Barce
Martuba
Jebel Akhdar
MEDITERRANEAN SEA
Benghazi
Mechili
Tobruk
Bardia
Sidi Barrani
Port Said
Msus
Mersa Matruh
Alexandria
Gulf of Sirte
Sirte
El Alamein
Ras Lanuf
Agedabia
Cairo
Nophilia
L I B Y A
Qattara Depression
El Agheila
Marble Arch
Siwa
Marada
Gialo
Great Sand Sea
E G Y P T
Nile
El Kharga

GREEN ROOM OPERATIONS

Codenamed Green Room, the direct-action operations of the Long Range Desert Group began on 8 May and ended on 27 July 1942. During this period, LRDG destruction of enemy equipment included two Italian Carro Armato M 13/40 medium tanks and their transporters, over 10 trucks, three trailers, one Guzzi motorcycle, and one unidentified troop carrier. Nine prisoners were taken and 28 enemy troops killed with a probable like number wounded. Participating in the operations were six patrols, including seven officers, 98 other ranks and 31 30cwt Chevrolet trucks. The logistics of mounting long-range raids in the Desert were very complex and the Green Room operations were hampered by difficulties. One patrol had to be aborted when a batch of faulty tyres overheated and blew out, and the final offensive sortie had to be abandoned prematurely when petrol consumption ran too high and the patrol's No.11 radio, set on receive only, could not be tuned in the field. There were also operational setbacks. For example, in order to maximise the damaging psychological effects of their raids on the enemy, two patrols set out to carry out unattributable, delayed-action attacks on trucks by attempting to lob satchel charges into them, to explode later in a random pattern. Unfortunately, the patrols' efforts were frustrated by the trucks' high sides and their Italian drivers' not unnatural habit of putting 'pedal to metal' when faced with unexpected 'road works', far from any assistance, in the middle of the night! However, the LRDG 'shoot and scoot' missions, combined with the depredations caused by the Special Air Service Brigade, seriously worried the Axis theatre commands, forcing them to increase rear area security measures and reduce unprotected transport movements at night – much to the satisfaction of Allied High Command, who learned of the units' successes via Ultra.

Below: A Chevrolet 1533X2 30cwt truck of Indian 2 Patrol, Indian Long Range Squadron, armed with two 0.303in Bren guns and a 0.303in Vickers machine gun.

and planning effort second to none. Some quite exceptional individuals emerged from the Group and the roll of honours and awards earned by them in the Desert is a long one, with over 50 Mentions in Despatches alone.

One such was George Garven, MM, a truly redoubtable man. On 31 December 1941 he was the senior soldier of a party of nine men from T2 who were stranded on 31 December 1941 when an air strike dispersed their patrol near Marble Arch. Jock Lewis, one of the founder members of L Detachment, was killed in this incident. The survivors, led by Garven and equipped with just three gallons of water, nine biscuits, an emergency chocolate ration for one man, a compass and a map, walked the 200-odd miles back to Gialo.

On 27 January 1943 Garven was involved in a road watch behind enemy lines in Libya. He reported the following event, one of only three minor compromises experienced by road watch forward observation posts:

'In company of Trooper R.J. Morgan I left base camp to take up road watch, arriving there at 0500 hours. The position which I took up was approximately 150 to 200yds from the El Agheila-Nophilia road. The trucks moved off eastward an hour or so later leaving troops whom we were unable to see but who we could hear working.

'At 1100 hours a large herd of camels with Arabs accompanying them came on the scene. The Arabs came and spoke to us, then retired 100yds or so and entered into a conversation. At 1200 hours an Arab who may have been in that group came up to us again and entered into a conversation with us... After a few minutes he walked to the road where by this time a truck and trailer coming by had stopped. He appeared to climb into the back of the truck accompanied by an Italian, to whom he pointed in our direction. The Italian immediately jumped down and the truck hurriedly departed.

'Fearing that we had been given away, and that capture was imminent, we destroyed all identification including road census, put a false bearing on the compass, and laid low. All was quiet again until about 1630 hours when traffic increased in both directions. Nothing of real importance happened until 1700 hours, when 27 Mk II German tanks on trailers proceeded east-

wards. Convoys going westwards then began stopping near us, appearing to be camping for the night. Believing the position I occupied to be a possible camping ground, I decided to take the risk of getting out to warn the patrol, hoping to be mistaken for natives.

'We put on our keffiyahs, also our coats inside out so as the white sheepskin lining would be showing, and then got up and made our way in the direction of some camels.

'We were definitely spotted by some soldiers who, however, took no action against us. We walked about three miles in the wrong direction before turning in the direction of our base camp, where we arrived about 1930 hours, warning my patrol commander of what happened.'

'The truck in front of us went up in the air at least four feet. We thought he had hit a coffin mine'

The patrol then abandoned its position and moved to an alternative rendezvous 40 miles away, again putting out its forward observation post at night and maintaining observation from a distance of two and a half miles.

Bill Johnson, REME, who served with S1 Patrol as its fitter, recalled an unusual expedient to keep his patrol operational:

'My role as patrol fitter was to keep the wheels turning – make do and mend. I also had to look after a 0.5 Vickers. Starting from Siwa – destination Benghazi to do a road watch – fitter's truck position last truck to pick up the cripples as they broke down. We had travelled many days trouble-free apart from a burst tyre and a burnt-out clutch. I was just congratulating myself on what an easy trip it had been when all of a sudden the truck in front of us went up in the air at least four feet. We thought he had hit a coffin mine at first. We drew alongside. They sat in the truck shaken and dazed. "What happened?" we enquired. The driver said he thought he'd hit a rock. I got down to see if he'd ripped off the exhaust system and noticed oil pouring from the gearbox. By the time the patrol skipper came to see what was wrong I could see the gearbox had cracked badly and we couldn't travel above another 20 miles, otherwise it would seize up solid.

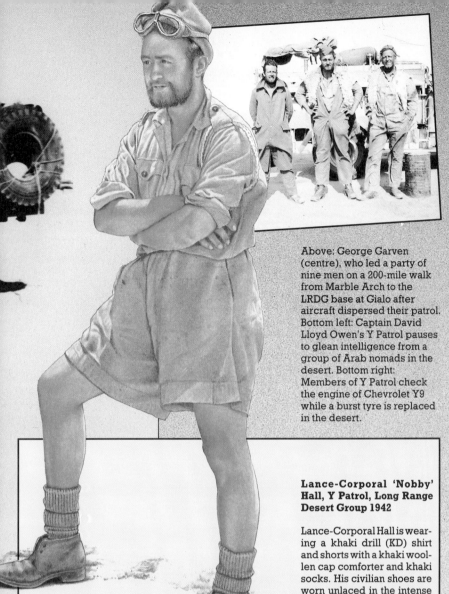

Above: George Garven (centre), who led a party of nine men on a 200-mile walk from Marble Arch to the LRDG base at Gialo after aircraft dispersed their patrol. Bottom left: Captain David Lloyd Owen's Y Patrol pauses to glean intelligence from a group of Arab nomads in the desert. Bottom right: Members of Y Patrol check the engine of Chevrolet Y9 while a burst tyre is replaced in the desert.

Lance-Corporal 'Nobby' Hall, Y Patrol, Long Range Desert Group 1942

Lance-Corporal Hall is wearing a khaki drill (KD) shirt and shorts with a khaki woollen cap comforter and khaki socks. His civilian shoes are worn unlaced in the intense heat. The goggles are those issued to despatch riders and were worn as a precaution against wind-blown sand.

'We did 20 miles, pulled up, brewed up, had some bully stew and off to kip. The following morning just breaking daylight I heard a voice and saw in the distance a Bedouin driving his flock of sheep and goats. I woke up my mate who could speak good Arabic. I told him to get the Arab to sell us some bananas in exchange for tea and flour. Sure enough, we got our bananas. I removed the top of the gearbox and stuffed it with the skins. This enabled us to continue our journey and we did almost 900 miles before a replacement gearbox was fitted at base.'

Bill Johnson typified the hardy, inventive and resourceful men who formed the backbone of the LRDG. The officers had other responsibilities: Ralph Bagnold summarised them in a directive written for his successor, Guy Prendergast, on 16 July 1941. He stated:

'OC LRDG is the officer finally responsible for the quality and quantity of the information supplied, and for the speed with which it is transmitted to those who want it.

'He will therefore make every effort both to instruct his officers in observation, reporting and map making, and to ensure that the LRDG earns its keep as an intelligence producing unit.'

That Prendergast and his men succeeded in fulfilling Bagnold's clear and remarkable vision may be seen in a note written by the Director Military Intelligence to the Director Military Operations at GHQ Eighth Army on 14 December 1942:

'LRDG road watch provides the only trained road traffic observers. Not only is the standard of accuracy and observation exceptionally high, but the patrols are familiar with the most recent illustrations of enemy vehicles and equipment.

'During periods of withdrawal and reinforcement of the enemy the LRDG road watch has provided and still provides an indispensable basis of certain facts on which calculation of enemy strength can be based.

'The road watch in rear of the El Agheila position has been of quite exceptional importance and the information which it has provided, in spite of interruptions due to a difficult and dangerous situation, has been invaluable. From the point of view of military intelligence the risks and casualties which the patrols have accepted and are accepting have been more than justified.'

THE AUTHOR David List is an historian with a special interest in the Long Range Desert Group. He and the publishers would like to thank Major-General David Lloyd Owen and the LRDG Association for their generous assistance in the preparation of this article.

At the end of the campaign in North Africa in 1943, the units of the Long Range Desert Group underwent considerable reorganisation for operations in the European theatre. The desert patrols were re-formed into 'sticks' of 12 men, and by December 1943 they were practised in insertion by parachute, boat, jeep or mule into anywhere within their area of operations.

Patrols now consisted of a captain or subaltern as patrol commander, a sergeant as second-in-command, two corporals, three signallers (one from the Royal Corps of Signals and two regimental), one medical orderly, one driver/mechanic and one general-duties soldier.

In the European theatre the Long Range Desert Group fielded two operational squadrons, A and B, each of eight patrols plus one reinforcement or training patrol. In addition, there was one signal squadron, under command of LRDG Headquarters, that provided all the communication links between patrols working behind enemy lines, the LRDG HQ itself, and the larger formations for which the patrols were working. The essential nature of the Group was maintained in that all the members were volunteers who joined the unit at the most basic grade and gradually received promotion. Every officer within the LRDG began as a patrol commander, and every man as a private soldier.

After retraining in the mountains of Lebanon, the Long Range Desert Group was sent with the British 234th Infantry Brigade to hold the Dodecanese islands in the Aegean

IN JANUARY 1943, some months before the final defeat in May of the Axis forces in North Africa, a question mark was already hanging over the future of one of the Allies' most specialised units of that campaign, the Long Range Desert Group (LRDG). Lieutenant-Colonel Guy Prendergast, assembling his men to let them know that their work in the Desert was nearly over, explained that they were due for a period of leave in Alexandria, prior to retraining for a new job.

Recalling that occasion, LRDG member 'Doc' Lawson remembers him saying: 'Those with a beard like the Doctor's or worse must shave them off and the rest can trim and keep theirs.' After over two years in the hot, waterless and inhospitable desert, the Group was bound for an entirely different terrain. The first step was a gruelling course at the Mountain Warfare School in Lebanon.

Not every member of the LRDG was to make the transition, however. At the end of the North African

Far left, above: Exhilarated members of the LRDG pause during ski training in the Cedars of Lebanon. Far left, below: Men of A and B Squadrons become accustomed to high-altitude climbing. Left: Captain David Lloyd Owen (left), who succeeded Lieutenant-Colonel Jake Easonsmith as commander of the LRDG in 1943, and 'Doc' Lawson, MC. Below: An LRDG patrol trains for operations in Italy.

peacetime a ski resort, and above their billet the mountains soared another 3000ft. Bill Smith recalled the training:

'At the time we took it for granted that we would do what was required of us. Looking back, it is astonishing that we achieved so much in such a short time, both in physical and mental adaptation to a new environment, and in testing and learning to use so many new items of equipment. But LRDG planning was, as ever, on the top line.'

'Doc' Lawson was asked to pick out patrols of men who liked hills and solitary conditions and who had no arthritis or chest diseases. He was warned that even the fittest men would take three weeks for their bodies to adjust to the high altitudes and that the training would need to progress slowly:

'The danger at that height was that over-exertion before you got adapted could bring on a dilated heart and also produce a severe depression from accumulated fatigue which took a long time to get over. The mountain warfare people suggested a five-month period of training ... At four weeks light packs of 15lb were taken on four-hour climbs. By 10 weeks there were daily climbs, with one or two days and a night up to 17 miles with 30lb packs, with practice in night camping, cooking, map reading and weapon training ... The fifth and final month was to find us doing 80 to 100 miles with 60 to 80lb packs and practising with aircraft for supply drops of rations and any other gear needed.'

Luftwaffe squadrons were rushing to take over the islands' airfields and reinforcements were brought in

Marching long distances in small patrols, the men speculated that they would soon be employed in clandestine operations behind German lines in the Apennines. When A Squadron departed from Haifa aboard the Greek destroyer HHMS *Queen Olga* on 22 September, however, it was finally confirmed that their destination was Portolago on the Dodecanese island of Leros. Arriving with three other destroyers the following day, the squadron landed, together with a detachment of the Special Boat Service (SBS), during an air raid. As little damage was done to the port, the squadron rapidly unloaded its equipment and transferred it to Alinda Bay on the eastern side of the island. Three days later, *Queen Olga* and another destroyer, HMS *Intrepid*, were sunk while still in harbour.

The situation into which the LRDG had been inserted was critical. Immediately after the Italian capitulation was announced on 8 September, the Germans, acting with admirable speed, had assumed control of an 'Iron Ring' of four important islands in the eastern Mediterranean; Cerigo, Crete, Scarpanto and Rhodes. Luftwaffe squadrons were rushing in to take over the islands' airfields and reinforcements were being brought in by convoys of troop carriers. Only the smaller islands to the north of the ring were still available for Allied exploitation,

campaign the New Zealand government, for example, insisted on the repatriation of the 1st, 2nd and 3rd Echelons of the New Zealand Division, from which most of the LRDG's A Squadron had volunteered. Although a number, to their great credit, decided to stay with the unit, many new recruits had to be found to bring A Squadron up to strength. There were also suggestions that New Zealander members of the LRDG should rejoin their parent division to replace men lost at Alamein and in subsequent fighting. Only the sudden collapse of Italy, coupled with urgent pleading by Special Force commanders, secured the postponement of their return.

The Mountain Warfare School, attended by the British and Commonwealth Squadrons of the LRDG in the summer of 1943, lay 6000ft above Beirut, high in a magnificent crescent of snow-covered mountains. The patrols were billetted at the Cedars Hotel, in

INTO THE IRON RING

and it was in the frail hope of holding some of these that the LRDG and SBS had gone to Leros. Island defence was hardly the role for which they had been trained, but at least, as one man observed, 'there was likely to be more company than on the road watch.'

The small British force that had been assigned the defence of the Dodecanese soon joined the advance units. Nearly 5000 men of the 234th Infantry Brigade arrived with jeeps and Bofors guns: some were left at Casteloriso, over 2000 men were distributed between Leros and Samos, and a company from the 11th Parachute Battalion with men of the RAF Regiment parachuted onto Cos. In order to make room for the influx of British troops, A and B Squadrons of the LRDG moved to the small island of Calino.

From Calino, LRDG patrols deployed onto such islands as Simi, Stamphalia and even Kithnos in the Cyclades, seeking information from local people on the islands' German garrisons and relaying a stream

Above: Y Patrol members 'Spud' Murphy and Jack Harris in Syria prior to the move to the Aegean. Murphy was captured on Leros and was involved in many attempts to escape. Background photograph: Officers and men of the LRDG transfer ashore at Portolago on the island of Leros in September 1943. Below: This wireless position, set up by R1 Patrol on a hilltop on Leros, was knocked out by a bomb during a raid on the island by the Luftwaffe.

of accurate reports of enemy shipping and air traffic to Alexandria. On 7 October a message from T1 Patrol brought four destroyers to the waters around Stamphalia, where they annihilated a German convoy consisting of an ammunition ship, an armed trawler and six landing craft laden with troops intended for the invasion of Leros. Only 90 of the enemy troops survived, and Leros was safe from invasion for a few weeks longer.

But just before this victory, the SBS and LRDG squadrons left on Calino had been forced to watch helplessly as the garrison on Cos, only six miles away, was reduced by an overwhelming invasion force of panzer grenadiers and assault engineers, supported by Junkers Ju 88s and Messerschmitt Bf 109s. Arriving on 3 October, this was Kampfgruppe (Battle Group) Mueller, making the first of a series of strikes that was to make the name of Generalleutnant (Lieutenant-General) Friedrich Mueller one of the

LRDG Operations
The Dodecanese, 1943

most feared in the eastern Mediterranean. In 24 hours of violent action the German forces overran the island. Six hundred British and 2500 Italian prisoners were taken, and the Italian commandant was shot with members of his staff.

With Cos in German hands. the island of Calino was virtually indefensible. On the night of 4/5 October a fleet of small boats returned the SBS and LRDG units to Leros. Anticipating air attacks at dawn, men and equipment were moved rapidly from the wharves, but they did not escape the first waves of a four-hour air

Below: In the shadow of the Greek destroyer *Kondouriotis*, men of the LRDG prepare a caique in Portolago harbour for the journey to a neighbouring island. Some of these ex-fishing craft were powered by tank engines from North Africa.

raid that came over at 0530 hours. More boats, including an Italian gunboat, were sunk, and many harbourside installations were destroyed. The garrison on Leros, now consisting of one battalion of the Royal Irish Fusiliers, one company of the Royal West Kents, 150 men of the SBS, 200 of the LRDG and members of 30 Commando, together with 4000 Italians, then prepared for the large-scale assault that must inevitably follow.

THE DODECANESE CAMPAIGN

In the months following the Allied invasion of Sicily in July 1943, Winston Churchill fought hard to gain the resources to implement a plan, codenamed Operation Accolade, to wrest the Dodecanese islands in the Aegean Sea from their Italian occupiers. From the islands' airfield and seaport facilities, he argued, the Allies could contain Axis forces in the eastern Mediterranean and, further, divert enemy aircraft from the imminent invasion of the Italian mainland. Following Italy's expected capitulation, the islands would offer an approach to southeastern Europe and a base from which to bomb German lines of communication and their annexed oilfields at Ploesti in Rumania. Hitler's supply of bauxite, copper and chrome from the Balkans could be interdicted, more effective support could also be given to Yugoslavian and Greek partisans, and a way would be opened to supply Russia via the short route of the Dardanelles.

Churchill's plan gained little support from his American allies, however, who saw it as peripheral to the main Allied thrust in Italy and also suspected it to be motivated by British expansionist aims in the Balkans. Finally, the British found one brigade to carry out a task that needed the strength of at least a division.

Early hopes of gaining Rhodes were dashed when a secret party from the SBS failed to persuade the island's governor to resist a German takeover following the Italian collapse. The brigade therefore occupied Cos, Leros, Calino, Samos, Casteloriso and Simi, while sending patrols out to many smaller islands.

On 1 October, Hitler ordered that the Aegean islands be retaken as part of the defence of Italy. Outnumbered and denied sufficient air cover, the British garrisons on Cos and Leros were defeated, after which the other islands were evacuated without a fight to avoid fruitless casualties. By the end of November the Dodecanese were in German hands.

As LRDG signallers set to work improving communications between the Italian artillery batteries on the island, which consisted of nearly 100 elderly and poorly emplaced guns, reinforcements began to arrive. On 25 October, for example, the 4th Buffs arrived after a destroyer bringing them was sunk en route, and 200 men of the Greek Sacred Squadron parachuted onto Samos to join the 2nd Battalion, Royal West Kents. Leros also received six 25-pounder guns with jeeps and trailers, submarines brought in an additional 12 Bofors guns, and mortars, machine guns, ammunition and radio sets were dropped by parachute. The island was being increasingly hard hit by bombing raids, however, and the new Beaufighters and Mitchells assigned to the defence of the area were operating at long range and were no match for the waves of Dorniers, Stukas and Bf 109s operating from bases on the islands and mainland Greece.

Just as the British garrisons on Leros, Samos and a handful of other small Dodecanese islands readied themselves for invasion, events were leading up to a disastrous operation that was to spell tragedy for the Long Range Desert Group. The focus of the events was the small island of Levita, some 20 miles to the southwest of Leros. A small naval craft, the *Hedgehog*, had called there with engine trouble while transporting 10 prisoners to Leros and had been destroyed by German gunfire. The Royal Navy was anxious to capture the island in order to secure the surrounding waters and Brigadier Brittorous, commander of 234 Brigade, ordered the LRDG to execute the task. But when time was requested to carry out a reconnaissance of the island, it was refused. In defiance of every military law, an amphibious attack was to be launched on an island without the most rudimentary knowledge of its defences.

The boats were pulled ashore and hidden, whereupon the party split into two patrols

For the purpose of the raid, the LRDG organised 'Olforce', a body of 49 men under Captain J.R. Olivey. Of the force, 23 were New Zealanders of Section 2, A Squadron, most of them from Lieutenant J.M. Sutherland's R2 Patrol, with a few men from R1 and T2 Patrols. The remaining 26 men were from B Squadron, including Y2 Patrol and part of S1 Patrol. Since it was unknown how the Germans were disposed, the plan of operation was to land two parties at opposite ends of the island, each keeping contact with the other by wireless. The B Squadron party, under Olivey, was to land to the southwest and sweep towards the centre of the island; the A Squadron party, under Sutherland, was to land on the northeast coast and sweep westward until the two parties made contact. Olforce was to leave Leros at dusk in two Fairmile motor launches, the men transferring to the Levita shore in canvas assault boats. These were found to have suffered damage in one of the air raids on Leros and required repair with sticking plaster before the mission could begin.

On the night of 21/22 October, the destroyer HMS *Dulverton* subjected Levita to a preliminary bombardment. At dusk on the 22nd, the Fairmiles left Leros and headed for their objectives. The B Squadron group, landing in the west, beached at 2200 and met no resistance. The boats were pulled ashore and hidden, whereupon the party split into two patrols in order to approach the centre of the island by way of wide arcs to left and right. Achieving their initial

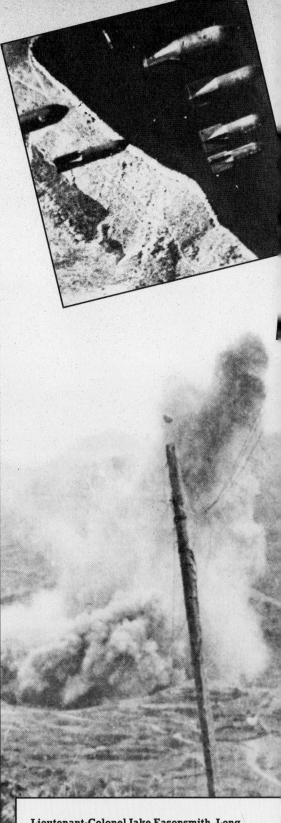

Lieutenant-Colonel Jake Easonsmith, Long Range Desert Group, Aegean 1943

Jake Easonsmith commanded the LRDG from October 1943 until he was killed by a sniper's bullet on Leros in November. He is wearing a denim version of British battledress, with the epaulettes of a lieutenant-colonel, and the blue-and-white ribbon of the Military Cross on his left breast. His attire is completed by khaki drill trousers and civilian suede boots, and he wears the black beret and silver badge of the Royal Tank Regiment.

Left: Standing with a uniformed member of the Yugoslav Army are two members of Olforce who were captured on Levita. Jim Patch (left) and Ron Hill jumped the train taking them to Germany as it passed through Yugoslavia, and eventually linked up with General Mihailović's Chetniks. Through the agency of the Special Operations Executive (SOE) they were reunited with the LRDG in February 1945. Jim Patch is now secretary of the LRDG Association. Far left: A stick of German bombs whistles down onto Leros, while (below) bombs explode on the island during an air raid.

rendezvous without incident, the men pressed on to a meteorological station standing on a hill. Finding it surrounded by trenches but unoccupied, the party established its radio in an outbuilding.

At dawn, two patrols sent to investigate a hill 600yds to the southeast encountered concentrated rifle and machine-gun fire. Then the party's HQ in the meteorological station came under fire from a heavy mortar concealed on the far side of the same hill. The patrols were ordered to make wide detours on either side of the hill to discover whether it was more practicable to attack from the flank or the rear. One of these moved round on the left flank and found that there was no possible means of approach without crossing 400yds of open ground up to positions set into a sheer hillside. Jim Patch, leader of the patrol, commented:

'I therefore decided to try an approach from the rear but at this, enemy aircraft appeared and began ranging the whole island. These aircraft numbered, as far as I could judge, eight Stukas and four two-seater seaplanes. We advanced with much caution in order not to be spotted by these planes and as we approached the rear of our objective a column of the enemy was observed filing in twos and threes and at very wide intervals along a ridge towards their position on the hill, our objective. They seemed to number about 30 men. We were then placed in an unfortunate position. We were 200yds from the enemy in very open country with bushes only one foot high and no rocks. The enemy planes now spotted us and the column had withdrawn to the other side of the ridge. The aircraft flew over us one by one, never firing but coming within 10ft of our heads while a machine-gun post was established among rocks on the ridge and kept us occupied with spasmodic fire.'

The patrol approached without caution, only to find itself covered by two German machine guns

The Olforce patrol had no option but to withdraw slowly, observed by the enemy and harassed by the machine-gun emplacement. Nearing the party's HQ and seeing men walking freely in the vicinity of the house, the patrol approached without caution, only to find itself covered by two German machine guns. The B Squadron party's HQ and both patrols were now all prisoners. Losses had been one man killed and one wounded.

The New Zealanders of the A Squadron party of Olforce had, if anything, suffered a worse fate.

Left: Photographed while a lieutenant and patrol commander, Alan Redfern later became the commander of B Squadron and participated in shipping watches in the Dodecanese islands. He was killed in action on Leros in November. Far left: Captain John Olivey, MC and Bar, who commanded 'Olforce' on Levita and was still on service in Yugoslavia when the war ended.

Arriving badly seasick at the eastern end of Levita, they had experienced much trouble launching the canvas boats from their tossing launch. Struggling onto a rugged, rocky shore, they had to wrestle their equipment up an unexpectedly steep cliff face, at the top of which were several enemy positions dug into the rocks. The motor launch remained in the area and gave covering fire but failed to prevent the party from receiving enemy machine-gun fire from the rear. Climbing down to deal with it, they captured 12 Germans near their landing place, but not before losing one man from mortal wounds.

Lieutenant Sutherland's party followed an advance patrol along the shore of the inlet where it had landed, climbed onto the ridge and eventually overran the German dug-outs. By now, two men had been seriously wounded, both by stick grenades exploding in their faces. As dawn broke it became apparent that enemy machine-gunners dominated all the routes leading from the ridge and the party, hampered by 35 prisoners, was too small to force a way to the German HQ positioned on a neck of land connecting the two main parts of the island.

'Eight Stukas and four seaplanes returned and machine-gunned our positions from low level'

At this point, Sutherland should have radioed Captain Olivey's group, which was now within 500yds of the German HQ. Unfortunately, his operator had found it impossible to raise Olivey. Sutherland knew only that his commander was somewhere in front, so he remained on the ridge in case movement would upset Olivey's plans, while Olivey could hear sounds of battle on the ridge and held his fire lest it should kill New Zealanders. Profiting from their foes' dilemma, the Germans concentrated first on the B Squadron party, encircling their positions and capturing most of them, and then turned to storm the New Zealanders on the ridge. Ron Hill of A Squadron described their fate:

'About 8am a seaplane took off from the inlet and flew over both our and Captain Olivey's positions on reconnaissance and was engaged by the Bren-gunner. Later the plane made off westwards and within an hour eight Stukas and four seaplanes returned and machine-gunned our positions from low level. Bombs were also dropped on Captain Olivey's HQ. This air cover and attack continued all day so that it was impossible to make any movement.'

Rapidly running out of water and burdened by prisoners, the New Zealanders came under heavy mortar fire and at about 1600 hours German infantry began to infiltrate forward, covered by Stuka dive bombers. As dusk closed in, the Germans made increasingly rapid progress, coming close enough to blast the New Zealanders with rifle grenades.

By now, the guns of Olivey's party were silent and the men were evidently killed or captured. The canvas boats that had offered the party's only hope of escape were in enemy hands, and with ammunition almost exhausted Lieutenant Sutherland decided that further resistance would be futile. At 1800 hours the Germans were informed by a prisoner that the party was surrendering. Four men who managed to slip away survived among the rocks for four days, but then thirst forced them to surrender. Of Captain Olivey's party, he and eight others evaded capture and were rescued by launch on the night of 24/25 October by Lieutenant-Colonel Easonsmith. No few-

The chequered history of the Long Range Desert Group contains more than its share of extraordinary episodes, and many members ended the war with remarkable stories to tell. Ashley Greenwood (below) joined the Group as a patrol commander in 1943 and went with his patrol to Leros. When the Germans overran the island he escaped to Turkey, and then immediately returned disguised as a Greek civilian to help men still on Leros. His commander, Lieutenant-Colonel David Lloyd Owen, credited him with great courage and the saving of a number of lives.

er than 40 members of the Long Range Desert Group had been lost in the raid on Levita.

When the New Zealand Command learnt of the costly failure on Levita it insisted that the New Zealander members of the LRDG should return to serve with the New Zealand Division, and in the event most joined the New Zealand Cavalry. In view of the superb work that they had done in the Western Desert and in the early weeks of the Dodecanese campaign, and the great potential of their squadron in the new role of mountain reconnaissance, it was for some members a sad and somewhat bitter ending to their illustrious history in the Long Range Desert Group.

THE AUTHOR Barrie Pitt is well known as a military historian and edited Purnell's *History of the Second World War* and *History of the First World War*. The publishers would also like to thank Major-General David Lloyd Owen, the LRDG association, and Mr David List for their generous assistance in the preparation of this article.

DESERT RAIDERS

The Long Range Desert Group operated behind Axis lines in North Africa, racing in, in jeeps and trucks with guns blazing, to attack enemy positions.

ACTIVE SERVICE

Although the LRDG gained widespread admiration for its daring raids against Axis supply dumps and airfields, most of its activities were concerned with the less glamorous, but equally important, aspects of information gathering. The LRDG was involved in reconnaissance, intelligence gathering, pathfinding and courier work.

In the field, however, the distinction between these roles was not clear cut. Any operation might involve all of these elements, either pre-planned or introduced as needs dictated. Although no two operations were ever identical, they all tended to have the same basic characteristics; long periods of boredom punctuated by short bursts of violent action.

Reconnaissance and intelligence gathering were by far the most useful contributions made by the LRDG to the war effort. These involved long cross-country drives to pinpoint enemy bases and positions, or 'road watches' to monitor the movement of Axis units.

Pathfinding operations identified routes through the desert interior capable of supporting heavy traffic, while courier running, or 'taxi service' as it was known, carried agents to their missions behind enemy lines.

Direct action, however, did bring more immediate and tangible results. Although often small scale engagements, they caused the Italians a great deal of anxiety in areas they believed to be secure from attack and, by forcing the diversion of troops and aircraft from frontline service, weakened their overall war effort.

THE ROLLING DUNES of the Great Sand Sea on the borders of Egypt and Libya shimmered in the merciless glare of the desert sun. A strange procession of vehicles, Chevrolet 30cwt trucks piled high with kit and machine-gun armed jeeps, struggled to advance against the grain of the land, grinding up the sides of the shifting sand hills before hurtling down the reverse slope to pick up momentum for the next, inevitable, climb. Progress was slow as trucks sank to their axles in the sand and, amid curses and the sound of racing engines, khaki-clad soldiers, some in Arab headdress and all sporting a week's growth of beard, climbed out to begin the back-breaking tasks of digging and shoving.

'Unsticking' (the extrication of vehicles from soft sand) was a regular and time-consuming operation. After a few experiments in which pieces of corrugated iron, beaten into channels, had proved to be effective, the ironworks of Cairo had been scoured for supplies of rolled-steel troughing normally used for roofing bunkers. When placed in front of a truck's wheels, these sections provided sufficient grip for a vehicle to escape all but the softest sands.

Suddenly, one of the jeeps disappeared over the top of a razor-backed dune and landed with a sickening thud. A few moments later, the driver, Captain Alastair Timpson, commander of G (Guards) 1 Patrol of the Long Range Desert Group (LRDG), staggered into view. His gunner, Guardsman Thomas Wann, lay paralysed seven metres below, his spine broken in the crash, and Timpson, his skull fractured, soon lapsed into semi-consciousness. The column ground to a halt and, as the injured men were carefully placed aboard one of the trucks, the

overall commander, Captain Jake Easonsmith, reassessed his position. He was en route to the Libyan port of Barce, recently captured by a triumphant Afrika Korps, and had been tasked to carry out 'Caravan', a raid which would be part of a large combined operation by the LRDG against Axis supply lines and airfields along the Mediterranean coast. The attacks were scheduled for the night of 13/14 September 1942: it was already the 7th and there were still 800km to go. It was not an auspicious start.

Despite this early setback and the delay it caused, Easonsmith remained confident that the column could reach the target at the agreed time. The qualities of his men would see to that. Drawn from all corners of the Commonwealth and every walk of life, they might look like a bunch of ill-disciplined misfits to the untrained eye, but Easonsmith knew that he could count on them in a tight spot. The men exuded an air of self-reliance, initiative and experience, and had the humour to mix well within a small group for long periods. Most were har-

THE DESERT RAIDERS

The formation of the Long Range Desert Group (LRDG) on 3 July 1940 was no new concept to desert warfare. During World War I the British Army in the Middle East had used Light Car Patrols (LCPs) against Senussi tribesmen, but their experiences were largely forgotten by the end of the war and it was not until the creation of the LRDG that the value of deep-penetration raids and reconnaissance missions was again recognised.

In the inter-war years, it was only the enthusiasm of Ralph Bagnold, a major in the Royal Corps of Signals, and some colleagues that kept the idea alive. Throughout the 1920s and 30s they carried out a series of desert journeys, so that, by the start of World War II, most of the problems of living and travelling in the desert had been solved.

Bagnold drew on his experiences to write a paper on the possible use of a long range reconnaissance force, but it was rejected by GHQ 'Middle East' in November 1939 and again in January 1940. With Italy's declaration of war on 10 June 1940, the British Army's most urgent need was for intelligence on the enemy's intentions and, given this chance, Bagnold set out to prove his theories.

Between December 1940 and April 1943 the LRDG saw almost constant service and only a handful of its 200 recorded missions failed. The LRDG was disbanded in August 1945.

Previous page, top: A desert rendezvous for members of Y and R Patrols of the Long Range Desert Group (LRDG) during a hit-and-run raid behind enemy lines. Patrols were expected to work in this bleak environment for weeks at a time and had to be self-sufficient. Their vehicles, in this case mainly 30-cwt Chevrolets, carried up to three weeks' supply of food, ammunition and petrol. LRDG units also carried a fearful array of weapons; (previous page, below) this Willys MB jeep is armed with twin Vickers Ks on the rear mounting and a 0.3in Browning. Below: Jeep-borne members of the Special Air Service (SAS), wait to join an LRDG raiding party. Both units allowed their men a degree of personal choice in the clothing they wore on missions.

dened professionals, chosen for their excellent driving skills, their ability to handle a wide variety of weapons, operate radios and navigate over long distances.

Easonsmith's LRDG column comprised three Patrols: S2, manned by men from Southern Rhodesia under Captain John Olivey; T2, consisting of New Zealanders under Captain Nick Wilder; and G1, now under Sergeant Jack Dennis who was accompanied by Major Vladimir 'Popski' Peniakoff and two of his Arab agents. S2 was to divert towards Benghazi on the other side of the Sand Sea, and act in support of the Special Air Service (SAS) raid on that port. For their part, T2 and G1 were to proceed directly to Barce to carry out an attack that, at this stage of the war, was unusual for the LRDG. By September 1942, the LRDG was feeling frustrated by the endless tedium of reconnaissance duties and the Barce raid was seen as a welcome opportunity for action. The patrols left Fayoum in the Nile delta on 2 September, aiming to cross the Sand Sea before turning north towards their objective. The distance was enormous, over 1600km across difficult terrain, and the raid itself, aimed at destroying Axis aircraft responsible for the attacks on Malta, was fraught with danger.

Travelling across the desert was always a tense, nerve-racking experience. Patrols had to make the best possible time, but there were the inevitable delays to repair damaged equipment or right an over-turned truck, and the need to make evasive detours often slowed them down. Straight runs were kept to a minimum, usually no more than 10km, and were periodically broken by right-angled diversions of up to two kilometres to confuse over-inquisitive enemy reconnaissance units. Approaches to supply dumps or rendezvous points had to be concealed by laying false trails.

The greatest threat to LRDG Patrols, however, came from the air. Disruptive camouflage, iron discipline and effective use of local terrain often meant that columns were overflown by enemy aircraft without being spotted, but, it these ploys failed, Patrols would reveal themselves and try to act like a friendly unit. Men would wave at the aircraft and the trucks, plastered with the white *beutezeichen* (booty mark) carried by Axis troops to indicate British equipment in German and Italian use, would be uncovered. Clothing was kept deliberately nondescript for the same reasons.

If none of these last ditch measures fooled the enemy aircraft, the column would mount up and then wait for the aircraft to make its strafing run before scattering. This tactic, however, often proved unnecessary as lone raiders, faced by the concentrated fire of dozens of machine guns, usually beat a hasty retreat.

Nothing disturbed the men as they checked their weapons and prepared special timebombs

Once Timpson and Wann had been placed on board the trucks and were receiving first aid, Easonsmith motored towards the 'Great Cairn', a distinctive landmark at the northern edge of the Sand Sea, from where the injured men could be picked up by an RAF bomber and flown to Cairo for hospital treatment. Leaving them with S2 Patrol and the LRDG doctor, Dick Lawson, T2 and G1 moved on, having lost a day. Fortunately the going was now much easier and late on 12 September, having been rejoined by Lawson, the column approached the foothills of the Jebel Akhdar. At Bir el-Gerrari, 96km short of the target, Easonsmith left a truck filled with rations, water and petrol to act as an emergency rallying-point, before pushing on into the more cultivated area of Barce itself. Arriving in the vicinity in the late morning of the 13th, the trucks took up defensive positions among the olive groves while Easonsmith and Peniakoff edged closer to town, despatching the two Arab agents to report on the state of enemy defences. Enemy aircraft buzzed continuously overhead, but the Patrols were well camouflaged and nothing disturbed the men as they checked their weapons and prepared special timebombs for use against the parked aircraft. As darkness fell, the column set off on the last leg of the journey.

Easonsmith was in the lead, on board a jeep armed with two Vickers K machine guns, and he was followed by a similar vehicle carrying Dennis and his gunner, Guardsman Duncalfe. A total of 11

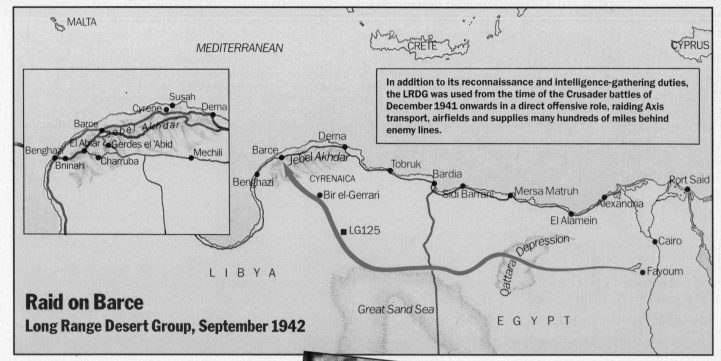

In addition to its reconnaissance and intelligence-gathering duties, the LRDG was used from the time of the Crusader battles of December 1941 onwards in a direct offensive role, raiding Axis transport, airfields and supplies many hundreds of miles behind enemy lines.

Raid on Barce
Long Range Desert Group, September 1942

trucks and a second jeep came behind, bunched up in the darkness. The going was rough as the column negotiated the Gerdes-el-'Abid track and approached an isolated police post at Sidi Raui. As they drove up, Easonsmith switched on his headlights, picking out a single Libyan policeman, Hamid, who ambled towards the jeep. He was quickly overpowered by Easonsmith and Dennis, who relieved him of his rifle and boots respectively, whereupon the column commander called for Hamid's officer to come out. When he did, he was shot down, causing the rest of the policeman to leave hastily by the back door. Dennis lobbed grenades into the building as he passed and then cut the telephone wires but, as the column started up again, two of the trucks collided. As there was no time to stop to carry out repairs, they had to be abandoned

Above: Major Peniakoff, one of the masterminds of the Barce raid. Below: 'Unsticking' was a frequent operation.

(the idea was to pick them up again on the way out), and this enabled the column to move swiftly to the main Barce road, ignoring a sudden burst of machine-gun fire. As they topped the escarpment, two Italian light tanks were silhouetted against the night sky, but the crews were asleep or lying low, and Easonsmith was able to motor past, raking the tanks with machine-gun fire as he went. Lawson and the T2 wireless truck were left at Sidi Selim as a forward rallying-point and, when a fork in the road outside Barce was reached just after midnight, the G1 wireless truck was also left behind as a back up. This left Dennis with one jeep and three trucks and Wilder with one jeep and four trucks. They split into attack groups; Dennis driving left towards the main Italian barracks and Wilder moving right towards the airfield. Easonsmith travelled separately into

town in his jeep, aiming to create a diversion. Surprise was complete, even though the Arab agents had failed to reappear.

Dennis paused only to cut down more telephone wires, this time by the simple expedient of throwing a tow-chain over the top to pull them down, and then pushed on. As he approached the barracks, two Italian sentries emerged from the shadows. Dennis slowed, rolled a four-second grenade towards them and raced on, intent on reaching his objective. Dennis remembered the ferocity of the attack on the barracks:

'We soon found it. A dozen or more soldiers had gathered on the low verandah in front of the building, anxious to find out the cause of all the noise. As we passed I tossed a grenade among them. Men on the trucks behind gave them one each, and a series of rapid explosions enlivened the party.

'I carried on as far as I could up the side of the building. Duncalfe emptied his twins (Vickers K guns) into the windows of the barracks as we swept past and the other guns picked out other windows for attention. In the meantime the (20mm) Breda gun was pumping shells through the front door of the building. Screams and yells, mingled with the sound of furniture being over-turned, came from inside the barracks and I called to my gunners to cease firing and to reload.

'Running to a low wall circling the barracks we began hurling bombs through the windows. When we attempted to scale the wall shots from troops who had managed to get out of the bar-racks into some slit trenches sent us back. We retaliated with Mills bombs and by the time our supply of grenades was exhausted all was quiet again.'

Meanwhile, Wilder had reached the airfield peri-meter. Opening the main gate, he drove in, hurling grenades into buildings and engaging the sentries with his machine guns. A petrol tanker was set on fire and in its glare Wilder turned his Patrol, in single file, along the landing strip, and then swamped each aircraft with a mixture of tracer and normal bullets.

Any that did not catch fire were left to the crew of the last truck in the line, who threw time-bombs towards them; in a matter of minutes, 20 aircraft had been wrecked and 12 badly damaged. The Italian reac-tion at this stage was confused, made worse by the sounds of battle from the barracks and by the actions of Easonsmith, who had spent some time 'beating up' the town before driving into a vehicle park and destroying 10 trucks, a tanker and a trailer. By 0400 hours on 14 September the raid had achieved its aims; all that remained was to withdraw safely.

This was no easy task. In the barracks, Dennis found his exit blocked by two light tanks. He tried to lure them in among the buildings, hoping to sneak out behind them, but the ruse did not work. Emerging from the back of one of the barrack blocks, he found a tank directly in his path; swerving violently, he tore the wing off his jeep as he scraped the tracks of the enemy vehicle, which was firing point-blank over his head. The Patrol filtered back into the darkness of the buildings, apparently stalemated, but at that moment one of the crews found a break in the boundary wall. The trucks squeezed through, emerging in the midst of tents and huts which they raked with fire. An anti-tank ditch was breached and suddenly the Patrol came out on the road, with no enemy tanks to be seen.

A second Chevrolet arrived, 'clanking like a tank' with one side of its body ripped away

Almost immediately, however, a T2 Chevrolet hur-tled past, guns blazing, and one of Dennis' trucks, commanded by Corporal Findlay, hastily took shel-ter in a side-street, losing contact with the Patrol. The remainder of G1 moved warily along the main road, only to witness the arrival of a second New Zealand Chevrolet 'clanking like a tank' with a mudguard and one side of its body ripped away. It contained a shaken Captain Wilder and three injured men, the survivors of a dramatic clash with more Italian tanks. As Wilder had emerged from the airfield, the tanks had blocked his path; driving his truck directly at

DESERT TRANSPORT

As the British-built vehicles available to the LRDG in Egypt were wholly unsuited to the rigours of prolonged desert driving, their first trucks were gathered from local sources. The best available was the Chevrolet WB 30cwt truck, of which 31 were commandeered from the Egyptian Army and the local branch of General Motors.

After a six-week operation in early 1941, these vehicles were in urgent need of repair, and over the next 12 months the LRDG had to make use of whatever transports they could lay their hands on.

In March 1942, however, a long-awaited consignment of 200 specially-ordered Canadian Chevrolet 1533X2 30cwt trucks arrived. Although these vehicles were standardised to the extent of having an open cab and steel bodies, they needed to be modified: windscreens were replaced by aircraft windshields, radiator condensers, gun mounts and compass brackets had to be fitted and the body was raised with wooden planking. After conversion, these vehicles were the mainstay of the LRDG until the end of the Desert War.

Patrols were initially issued with a variety of weapons, most of which were mounted on their trucks. Ten Lewis Mark 1 machine guns, four Boys anti-tank rifles and one 37mm Bofors gun gave them a good mix of weapons, but the arrival of the new Chevrolets heralded the introduction of several new weapons. Henceforth, each Patrol carried five Lewis guns, six medium and heavy Vickers machine guns and one dual-purpose 20mm Breda.

The normal range of the LRDG's vehicles was over 1600km , but this could be increased by the establishment of petrol and supply dumps in forward areas. Each truck carried sufficient supplies of food and water for three weeks of active service.

ORGANISATION

The forerunner of the LRDG, the Long Range Patrol Unit (LRPU), had an establishment of eight officers, 112 men and 16 reinforcements, divided equally between a Headquarters and three Patrols. Altogether, 44 vehicles were available for transport purposes. On active service, each Patrol was sub-divided into four troops, although experience soon showed that a Patrol could operate more effectively when divided in half, with the smallest viable sub-unit being two trucks.

In the light of these early experiments, the Provisional War Establishment of the LRDG, authorised in July 1940, called for a strength of 11 officers and 76 other ranks, carried in 43 vehicles. In November 1940, however, it was decided to double the strength of the unit to 21 officers and 271 men, divided between Headquarters and two squadrons. Each squadron consisted of three Patrols transported in 10 vehicles.

The process of reorganisation began on 5 December with the arrival of the Guards (G) Patrol, and over the following three months, Rhodesian (S) Patrol and Yeomanry (Y) Patrol arrived in Egypt. A sixth Patrol was never created, the authorisation for its establishment being used to form a Royal Artillery Section instead. The LRDG had reached full strength by March 1942; some 25 officers and 324 other ranks of which 36 were Signal and 36 were Light Repair personnel, equipped with 110 vehicles. The growth of the LRDG was matched by reorganisation. The Group was divided into two squadrons; A Squadron consisted of R, T, and S Patrols and B Squadron G and Y Patrols.

This organisation survived until March 1943, when the Group was withdrawn to Cairo to re-equip for later operations in Greece, Italy and Yugoslavia.

them, Wilder had cleared a way, wrecking his vehicle in the process. He transferred to the Patrol jeep, manning the twin Vickers with such fury that he obscured the vision of the driver, causing him to hit the kerb and overturn. Unconscious, Wilder was hastily bundled aboard another truck, where he came to just in time to link up with Dennis. The fourth T2 truck, cut off by the tanks, was never seen again.

Wilder and Dennis headed out of town, linking up with Easonsmith on the outskirts and picking up the wireless trucks left behind the previous evening. They reached the police post without incident, taking the abandoned trucks in tow, but as dawn broke they came under fire from a carefully-laid Italian ambush. Three LRDG men were wounded and the doctor's truck was disabled by a bullet-punctured tyre but, as Dennis circled the stricken vehicle, firing wildy at the enemy, the crew changed the wheel in less than three minutes. Extricating themselves from the ambush, some progress was made, only to be nullified when the G1 wireless truck suddenly ground to a halt on an exposed slope, its rear axle broken. The column was still only 40km from Barce and was continuing to come under fire from members of the original ambush who had caught them up.

Easonsmith, with Duncalfe as gunner, forced the Italians to pull back, but at 1030 six enemy aircraft appeared. For the rest of that day Axis fighters strafed the stalled column, destroying vehicle after vehicle. LRDG casualties were light as the men sought shelter among the rocks, but by dusk only two jeeps, a Chevrolet and the T2 wireless truck remained intact.

33 men were expected to travel nearly 1300km through a hostile wasteland to reach safety

Easonsmith supervised the loading of salvaged supplies aboard the latter, just in time to see it destroyed in a final fighter sweep. The column was reduced to three vehicles in which 33 men, six of them wounded, were expected to travel nearly 1300km through an inhospitable and hostile wasteland to reach safety.

The only hope was to reach the spare truck at Bir el-Gerrari. Easonsmith split his force: Lawson, with the wounded, was to take the last Chevrolet and one of the jeeps and head for LG 125, a temporary airstrip to the north of the Great Cairn, while the 'walking party', with the other jeep, was to aim for Bir el-Gerrari. It was a difficult journey, behind enemy lines the whole way, and water was in short supply. Lawson had to abandon his jeep, although his group did reach the landing strip without further incident; the walking party would probably have been lost if they had not stumbled on a Bedouin camp on 15 September. By then, however, other LRDG Patrols, alerted by the lack of radio contact, were out searching for Easonsmith's column and at dawn on the 17th the walking party was found. Another Patrol rushed towards LG 125, whence Lawson and the wounded were airlifted out by a Bombay transport of No.216 Squadron, RAF. The other members of the raiding force were taken south to Kufra.

Despite the loss of 10 men (all POWs) and most of

Soldier, LRDG, North Africa 1942

The Long Range Desert Group was famed for its less than parade-ground appearance, although the 'scruffy' dress of the Group was often used to advantage on operations. Out in the desert an LRDG column was highly vulnerable to aerial attack, so that when German aircraft were near, LRDG troops would attempt to confuse the enemy with their nondescript uniforms and multitude of unorthodox vehicles. This soldier wears serge battledress trousers and jacket plus a drill shirt. Distinctive headgear comprises the Arab *kifir*, which was worn alongside balaclavas and 'cap comforters'. Goggles were an essential item of equipment when crossing the sands of the Sahara.

the vehicles, the raid had been an undoubted success, made more dramatic by the concurrent failure of the attacks on Tobruk and Benghazi. Easonsmith and Wilder both received DSOs, Lawson an MC and Dennis a richly-deserved MM. In terms of the overall strategy of the Desert War, the loss of 32 aircraft may have been little more than a pinprick to the Axis forces, but the psychological effects were significant; undermining Italian morale and forcing them to concentrate on rear-area security at a time when Rommel needed all the troops he could find at the Alamein front. The raid may have been less than typical of the normal reconnaissance duties performed by the LRDG, but its success acts as a fitting tribute to the resourcefulness and raw courage of one of the more colourful elites of World War II.

THE AUTHOR John Pimlott is Senior Lecturer in War Studies and International Affairs at the Royal Military Academy, Sandhurst. He has written *Strategy and Tactics of War* and edited *Vietnam: The History and the Tactics.*

NOT BY STRENGTH BY GUILE

Above: This silver badge of the New Zealand Long Range Patrol was later superseded by the bronze insignia of the Long Range Desert Group, which consisted of a circle containing a scorpion and the letters LRDG. Left: Wrapped in Arab head-dress and wearing goggles as protection against the harsh winds of a desert sandstorm, LRDG men shelter in the lee of their vehicle.

Covering thousands of miles of arid wilderness, the Long Range Desert Group became one of the legends of the campaign in North Africa

ON 23 JUNE 1940, 13 days after Mussolini brought Italy into the war, a 44-year old major from the Royal Corps of Signals walked into the Cairo office of General Sir Archibald Wavell, Commander in Chief Middle East. With him he brought a slim document, a series of proposals for the raising of a special long-range reconnaissance unit for operations in the vast expanses of the Libyan Desert. The author of the proposals was Major Ralph Bagnold, a seasoned explorer and desert expert, who probably knew more about the Libyan Desert than any man on earth.

It was not the first time that Bagnold had approached GHQ Middle East with his proposals. In November 1939, and again in January 1940, he had lobbied for a clandestine reconnaissance force to be raised to investigate the desert interior of Libya and obtain a clear picture of Italian dispositions in the region; but his words went unheeded – that is until he met Wavell. Wavell, now at war with Italy and threatened with possible attack from Italian forces in southern Libya, Eritrea and Abyssinia, realised the necessity of obtaining intelligence on any plans for an offensive against Egypt, and its lines of communication with Sudan, that the Italians might be harbouring. With southern Libya well beyond the range of aerial reconnaissance, he immediately authorised Bagnold's plans for an overland reconnaissance unit to be formed. Bagnold was given a mere six weeks in which to be ready.

The men were hardy characters, used to the rigours of outdoor life and good with vehicles

With Wavell behind him, and a completely free hand to draw whatever equipment he deemed necessary, Bagnold launched himself into the task with his customary combination of imagination and an eye for practical detail. It was during this period that he drew up his now famous *Training Notes*, which outlined the role, organisation, operational procedures and equipment to be issued to the unit:

'OBJECT: The principal object is to provide long-range ground reconnaissance patrols in the Libyan Desert. Patrols are organised so that they can be used offensively if required.
CHARACTERISTICS: Great mobility and staying power. Each patrol is an independent body, capable of travelling entirely self contained for a minimum of 2000km in distance, and capable of finding its way over unmapped country.'

These were tall orders for a unit with only six weeks to prepare. Bill Kennedy Shaw, a fellow desert explorer of Bagnold's from before the war, was one of Bagnold's first recruits and became the Group's intelligence officer. He describes their hectic days of preparation:

'It was just like the preparations for a "Bagnold Trip" in the 'thirties and the same friends helped us as they had helped us then. Since maps of Libya and suitable technical equipment were not at the time available from Army resources, Rowntree printed the maps for us at the Survey Department in Cairo... Harding Newman "wangled" sun-compasses for us out of the Egyptian Army... Shapiro at Ford's did rush jobs on the cars .. schoolmis-

Left: A patrol struggles to 'unstick' a vehicle bogged down in loose sand. Below and below left: Tough and rugged, the New Zealanders were ideal material for the rigorous duties demanded of the LRDG. Bottom: A Chevrolet WB 30cwt truck of R Patrol. This vehicle mounts a 0.303in Lewis gun beside the driver and a 0.5in Boys anti-aircraft rifle in the back.

tresses gave us books of Log. Tables and racing men their field glasses, and in half-forgotten shops in the back streets of Cairo we searched for a hundred and one unorthodox needs.'

The initial volunteers for the Long Range Patrols, soon to become known as the Long Range Desert Group, came from the ranks of the New Zealand Divisional Cavalry Regiment. These men were hardy characters, used to the rigours of outdoor life and good with vehicles. Each patrol fielded two officers and some 30 men, mounted in a 15cwt Ford pilot car and 10 30cwt Chevrolet trucks, heavily armed with Lewis machine guns, Boys anti-tank rifles, a 37mm Bofors and various smallarms.

In August 1940, preparations complete, there were three Long Range Patrols under Bagnold's overall command: T and W Patrols, the fighting elements, were commanded by British Captains Pat Clayton and E.C. Mitford respectively, while R Patrol, tasked with supply carrying, was led by a New Zealander, Second-Lieutenant D.G. Steele.

On 7 August the first cross-border mission of the new formation was launched. Under the command of Captain Clayton, who had explored the desert with Bagnold in the pre-war years, a small patrol set out to reconnoitre the track running between Gialo and the Kufra oasis, the Italian line of communication between the port of Benghazi and the southern garrisons. Four days later, he had crossed the Egyptian Sand Sea and was heading out into unexplored territory. Reaching the track, they kept up a 24-hour a day watch for Italian traffic for three days, but saw nothing. On 19 November Clayton and his men were back in Cairo. Although they had little to report on the military situation in southern Libya, Clayton's reconnaissance of the previously uncharted areas of

RALPH BAGNOLD

Brigadier Ralph Alger Bagnold was born on 3 April 1896. After an education at Malvern College, the Royal Military Academy at Woolwich and Cambridge University, he was commissioned into the Royal Engineers in 1915. He served on the Western Front during World War I, rising to the rank of captain, and then, in 1920, transferred to the Royal Corps of Signals. In 1930 he served on the Northwest Frontier of India.

During the years that followed before the outbreak of World War II Bagnold became a leading authority on the Desert, making numerous large-scale expeditions into the heart of Libya. Some of his journeys covered more than 5000 miles. An explorer by nature, Bagnold perfected the sun-compass for desert navigation during his researches and various methods for 'unsticking' vehicles bogged down in loose sand.

In October 1939 Bagnold was on his way to take up a post in Kenya when his ship stopped in at Alexandria for repairs. His presence in Egypt came to the attention of General Wavell, who immediately had him transferred to his command.

In June 1940 he raised the Long Range Desert Group and commanded the unit until August 1941 when he was appointed Inspector of Desert Troops, tasked with planning additional long-range reconnaissance units. He later served as Deputy Signal Officer in Chief, Middle East, and was released from Army service in 1944. Bagnold was Mentioned in Despatches and received an OBE.

In the years after the war, Bagnold continued his researches into deserts and sand and received a number of awards for his distinguished work.

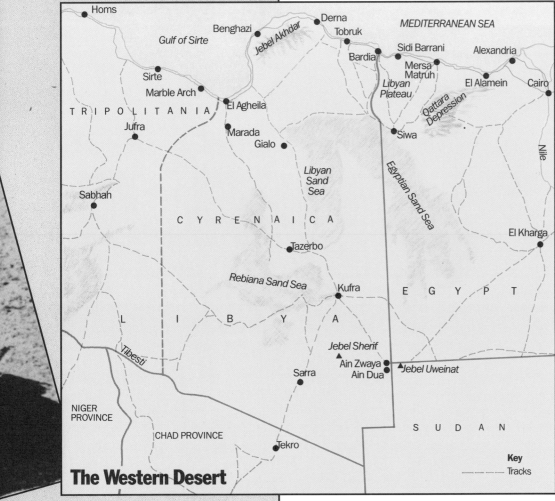

The Western Desert

Key
------- Tracks

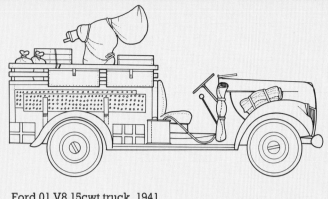

Ford 01 V8 15cwt truck, 1941

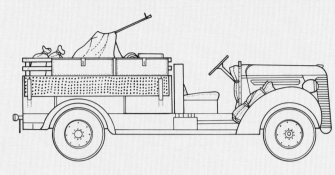

Chevrolet WB 30cwt truck, 1941

Ford F30 30cwt truck, 1941

Chevrolet 1533X2 30cwt truck, 1942

sand and gravel to the west of the Egyptian Sand Sea was to prove extremely useful to the LRDG in later operations.

The Long Range Patrols were soon in action, harrying the Italians between Gialo and Uweinat with good results. On 5 September all three patrols left Cairo and headed into the desert where they attacked Italian fuel dumps, captured a convoy and calculated the level of enemy traffic in the area, in addition to their reconnaissance work.

Further expeditions followed in which the 'offensive' aspect of Bagnold's original brief was put to the test. In late November Mitford's W Patrol approached the mountain of Uweinat where the Italians had two posts at Ain Zwaya and Ain Dua. The patrol soon ran into trouble from three enemy bombers. For over an hour Mitford and his men were

Above left: Mounted on their Ford F30 trucks, Rhodesian members of S Patrol pose for the camera. S Patrol was formed in January 1941. **Above right:** An LRDG Chevrolet truck, equipped with a 37mm Bofors gun, makes its way down a rough incline.

bombed by the aircraft but fortunately they suffered no casualties. They then investigated the post at Ain Dua, which at first sight appeared to be deserted, but a round fired from the patrol's Bofors elicited a volley of machine-gun and rifle fire. The garrison was well entrenched among huge boulders, so eight men, under Lieutenant J. Sutherland, were despatched to attack the enemy on the left flank. Using grenades and smallarms at close range, Sutherland and his men forced the garrison out of their positions and up the slope. A fresh attack was then launched, this time on both flanks, and after more close-quarters fighting the patrol withdrew, leaving six enemy dead and several wounded. Sutherland and Trooper L. Wilcox had been in the thick of it throughout the

battle and were awarded the first New Zealand Military Cross and Military Medal of the war for their courage and determination.

By December 1940 the Long Range Patrols had proved their worth beyond doubt. On 5 December the patrols were redesignated the Long Range Desert Group, and with the new title came an increase in strength: W Patrol was disbanded, its equipment going to the newly formed Guards (G) Patrol while some of its personnel were assigned to R and T Patrols. Then, in early 1941, two further patrols were added to the Group – a Southern Rhodesian (S) Patrol in January and a Yeomanry (Y) Patrol in March. After the new intake had received desert training the Group was divided into two squadrons, A and B.

Above: One of the two WACO aircraft that formed the LRDG 'air force'. Guy Prendergast (bottom), who later commanded the LRDG, was an experienced desert explorer and airman and joined the Group in February 1941. He soon realised the contribution that aircraft could make to the LRDG's various operational roles. The air element was created during the LRDG occupation

raids against strategic targets such as airfields, going in with all guns blazing, required a certain brand of courage, to operate behind enemy lines in the Desert for long periods of time was equally, if not more, taxing on the men.

The prevailing conditions in the endless expanses of the Libyan Desert were hardly conducive to human survival. Apart from the searing heat and the absence of water, there was also the Libyan *qibli* to contend with. Kennedy Shaw describes this wind:

'Many countries have their hot winds; the *khamsin* of Egypt, the *sherqiya* of Palestine, the *harmattan* of West Africa. Add all these together and blow them, with sand to taste, northwards out of the gates of Hell and you may begin to know what the *qibli* is like at Kufra in the summer. You don't merely feel hot, you don't merely feel tired, you feel as if every bit of energy had left you, as if your brain was thrusting its way through the top of your head and you want to lie in a stupor till the accursed sun has gone down.'

Kennedy Shaw goes on to describe the effect this could have on a patrol:

'Having judged from the car tracks the amount of traffic on the Gialo-Kufra route we moved on westwards to examine that between Tazerbo and Marada. That afternoon was, I think, the worst of all. At camp, Beech was slightly delirious from heat-stroke and I remember Croucher, who was navigating in the second car behind Mitford, telling me that for the last 20 miles he found himself saying to the rhythm of the tyres on the sand, "If he doesn't stop I shall go mad. If he doesn't stop I shall go mad. If he doesn't ..." After supper on days like this many men would be sick, for

   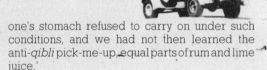

The organisation of the Long Range Desert Group underwent a number of changes during the war as the practicalities of desert operations made their mark and lessons were learnt. In the autumn of 1941, for example, the patrols were all divided into two 'half-patrols', each consisting of one officer, between 15 and 20 other ranks and five or six vehicles. Specialist formations were also added to the LRDG order of battle: a Signals Section, Light Repair Section, Heavy Section and even an LRDG 'air force', consisting of two specially adapted WACO bi-planes, came on strength. By March 1942 the LRDG had reached the level of establishment set in November 1940 with 25 officers, 324 other ranks and 110 vehicles, now under the command of Lieutenant-Colonel Guy Prendergast, who succeeded Bagnold as the Group's CO in September 1941. Despite this increase in manpower and equipment, however, the patrol and half-patrol remained the basic operational unit of the Group during the war in the Desert.

Contrary to the popular romantic image of the Group, they were, first and foremost, an intelligence gathering organisation; raids (or 'beat ups', as they were popularly known) were more the propriety of David Stirling's Special Air Service (SAS), but this did not mean that the LRDG was not a fighting unit! Offensive harassment of the enemy when the opportunity presented itself, or on the way back from an intelligence mission, was a frequent task on the Group's operational agenda. But while lightning

of Kufra in 1941 and the machines were adapted for long-distance flying. Prendergast flew one while the other was piloted by Sergeant R.F.T. Barker (shown top, second from right). The two planes were used for reconnaissance work and patrol liaison, for bringing in wounded LRDG men, and for making flights between Kufra and Cairo. Above: A column of LRDG vehicles sets out across the barren wastes of the Libyan desert on an operation during 1941.

one's stomach refused to carry on under such conditions, and we had not then learned the anti-*qibli* pick-me-up, equal parts of rum and lime juice.'

It was in conditions like this that the LRDG conducted their operations in the Desert. Generally speaking, their intelligence role comprised reconnaissance of an area in advance of action by another force, and the painstaking observation and logging of enemy movements. In addition to this, the exploration and detailed mapping of the areas in which they operated was part of their brief. This type of work reached its peak in 1942, when the LRDG conducted the famous 'road watch' – a four and a half month vigil along the 600 miles of road between Tripoli and Benghazi. Every vehicle, artillery piece, tank and troop formation was noted and the information reported back to HQ by LRDG men operating in pairs for 24 hours at a stretch.

Experts in the field of desert navigation, armed with a broad knowledge of the geography and ways of the desert, the LRDG was also used in the pathfinder and courier roles. Perhaps their most famous 'find' was the reconnaissance of a previously uncharted passage through the Matmata Hills by Captain N.P. Wilder and the men of New Zealand T1 Patrol. 'Wilders Gap', as the route became known, allowed General Freyberg to outflank the Axis defences on the Mareth line in March 1943.

LRDG courier work took on many forms but best

Far right: A patrol MO bandages an injured finger while a colleague prepares a meal for the men (right). On operations, all rations had to be carried with the patrol and the cooks became quite adept at providing a variety of meals from the tinned goods available. Left: A group of LRDG men gather around one of their trucks to listen to the news on the radio. Left, below: One of the most crucial aspects of long-range operations was keeping the vehicles going in the harsh desert environment. Here two fitters tinker with a faulty carburettor.

Lieutenant-Colonel David Lloyd Owen, Long Range Desert Group

Colonel David Lloyd Owen served with the LRDG during the war in the Western Desert and later took over command of the Group when the CO, Lieutenant-Colonel Jake Easonsmith, was killed in action on Leros in November 1943. Colonel Lloyd Owen is dressed in army shirt and khaki drill shorts, with suede desert boots and woollen socks. His beige beret bears the scorpion in a wheel cap badge of the LRDG.

known is the working relationship that evolved between the SAS and the LRDG. To attack enemy airfields, which was one of the primary missions of the SAS, the troopers had to be inserted near the target as inconspicuously as possible, and then got out again when their destructive work had been completed. With their variety of desert-adapted vehicles and their navigational expertise, the LRDG were perfect candidates for the job and the two units operated hand-in-hand on many occasions.

In addition, the LRDG's courier role also included the insertion and collection of undercover agents from a number of organisations, and the rounding up of escaped Allied POWs. Whatever their task, the men of the LRDG were the acknowledged experts on the Desert and their assistance was sought whenever such knowledge could prove useful.

The ability to navigate precisely by sun-compass and theodolite, and a sound knowledge of Libyan geography, were not, by a long chalk, the only areas of expertise within the LRDG. Out in the desert for long periods of time, the men had to know how to survive the rigours of the desert environment, to pace their consumption of water, and be ready to improvise at a moment's notice to meet any unexpected situation – this was especially true in dealing with their vehicles, the key to LRDG mobility and their very lifeline when far from base. Bill Johnson, an LRDG patrol fitter, describes a typical hiccup:

'In the desert all patrol fitters had to carry a variety of spares... clutches, carbs, water pumps, fan belts, plugs, coils etc. Now there was one driver in my patrol who persisted in tuning and tampering with his engine. Every night when we stopped he had the bonnet up. I told him many times that if his engine wasn't running properly to let me know and I would fix it. He took no notice... One night I saw him sifting through a lot of sand under his truck. He had been making an adjustment to the ignition points and had lost his rotor arm. Eventually he came to me and asked if I had one. I had three distributors, but not one with a rotor arm.

Next thing, the skipper came to me and said we

Whereas reliable maps were freely available for the Allied campaign in Europe that followed the invasion of June 1944, much of the war in the Western Desert was fought over terrain recorded only by a few inaccurate charts produced by Italian surveyors before the war. Knowledge of such features as oases and navigable routes was indispensable to both offensive and defensive planning, and in 1941 the Survey Section of the Long Range Desert Group was formed to reconnoitre and chart areas likely to assume strategic importance. The LRDG's field maps were made to a scale of 1:400,000, later to be reduced and printed to a scale of 1:500,000. Each sheet covered two degrees of latitude and longitude, an area of approximately 19,000 square miles. The LRDG surveyed five sheets, all in the Libyan southern desert, including Calansho Serir, Calansho Sand Sea, Big Cairn, Kufra and El Riquba.

Survey patrols consisted of two vehicles, a navigation truck and a radio truck. The former would be fitted with two sun compasses, one for the driver and one for the surveyor. These were of a type designed by Ralph Bagnold and produced by the Department of Survey of Egypt, and some of the surveyors' compasses were modified for use on the move in order to speed up the mapping procedure. Since triangulation was not possible in the time available, the maps were oriented with fixes on the stars. In daylight, a fix could be made on Venus by computing its position with an Air Almanac and then detecting its small white crescent with a telescope. The scale of 6.3 miles to an inch allowed little detail. The LRDG divided the desert into different topographical areas and each land type was described and delineated. Beyond that, only such landmarks as isolated rocky hills could be shown.

weren't leaving a truck behind and I'd have to think of something. So I thought. And from my thoughts emerged a cork out of a beer bottle and a safety pin out of the first aid kit. With a razor blade I fashioned the cork and with a pair of pliers I bent the safety pin. The engine leapt into life. The driver was very pleased...he gave me his rum ration for a week.'

They were left behind with less than two gallons of water, no food and only the clothes they stood in

Sometimes, however, it was not the fault of the vehicles that the men were stranded without any means of transport – and in the hostile desert this was more than an inconvenience! In late January 1941 T Patrol, under Clayton, ran into an Italian motorised patrol at Djebel Sherif, 60 miles south of Kufra. The enemy force, directed by three aircraft circling overhead, opened up on the patrol and knocked out several of the trucks. The aircraft then proceeded to bomb and strafe the Group, which withdrew as best it could towards Sarra. But not all the vehicles got away. One, driven by Trooper R.J. Moore, caught fire and the men on board abandoned it as their ammunition began to explode. Presumed either dead or captured by the rest of the patrol, they were left behind with less than two gallons of water, no food and only the clothes they stood in. Their options were either to walk the distance to Kufra and surrender to the Italian garrison, or to follow the tyre tracks of their patrol towards Sarra. They chose not to surrender. Moore and three others, Easton, Tighe and Winchester, set out on 1 February on a march across the desert that was to become an epic of LRDG desert survival and determination.

On the 6th they reached Sarra, 135 miles away, but they had been forced to leave Tighe behind when he failed to keep up. Tighe reached Sarra on the 8th. On the evening of the 9th a French party, returning from a reconnaissance at Kufra, dropped in at Sarra where they found the exhausted Tighe. He was able to alert them to his erstwhile compan-

ions' predicament. On the 10th the French found Easton 55 miles out from Sarra, and 10 miles further on they located a semi-delirious Winchester. Finally, they found Moore, marching steadily onwards, 210 miles from the point at which the group set out. It is said that he was irritated at not being able to prove that he could reach the nearest water, 80 miles away at Tekro! Such is the stuff of LRDG legend.

But behind such tales of individual heroism lay a remarkably cohesive unconventional warfare unit whose operational record during the war in the Desert has set them apart as one of the greatest units of their kind ever to be raised. Never numbering more than a few hundred men, the LRDG certainly lived up to its unofficial motto, 'Non vi sed arte' – 'Not by strength, by guile'.

THE AUTHOR Jonathan Reed is an historian with a special interest in the techniques of counter-insurgency and unconventional warfare. The author and publishers would like to thank Major-General David Lloyd Owen, the LRDG Association, and Mr David List for their generous assistance in the preparation of this article.

Revitalised in late 1943, the Long Range Desert Group proved itself an exceptional unit fighting against German forces in the Balkans

FIVE MONTHS AFTER the last operator of the Long Range Desert Group (LRDG) exfiltrated from Leros following the disastrous campaign in the Aegean Sea, a campaign which had cost the unit its commanding officer, the brilliant Jake Easonsmith, and over 50 of its men taken prisoner, the LRDG once more went into operation against the forces of Germany. At 2150 hours on 30 May 1944, the Rhodesian S Patrol, led by Second-Lieutenant C.J.D. 'Jacko' Jackson, jumped into the night sky over Albania. The force included Sergeant C. Ryan, Corporals D. Moyes and R. McCullough, Privates T. Scott and J. Evans, Gunner J. Le Grange, Signalman J. Whale, and two men from No.9 Commando, Lieutenant Bassett Wilson and a corporal. Their mission was to reconnoitre the garrison at Himara for a commando strike. Re-equipped, retrained, and now under the command

Below: Parachute training was an important element of Lieutenant-Colonel David Lloyds Owen's training regime for new recruits of the Long Range Desert Group. Here, men step into space for the first time over an airfield in Palestine. Below right: Raiding operations against coastal installations in Yugoslavia and Albania were mounted in such craft as this, MFV *Kufra*. Below far right: Officers of the LRDG are photographed in Azzib during the working-up period of Christmas 1943. David Lloyd Owen is standing at the far left of the middle row.

of a veteran patrol commander, Lieutenant-Colonel David Lloyd Owen, MC, the group would go on to mount 42 more operations before disbandment on 1 August 1945.

The LRDG that resumed operations in the Balkans was a much-changed unit. The well-tried New Zealander squadron had been withdrawn on the instructions of the New Zealand government after the latter had learned of its deployment on the disastrous operation on the island of Levita in October 1943, when most of the raiding force had been captured. Though now without many of its experienced and highly trained men, the LRDG re-formed by David Lloyd Owen was to lack none of the capability of its earlier incarnations to mount strike and reconnaissance missions deep within enemy territory.

S2 Patrol and the two commandos spent six days operating with the partisans in the Himara area

The LRDG's first operation in the Balkans, Operation Landlubber, was to be the first of a highly successful series of reconnaissance and pathfinder operations mounted by men of the newly formed Rhodesian A Squadron, under Ken Lazarus, raised to replace the sorely missed New Zealanders. S2 Patrol and the two commandos spent six days operating with partisans in the Himara area, photographing the defences and surveying a beach at Zal Jalje for a later commando landing. On 5 June, Jackson was extracted by sea with the first reports for the planners of the main attack, leaving his patrol behind to act as a future reception party for the incoming raiders. Unfortunately, the projected raid had to be postponed due to heavy commando casualties in Operation Flounced

BALKAN FIREFORCE

against Brac, mounted at short notice to dislocate the German forces attacking Marshal Tito's HQ at Drvar. The rest of S2, under Sergeant Ryan, was extracted some two weeks later without incident. On 25 July Jackson and his men returned to the area by sea on Operation Healing I, and after another successful recce received 700 men of Nos. 2, 9 and 40 Commando, the Highland Light Infantry, and the Raiding Support Regiment, backed up by two destroyers and Spitfires from Nos. 249 and 253 Squadron. In Operation Healing II S2 landed on the night of 28/29 July to reopen the coastal road to the partisans and force the Germans to fight at a disadvantage.

While A Squadron was committed to trans-Adriatic operations, the British B Squadron, under Moir Stormonth-Darling, was preparing for a ground recce operation in jeeps under the Eighth Army. However, events moved more rapidly than anticipated and the operation was first postponed and then cancelled. Later in May, Operation Jump was planned, involving the insertion of four patrols by air onto drop zones (DZs) north of Rome to watch for the enemy redeploying as the Eighth Army renewed its offensive operations.

The operation was originally planned as a two-phase drop beginning on the night of 11/12 June. Bad weather and heavy enemy anti-aircraft activity delayed its start until 13/14 June, when Fleming's M2 and Bramley's W2 Patrols were dropped, followed by Greenwood's M1 and Rowbottom's W1 on the night of 14/15 June.

Each patrol was inserted with B Mk I radio sets and seven days' rations per man, plus a further 10 days' rations in canisters. W2, M1 and W1 Patrols all had problems on exit, one with a jammed container, the others with men slipping or jamming in the door, causing widely spread sticks. Corporal Aspden of W2 was badly concussed on landing, Greenwood landed on the roof of a church in Lama village, 12 miles wide of the intended DZ. Corporal Burgess landed in a tree and, to cap it all, M1 were right on top of an aroused German position. Rowbottom's men landed safely among trees at 10-20yd intervals with one rucksack container 'roman candling' and Trooper Heymans hung up in a tree. Fleming's men fared worst of all. Dropped, like the others, wide of their planned DZ, the patrol landed in a cornfield in the vicinity of another German unit, and there followed a deadly game of hide-and-seek as the patrol attempted to regroup and recover its equipment canisters, while being harassed by shouts of 'Hey Johnnie, over here' and the occasional burst of fire.

Fusilier G.W. Ford of M1 Patrol, evading on his own, fell headlong down a ravine on 9 July

Simon Fleming was never seen alive again after he exited the aircraft. Corporal J. Swanson, the last man of the stick, saw nine or 10 deployed parachutes and four shots were heard coming from the area of Fleming's landing. With the patrol scattered, another man dead and Corporal Parry-Jones captured on the DZ, Operation Jump was in a bad way. There was worse to follow.

Fusilier G.W. Ford of M1 Patrol, evading on his own, fell headlong down a ravine on 9 July and was looked after by friendly Italians for 20 days before he recovered. Rowbottom and his men bumped into German posts on two successive days and were forced to split up as they tried to get to their

JOINING THE LONG RANGE DESERT GROUP

Before passing out as fit for operations, LRDG recruits underwent a basic parachute course, followed by four weeks on weapons and explosives. They were familiarised with all standard enemy smallarms and trained in driving, boat and animal handling; once in 1943 and again in 1945 the squadrons were put through ski courses.

Two men in each patrol were trained as photographers, and one man per patrol as a medic. All men were trained in the information-handling skills of message and report writing, observation, recognition and description of enemy troops and equipment, field sketching and the use of aerial photography. Field signallers were always at a premium and learnt how to use, maintain and carry out 'running repairs' on B Mk I and B Mk II suitcase wireless sets.

In the field, the patrols adopted American M1 carbines, Thompson sub-machine guns and Colt automatics as personal weapons. Bren guns and Piats were taken only on offensive action missions. Every man was issued with IS9 escape aids and a Bergen rucksack, and the Thomas Black or heavier Baxter, Woodhouse and Taylor sleeping bag with waterproof cover.

Clothing was a mixture of British and Commonwealth issue, supplemented by American items. Steel helmets were never used and jumps were carried out in the original British-style sorbo rubber helmets, discarded on the ground for cap comforters or the distinctive LRDG sand-coloured beret, although some men retained the old black beret originally worn in the desert campaign. Above: The shoulder patch of the Long Range Desert Group.

surveillance positions. Rowbottom himself was captured. Incredibly, the truck in which he was taken away crashed, whereupon W1's commander grabbed his carbine and pouches and made off. He was later awarded the MC for his activities in this operation.

Of the four patrols dropped blind, only Bramley and W2 managed to carry out their surveillance as planned, that is, until their radio batteries ran out. The other three patrols, individually or collectively, linked up with Italian partisans and continued to fight and collect information until they could infiltrate back to the advancing Allied forces, where their information was put to good use.

Sergeant L. Morley of W1, in particular, distinguished himself, winning the MM for leading the 1st/9th Gurkha Rifles of the 4th Indian Division onto their objectives. His success was based on two and a half months of methodical and thorough reconnaissance of the German dispositions in his area. He had been walking around the enemy positions in broad daylight dressed in an American shirt, shorts, Arctic knee boots and carrying an M1 carbine.

At 100yds they opened up with a Piat, two Bren guns, Thompsons and M1 carbines

Four days after the beginning of Operation Jump, the LRDG deployed its first patrols on Operation Allah, a standing shipping watch based on the north Dalmatian Islands and serviced by their latest acquisition, the MFV *La Palma*. This watch was to be maintained well into 1945. On 20 June 1944, T1, S1 and S2 Patrols deployed on two more Landlubber operations against an enemy coast-watching station at Orso Bay in Albania.

On the night of 20 June, Stan Eastwood, two of his men, and an Albanian guide were landed from the sea to size up the position. It proved to be a single storey building on Height 361, camouflaged to look like an ordinary house with a pitched roof, the eastern portion having gone with the appearance of having fallen in. On top was an Observation Post (OP) tower, and at the northeast and southwest corners were seven-foot high pillboxes. The entire complex was surrounded by wire and manned by about 10 enemy troops.

It was too good a chance to miss. Eight days later, Tony Browne, MC, DCM, newly returned from the New Zealand Division, landed from Italian-manned MAS boats. He was in command of a strike force of three patrols, with Captain P. Wardroper, RA, along to control the guns of three Tribal-class destroyers. At the last minute, David Lloyd Owen joined the party to 'get a breath of fresh air'. At 2344 hours the guns of HMS *Terpsichore*, *Tumult* and *Tenacious* began to blast the position.

S1, followed by T1 in line abreast, advanced on the smoking target. At 100yds they opened up with a Piat, two Bren guns, Thompsons and M1 carbines, and called for more naval gunfire on their SCR 194 Walkie Talkies. Three Germans were seen to run out and vanish in the ensuing salvo. Three more tried to oppose the advancing patrols but thought better of the idea when they found they had to break cover to use their weapons effectively. Stan Eastwood then took one of the men, who claimed to be the station's OC, inside the building to check for further opposition and any papers of intelligence value. Mike Reynolds and three of his men from T1 acted as a covering party. Finding nothing, the building was

finished off with grenades and they withdrew to their rendezvous with the boat, only to find it unmanned due to their Italian-crewed transports' reluctance to close with the shore. Hasty signalling ensued, producing a destroyer and the shamed MAS boats, which had been bullied into completing the pick-up by their onboard British liaison officer. The assault and OP parties recovered safely, along with the three enemy survivors of the decimated post.

Mike Reynolds, a signaller and two Albanians returned to the area in Operation Landlubber V in July to find the post being rebuilt and the garrison up to 30 men. Strangely, while Reynolds was still watching the position, the Germans demolished the place!

Further operations in the Balkans were to follow as both LRDG squadrons were committed to this area following cancellation of yet another Italian theatre operation. On 9 August 1944 Stan Eastwood's S1, plus Spiro, a Greek fisherman recruited into the patrol during a previous mission on Corfu, dropped onto a prepared DZ at Leshnje in Albania, tasked to recce the area north and south of Durazzo on Operation Lithograph. Four months and much fighting later, the patrol would extract in style in two Dakotas flying out of the newly captured capital of Tirana.

Linking up with the partisans' General Enver Hoxha, who later became Albania's first communist president, S1 obtained mules and guides and started the long infiltration march north to their operational area. Direct insertion had been ruled out due to strong defences and extensive minefields. In September the Germans started to pull out of Greece and the opportunities for effective direct action against their withdrawal routes through Albania markedly increased.

'Kenforce', comprising T2, S3 and M1 Patrols, was deployed on Operation Lochmaben

After much planning and political manoeuvring with the partisans, who after years of fighting and reprisals against their population were keen for the Germans to leave as speedily as possible and were not happy at the prospect of British troops arriving to delay them, Lloyd Owen obtained permission to put LRDG offensive action plans to Hoxha himself. An attempt to parachute onto his HQ on 21 September failed as S1, who were to sponsor their CO's DZ, were being shelled at the time. Nevertheless, the partisan command acceded to Allied pressure and 'Kenforce', comprising T2, S3 and M1 Patrols, was deployed on Operation Lochmaben. Inserting from six American aircraft at hourly intervals onto a landing zone at Pajanja on 24 September, only one man actually landed on the DZ.

Of the 35 other officers and men dropped that night, plus canisters of equipment and rations, all were despatched too high. Robin Marr of T2 and two of his men were hurt in the drop and the LRDG's CO, who landed safely in a bush well away from the DZ, fell 30ft down a ravine and fractured his spine as he attempted to link up with the DZ party. Operation Lochmaben, like Operation Jump before it, was off to an inauspicious start.

Within 48 hours, despite pouring rain and poor visibility, a Halifax II of No.148 (Special Duties) Squadron, RAF, flown by Warrant Officer G.P. Bowser, RCAF, delivered the LRDG's medical officer, Michael Parsons, with all necessary medical supplies, adding lustre to the squadron's already high reputation for Special Duties flying Lloyd Owen was

Below: 'Tiny' Simpson and Stan Eastwood await their next move during Operation Lochmaben in Albania. Bottom: German positions in Tirana, Albania, are subjected to rocket attack from the air in support of an LRDG raid.

Centre left: Moir Stormonth-Darling, officer commanding the British B Squadron, Long Range Desert Group. Centre right: Ken Lazarus, the officer commanding the Rhodesian Squadron during Balkan operations.

Long Range Desert Group
The Balkans, May 1944-March 1945

Key
▲ Reconnaissance missions
■ Road/air/sea watches
✳ Raids

Hoyden
Zagreb
Trieste
ISTRIA **Bicknell**
Bertram
Fiume **Adair I**
Krk
Bakerlake
Rab **Anglefish**
Gradient I **Ballindon**
Cherso Jablanac
Presto II **Ashington**
Presto III
Ist **Facade II**

Y U G O S L A V I A

Sarajevo

A D R I A T I C

Split

Brac **Behemoth**
Allah Mostar

Pescara

Dubrovnik

Health Able
Budva
Health Baker
Gulf of ▲ Scutari
Kotor
Concord II ✳ Lesh
Concord

I T A L Y

Lithograph Tirana
Durazzo ▲
Lochmaben
Elbasan

Landlubber Leshnje
III
Landlubber IV
Orso ALBANIA
Bay

Bari

Brindisi

Taranto

Gulf of
Taranto

Himara ✳
Landlubber
Healing I **Healing II**
Corfu ▲

Independence I

Inset (Greece)
G R E E C E
Gulf of Corinth
Athens
Argos **Geography II**
Navplion
Cerigo Kithira
Geography

CAPTAIN STAN EASTWOOD

Along with Second-Lieutenant C.J.D. 'Jacko' Jackson, Stan Eastwood was a Rhodesian recruited into the LRDG as a private soldier during the North Africa campaigns. His ability soon saw him commander of S1 Patrol, and he gave distinguished service as patrol commander on five named operations. For his work he was awarded the Military Cross, while his patrol sergeant, Andy Bennet, won the MM.

Eastwood was captured with one of his men on a recce mission on the island of Calinos during the Aegean campaign. Within a month both men had managed to escape and return to their unit via Turkey, and in May 1944 Eastwood was back in action, reconnoitring a German radar station on Corfu as part of Operation Independence I.

Slightly wounded by naval gunfire at Orso Bay, Eastwood also contracted malaria during Operation Lithograph. Recovering, he was part of the two-patrol effort to deny enemy movement on the main Elbasan-Tirana road in Albania, and was responsible for the destruction of German forces attempting to reinforce Tirana in November 1944.

In April 1945, Eastwood and his patrol were inserted by sea into Istria for the reconnaissance mission Operation Bertram. Unfortunately, Yugoslavian partisans were arresting LRDG and SBS patrols in Istria, seeing them as compromising Marshal Tito's claims to the area. Eastwood and his men were withdrawn, and their LRDG service was finally over.

placed in a plaster jacket and, despite his injuries, he remained in Albania to co-ordinate operations until the end of October, when he was exfiltrated by sea and hospitalised. He later made a full recovery.

'Kenforce', despite the initial setback, soon began to make its presence felt. S1 and S3 Patrols, operating with the 1st Battalion, 4th Partisan Brigade, as their covering force, denied movement along the Elbasan-Tirana road for four days in October, stirring up a hornet's nest in the process. Having blown up the road in two places on successive days, the patrols' Piats and Bren guns provided trained firepower to back up the partisan infantry as they killed 80 of the enemy, beating off attacks by 200 German troops who later received the support of three tanks.

On 12 October, still maintaining his stranglehold on the road, Eastwood called in an air strike and neutralised a key German OP at Cafa Krabs. On 17/18 October, M1 and T2 under Ron Tinker blew the Ljabinoti-Sip road, but were ordered to withdraw by the partisans. Their camp was later shelled, fortunately without casualties.

Running short of explosives, 'Kenforce' was re-supplied by brilliant pinpoint drops from the Halifaxes of No. 148 Squadron. On 31 October, S1 and S3 blew the Shijak road in the face of a German cavalry patrol, having waded through a marsh to get their 250lb pressure charge in a good position. Then, having stopped all movement on the Elbasan-Tirana road for three weeks, the patrols had to be called off as partisan interests switched to the re-occupation of their capital. Unable to maintain the offensive on the roads without partisan assistance, Stan Eastwood's patrol switched to calling up air strikes in Tirana itself in support of the 1st Partisan Division.

On 11 November, hearing that German reinforcements were moving on Tirana, the Rhodesians blew the river bridge at Mysgete on the Elbasan-Tirana road and awaited developments. The following day a few tanks, artillery, transport vehicles, horse-drawn wagons and some 1500 men built up around the choke-point. On 15 November, multiple RAF air strikes called in by the patrols worked over this lucrative target, and with no further effective reinforcement Tirana fell to the partisans on 17 November.

Despite misfortune, frustration and conflicts of interest with the partisans, Operation Lochmaben had achieved its objective, denying the Germans an orderly withdrawal and causing them considerable casualties without a single loss to 'Kenforce'.

With the bulk of the German forces clear of Albania, the tired patrols were airlifted out of the newly cleared airstrip at Tirana for redeployment

Bottom right: Men of the LRDG wait to embark on MFV *La Palma* as the last items of equipment are stowed aboard. The tarpaulin in the bow covers a jeep, the standard vehicle of LRDG raiding missions in the Balkan area. The vessel is being prepared in June 1944 for her maiden voyage, the journey from Rodi Garganico harbour on the eastern Italian coast to the Yugoslavian island of Vis. Bottom left: Leaders of the partisan forces in Albania gather at Tirana to celebrate victory over the German garrison in December 1944.

elsewhere. From the Balkans the LRDG's operations would take them to the Dalmatian Islands, Istria, and finally to Greece.

Operation Lochmaben, the last major LRDG parachute operation of the war, demonstrated what a handful of highly trained specialists could achieve with good communications, effective air support and liaison with indigenous forces. Although the unit insignia, the 'scorpion within a wheel', does not survive in any Commonwealth forces of today, it remains a potent symbol of what may be achieved by a special force of dedicated professional soldiers.

THE AUTHOR David List is an historian with a special interest in the Long Range Desert Group. He and the publishers would like to thank Major-General David Lloyd Owen and the LRDG Association for their assistance in the preparation of this article.

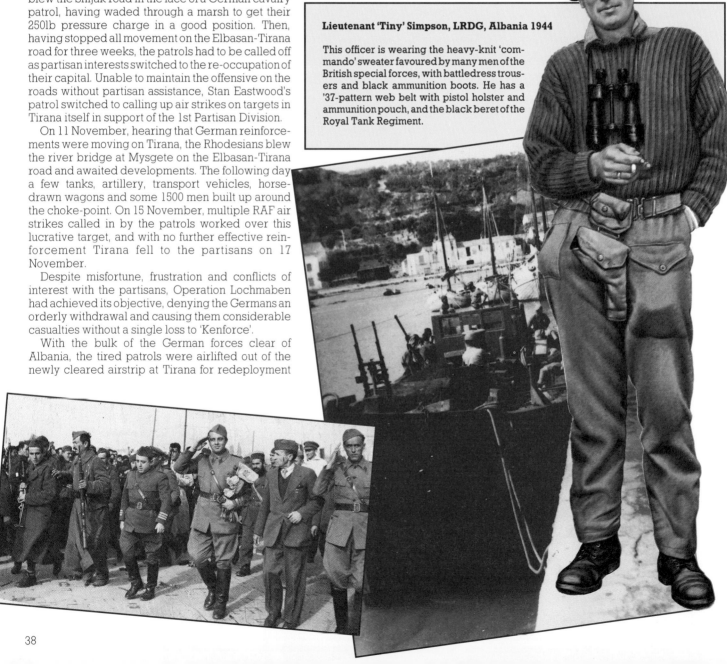

Lieutenant 'Tiny' Simpson, LRDG, Albania 1944

This officer is wearing the heavy-knit 'commando' sweater favoured by many men of the British special forces, with battledress trousers and black ammunition boots. He has a '37-pattern web belt with pistol holster and ammunition pouch, and the black beret of the Royal Tank Regiment.

SAS

BIRTH OF A LEGEND

Left: Lieutenant Edward McDonald, with Corporal Bill Kennedy manning the twin-barrelled Vickers K, leads an SAS jeep patrol into the desert. Below: David Stirling, founder and guiding light of the wartime SAS and (bottom) three members of his original 'L' Detachment – left to right: Jeff Duvivier, 'Gentleman Jim' Almonds and Bob Tait, all participants in many of the early desert operations.

In late 1940 a commando brigade, known as Layforce, was dispatched to North Africa to carry out raids against the Italian Army. By mid-1941, however, Layforce had been severely mauled and was earmarked for disbandment. At this stage, David Stirling, a Scots Guards subaltern in No.8 Commando, received permission to recruit a small force for raids deep behind enemy lines.

Some 65 men, drawn from Layforce and known as 'L' Detachment, assembled at Kabrit on the Suez Canal for para training. The first jump, on 16 November, was a total disaster with the detachment losing nearly 70 per cent of its strength.

Stirling immediately abandoned the para concept and opted to use the Long Range Desert Group to get his men to and from their targets. Success was almost immediate and Stirling, by this time a major, was allowed to expand his force. New recruits flocked in: 50 French paras, later known as the French Squadron SAS; men from the Special Boat Squadron (SBS); in March, the Greek Sacred Squadron; in June, the Special Interrogation Group of anti-Nazi Germans; and in August, more SBS men. Stirling's force had grown to regimental size and was renamed 1 SAS. Total strength was around 750 men.

The successes of 1 SAS did not go unnoticed and David Stirling's brother, William, was allowed to form 2 SAS from men of 62 Commando, but the new regiment was only officially inaugurated in May 1943.

In early 1943 David Stirling was captured in Tunisia and command of 1 SAS passed to Paddy Mayne who led the regiment until the end of the desert campaign in May.

David Stirling formed the Special Air Service (SAS) in difficult circumstances, but his force proved itself in the cauldron of the desert

DAVID STIRLING, creator of the SAS, has always insisted on two things. First, that the SAS was created essentially to carry out strategic tasks, second, that the nature of these tasks demanded men of exceptional character, skills and training. At the time when Stirling developed and put over his ideas to General Sir Claude Auchinleck, the Commander-in-Chief, Middle East, in July 1941, the strategic circumstances in the desert war were peculiarly favourable to the adoption of such ideas. Rommel's forces were stretched out across Cyrenaica to the Egyptian frontier; Auchinleck was planning and preparing for his Crusader offensive, timed for November; and Germany had more or less turned away from the Mediterranean and was concentrating on the Drang nach Osten (Eastward Expansion) to destroy the Soviet Union. Any idea offering offensive action, which had the great virtues of originality and daring, which promised much and asked for little, was bound to be welcome. Stirling's proposals were eagerly accepted.

The operations which he proposed were quite different from those which any other units undertook. In the first place, they were to be raids behind enemy lines in order to attack vulnerable targets like airfields, military headquarters and supply lines. What is more, they were to be carried out by very small groups of men. Stirling argued that 100 men, divided into groups of four or five, could attack 20 targets simultaneously and with far more chance of achieving surprise by their very size. Further, such a group, infiltrating by air or sea or land, could, with the proper explosives, do a great deal of damage to the enemy, escape detection – and return to do it all again. The nature of the desert war was such that unprotected targets well behind enemy lines were in profusion. Rommel's immensely long lines of communication and scattered airfields would be especially vulnerable to this form of attack.

However, Stirling's strategic vision did not end there. Picturing occupied Europe as it was, he recognised the potential worth of mounting offensive operations from clandestine bases in enemy territory both by his own men and by local guerrillas, raised, trained, armed and directed by the new force. It was, therefore, clear why Stirling insisted from the outset on the highest possible standards of selection, training, versatility and discipline for the men of his Special Air Service.

Closely allied to these ideas as to how the SAS should be used was Stirling's notion of how opera-

Below: David Stirling (standing) photographed with members of a jeep-borne raiding party, shortly before his capture in Tunisia. Stirling's unorthodox and highly flexible approach to the war in the desert achieved many spectacular successes and, with only a handful of men, he was able to inflict massive damage on the Axis war effort in North Africa. Central to the SAS 'style' from July 1942 was the four-wheel-drive, heavily armed jeep, and on many an occasion raiding parties would blast their way in and out with all guns blazing. Firepower was crucial and the jeeps were fitted with ex-RAF Vickers K and Browning machine guns. Stirling's desert warriors were highly individualistic men, selected for their initiative, imagination and élan, combined with a tough and professional approach to soldiering.

tions should be planned and directed. He was determined to outflank the stifling bureaucracy of staff officers, and made it plain that he should be responsible directly to the Commander-in-Chief himself. Fortunately, Auchinleck shared this view, with the result that Stirling was placed in charge of all training and operational planning. Having got his broad ideas approved, Stirling then proposed some specific operations – raids on the Axis airfields at Tmimi and Gazala – designed and timed to support Auchinleck's forthcoming offensive, code-named Crusader. As a result of his proposals he was authorised to raise his new unit, train it, and continue to plan for the raids. In this way the SAS was born in July 1941.

To start with, Stirling's force was quite small, and was named quite by chance. It so happened that at this time Brigadier Dudley Clarke, on the staff of HQ Middle East, was attempting to deceive the enemy as to the exact British order of battle and wanted to convince enemy intelligence that the British possessed a complete airborne brigade of parachute and glider troops. When he heard of Stirling's proposal to form a special unit, whose skills would include parachuting, he persuaded Stirling to call it 'L' Detachment, Special Air Service Brigade. To start with 'L' Detachment would have seven officers and

60 men, many of whom would be NCOs. Stirling recruited them largely from the Guards Commando, which had been part of a special force under Robert Laycock, and from the Scots Guards. Two of Stirling's initial officers, still renowned in the SAS, were Jock Lewis and Blair 'Paddy' Mayne.

By August 1941 Stirling had established his force at a camp at Kabrit, some 100 miles south of Cairo in the Canal Zone. Training then began in earnest and Stirling aimed to develop two qualities, which have endured to this day – the pursuit of excellence and the highest possible self-discipline. To achieve such standards demanded a combination of the right character and sheer physical fitness. One of Stirling's recruits, Fitzroy Maclean, recalled that:

'for days and nights on end, we trudged interminably over the alternating soft sand and jagged rocks of the desert, weighed down by heavy loads of explosive, eating and drinking only what we could carry with us. In the intervals we did weapon training, physical training and training in demolitions and navigation.'

In addition, everyone joining the SAS had to be a parachutist, and one of the more colourful instructors in this technique was Peter Warr, who, contrary to the actual need for quiet, assured competence,

A MAN OF VISION

David Stirling, DSO, MC, the creator of the SAS, was born in 1915, the son of Brigadier-General Archibald Stirling of Keir. After three years at Cambridge, he joined the Scots Guards in 1939, serving with the regiment for six months before joining No.8 (Guards) Commando in mid-1940. As part of Layforce, No. 8 Commando sailed for the Middle East in 1941 to carry out hit-and-run raids against Axis supply lines.

Because of the failure of Layforce's attempted attacks against enemy targets on the Cyrenaican coast, Stirling began to think of other means of mounting commando raids. In mid-1941 Stirling, with Lieutenant Jock Lewis of the Welsh Guards, began experimenting with parachutes at Mersa Matruh airfield. Following a parachute accident Stirling spent two months in hospital at Alexandria, and had time, as he put it, 'to evaluate the factors which would justify the creation of a special service unit to carry out the commando role'. After his discharge in July, Stirling presented his case to HQ Middle East Command and received permission to recruit 66 men from Layforce.

Despite a measure of official indifference and a disastrous first raid, Stirling's force, known as 'L' Detachment was gradually expanded over the following months. Many men fell under Stirling's spell. David Lloyd Owen of the Long Range Desert Group recalled his character: 'He had a power over men which I had never seen before. I was carried away by his enthusiasm, sheer determination, courage and endurance.'

Stirling was never a man to stand back from a fight and he took part in many of the SAS raids during the North African campaign. On one occasion, a raid on Bagush airfield in mid-1942, Stirling developed a new means of attacking enemy aircraft. After several bombs had failed to explode, Stirling ordered his men to drive their jeeps down the runway with their guns blazing. The attack was successful and the SAS continued to use jeeps throughout the war.

Stirling was still leading from the front at the close of the desert war, and in January 1943 he paid the price. Captured by the Germans, he subsequently made several unsuccessful escape attempts and ended the war in Colditz.

would dramatise the whole process into one of frenzied excitement.

As Stirling had decided that the SAS would operate in small four-man groups, it was necessary that the different team members, apart from all the general skills common to everyone in the SAS, should have a particular proficiency in either navigation, explosives, radio or weapons. And then the nature of operations, based often on extremely sensitive sources of intelligence, required absolute security. So insistent was Stirling on the highest standards that any man recruited who did not come up to them was instantly returned to the unit he had come from. He also demanded that the discipline, cleanliness, turnout and behaviour of his detachment was to be as high as that in the Brigade of Guards. He had no time for displays of ill-disciplined toughness by his men when they were on leave in Cairo. Toughness was to be kept for the enemy.

The whole idea of attacking enemy airfields and destroying aircraft on the ground depended on having the right sort of explosive device, and this was something that Jock Lewis invented: a small, light, incendiary bomb made of plastic, oil and thermite. To test the device before the SAS's first operation, they staged a dummy run at Heliopolis airfield. After marching 90 miles across desert by night and hiding up by day, they placed labels representing bombs on RAF aircraft. Despite all the RAF's scepticism and security precautions, 'L' Detachment proved that the thing could be done.

Alas, the actual raid on Tmimi and Gazala airfields on 16 November, just before Auchinleck's offensive, went badly wrong, but some invaluable lessons for the future emerged. David Stirling has himself explained that the night in question, with no moon and a strong wind, was totally unsuitable for a parachute operation. Desert sand and dust made navigation very difficult; one aircraft was forced down by German fighters, some men were killed on landing, and no-one got anywhere near their objectives. Only 18 men and four officers, out of the 64 taking part, reached the Long Range Desert Group (LRDG) rendezvous (RV). It had been, as Stirling later put it, a complete failure.

The trials of Kabrit. During the early days of parachute training, the SAS men were put through a gruelling programme to acclimatise them to the rough and tumble of their trade. Right and far right: Bob Bennet, one of the 'old hands' from 'L' Detachment, leaps from the scaffolding tower. This was a relatively gentle experience compared with a heavy landing on the backside from a truck moving at 30mph! (far right centre). Training progressed to jumping with kit from a static aircraft (far right) demonstrated here by Pat Riley whose operational SAS breast wings bear witness to his successful passage through the traumatic course. The regime at Kabrit was overseen by Army PTIs who gave no quarter in the business of battle training.

Yet, the historic meeting which took place a few days after the first raid, at dawn on 20 November 1941, between Stirling and David Lloyd Owen of the LRDG was to lead to some astonishing exploits and successes. Lloyd Owen proposed that his patrols should get the SAS parties as near their targets as they wanted to be, and then lie up at an agreed RV to pick them up again afterwards. Before long, Stirling had established 'L' Detachment at Gialo, a Saharan oasis well away from the main battle arena, where the SAS and the LRDG could work together and achieve great things.

The two groups, the experts in raiding and the experts in desert navigation, complemented each other perfectly. Before long, Stirling's SAS idea had been wholly vindicated. In early December an SAS group under Paddy Mayne destroyed 24 enemy aircraft at Tamet airfield, while Bill Fraser's party destroyed 37 at Agedabia. Two weeks or so later, a six-man group led by Paddy Mayne went back to Tamet and accounted for a further 27 aircraft. Daring, surprise, skill and determination were paying great dividends.

The way in which the SAS achieved these results was admirably summarised by Fitzroy Maclean, who explained that the best targets were aerodromes. A long way behind the front line, inadequately defended by a wire fence and a few patrols with machine-gun posts, it was relatively simple for the SAS groups, having studied the position, to slip through the defences to plant their incendiary charges on the aircraft. The time delay gave the attackers the opportunity to get away before the bombs exploded. They would then make their way to the LRDG RV.

KABRIT

After receiving permission to raise 'L' Detachment, David Stirling gathered his recruits and then set up a base camp at Kabrit on the Suez Canal. Arriving in July 1941, the men had until their first raid, scheduled for the following November, to learn the skills of their new trade. Bob Bennett, a member of Stirling's original team, later recalled the hectic routine:

'When we finally arrived at Kabrit it was totally deserted and one chap asked: "Where's the camp?" David Stirling immediately replied: "That's your first mission." When it was dark we went down to a New Zealand camp and stole the whole works including pianos, marquees and enough tents for everybody.

'Then the intensive training started. Training was taken care of by Lieutenant Jock Lewis of the Irish Guards – a very tough man who worked us into the ground. We did everything: physical exercises, canal crossings, night marches, map reading and

firing practice.

'After a while, we began our parachute course. We started with jumping from platforms 12ft from the ground but then someone had the bright idea of getting us to leap off trucks moving at 30mph. After three attempts, we were all battered and bruised, so that was stopped. Our first live jump from two British Bombay aircraft was cut short after two men were killed. That night we all went to bed with as many cigarettes as possible and smoked until morning. Next day, every man jumped; no-one backed out. It was then that I realised that I was with a great bunch of chaps.

'Just before we went on the first mission, we did a four-day route march across the desert from Kabrit to Heliopolis airfield.

'When we reached Heliopolis, we plastered the RAF aircraft with stickers – as a calling card. David Stirling had had a bet that the detachment could sneak into the airfield and then escape without being detected. Our success did much to prove his ideas.'

DESERT JUMP

After months of exhaustive parachute training at Kabrit, David Stirling's men made their first operational jump during the night of 16 November 1941. The objective of the mission was the destruction of enemy aircraft at five airfields between Tmimi and Gazala. Some 64 men in five parties were to land behind enemy lines, hit the targets and then rendezvous with the Long Range Desert Group (LRDG) for the return trip. Unfortunately, the night chosen for the jump was totally unsuitable: there was no moon and high winds whipped up dust clouds which made accurate navigation impossible. None of the parties landed within 10 miles of the pre-arranged drop zones.

One aircraft was forced down with engine trouble and, after being repaired, the pilot's request for directions was intercepted by the Germans who guided him to one of their own airfields. The other parties had mixed fortunes: at least two men were killed on landing, dragged to death by their parachutes, and those who survived suffered broken limbs or cuts and bruises. To make matters worse, only a handful of the supply canisters was found and these contained insufficient supplies to mount the raids. Reluctantly, Stirling was forced to call off the mission and head for the rendezvous with the LRDG. Only 22 men, four officers and 18 other ranks, made it to safety. Although the jump had been a disaster, the meeting with the LRDG was to have a profound effect on future SAS operations. In a convivial meeting with David Lloyd Owen of the LRDG it was suggested that the LRDG should transport the SAS to and from their targets. Although Stirling was a little sceptical at first, the seeds of an idea, that was to prove a dazzling success, were sown.

INSIGNIA

By early 1942 the future of the SAS seemed assured and, despite some official hostility, David Stirling set about devising a badge for the unit. The colours of the new insignia were dark and light blue, reflecting the Oxford and Cambridge rowing background of two SAS officers.

Originally, the cap badge was to be a flaming sword of Damocles with the motto 'Who Dares Wins', but a local tailor produced a design more reminiscent of a winged dagger. Parachute wings in white with two shades of blue, were also produced. Worn on the upper arm they were presented after seven jumps. Men who performed with particular gallantry were permitted to wear the wings on their left breast.

The cap badge was displayed on a bewildering variety of headwear. In the early days the men experimented with field caps, dress caps and kepis. At one stage, they took to wearing a white beret, but this provoked a number of fights in Cairo and it was hurriedly replaced by the beige beret! The SAS continued to wear the beige version until early 1944 when the SAS Brigade was attached to the British 1st Airborne Division and adopted the paras' maroon beret. However, many men continued to wear the 'unofficial' beige beret when in action. The four SAS regiments (numbered from one to four and which included two French regiments) also wore shoulder titles in pale blue and maroon. After D-day, the SAS was involved in operations behind enemy lines and, as Hitler had issued orders that any SAS man captured was to be executed, the men wore the beret of the Royal Tank Regiment to hide their true identity. However, the beige beret was still worn on more formal occasions.

Maclean later wrote of the overwhelming success of most raids:

'Working on these lines, David achieved a series of successes which surpassed the wildest expectations of those who had originally supported his venture. No sooner had the enemy become aware of his presence in one part of the desert than he was attacking them somewhere else. Never has the element of surprise, the key to success in all irregular warfare, been more brilliantly exploited. Soon the number of aircraft destroyed on the ground was well into three figures.'

But it was not only aircraft that were to receive the attention of the SAS. The battle for North Africa was always a battle for supplies, and Stirling was quick to see that Rommel's logistical services – ports, depots, railway lines, vehicle convoys – were equally important and equally vulnerable to surprise attack. Between January and May 1942, several raids were mounted to destroy shipping in the harbours of

Bouerat and Benghazi. They were more remarkable for the ease with which the SAS penetrated enemy-held ports than for the damage done, but a number of supply dumps and many vehicles were destroyed.

On one of his 'visits' to Benghazi, Stirling took with him both Fitzroy Maclean and Randolph Churchill, the Prime Minister's son. They spent two days there on a useful reconnaissance; with Maclean speaking fluent Italian, boldly demanding an interview with the guard commander when sentries became too interested in their activities. He later recorded that during such exploits, nobody paid any attention provided one's manner was right. Behaving naturally, avoiding any form of furtiveness, was better than any number of disguises or false documents.

Although the SAS teams were continuing to enjoy success, the Eighth Army was not doing so well and by June 1942 had withdrawn to the El Alamein line. It was then that Stirling decided to mount a series of raids early in July to destroy aircraft on five airfields close behind the German lines. For these raids, he would use his whole force, some 100 men, and having got hold of 20 trucks and 15 jeeps, he could take supplies and be able to keep going for some time without returning to base.

It was during a raid on Bagush airfield on the night of 7/8 July that Stirling, accompanied by Paddy Mayne, developed a new method after several bombs failed to explode, leaving some 20 aircraft undamaged. There and then, he led his men in three vehicles back onto the airfield to shoot up the

Above left: 'Spud' Taylor reloads a mag. Left : Into battle. Corporal John Henderson mans a Browning. Below left: En route to a raid. Right: Stirling snatches a well-earned kip.

remaining aircraft. Speed and surprise once more succeeded and later in July, having armed 18 of his new jeeps with Vickers machine guns, Stirling led another jeep-mounted raid on Sidi Haneish, near Fuka, destroying some 40 enemy aircraft.

Soon after this last raid there was a new name and a new style to be reckoned with in the desert war. Although the effect was extremely beneficial in terms of ultimate victory, initially it had a cramping effect on Stirling's own way of going about things. The name was Montgomery and, while Montgomery was preparing for what he called the 'last offensive', he was anxious further to deplete Rommel of the sinews of war by destroying harbour installations, shipping and supplies. As part of a larger plan, including a raid

Desert Raiders
SAS, 1941 - 1943

On 4 November 1942 Rommel's forces in North Africa began their retreat after the defeat inflicted on them by the British Eighth Army at El Alamein. As the Axis armies were pushed back by the Eighth Army to El Agheila, Bouerat, Tripoli and eventually to the Mareth line in southern Tunisia, their communications were harassed relentlessly by the raiders of the SAS.

MEDITERRANEAN SEA

Mareth line
Tripoli
Bouerat
Tamet
Sirte
GULF OF SIRTE
Nofilia
El Agheila
Agedabia
Benina
Benghazi
Berca
Barce
Slonta
Derna
Tmimi
Jebel Akhdar
Gazala
Tobruk
Bardia
Mersa Matruh
Fuka
Sidi Haneish
Bagush
El Alamein line
Alexandria
Cairo
Kabrit
Port Said

CYRENAICA

Gialo oasis
Gialo

Siwa Oasis
Qattara Depression
Great Sand Sea
Nile

L I B Y A   E G Y P T

Key
→ Allied Forces
✳ SAS raids
— Allied defensive line
— Axis defensive lines

on Tobruk, Stirling was required to attack Benghazi with a large party and many vehicles in order to destroy as much as possible.

'The whole plan,' he later recalled, 'sinned against every principle on which the SAS was founded.' Nevertheless he was persuaded to do it, with promises of an expansion of his command and a much freer hand in executing later operations. As events showed, not only was the concept at fault, but security had been appalling. The Benghazi garrison had been reinforced, and there were minefields and defences protecting the town. Even the date of Stirling's proposed attack seemed to be known in the bazaar. Small wonder that when, after an 800-mile journey across the Great Sand Sea to a point some 600 miles behind enemy lines, they eventually advanced towards the town, 'pandemonium broke loose'. Mines, wire, machine-guns, 20mm Bredas, mortars, snipers – everything opened up. All surprise was gone, and there was no alternative but to retire and

Right: Warhorse of the SAS, the raiding jeep. Below: SAS men relax in the mess tent at Kabrit. Bottom: Scruffy but professional, faces bear witness to months of hard campaigning.

STRIKE ON BERCA

On 15 March 1942 a 20-strong SAS party left Siwa, a large oasis in the southwestern corner of the Qattara Depression, and struck out for Benghazi. Transported by S (Rhodesian) Patrol of the Long Range Desert Group (LRDG), the SAS men, led by David Stirling and Paddy Mayne, were out to hit four Axis airfields at Berca, Benina, Barce and Slonta.

After travelling a distance of some 400 miles, the SAS party split into four teams and headed for their respective targets. Mayne's team, consisting of Bob Bennett, Johnny Byrne and Johnny Rose, marched to Berca, lying eight miles to the south of Benghazi. Bennett recalls:

'We hit the perimeter at about midnight and saw German sentries strolling along the road. As usual, we waited until they had walked by our position and then shot across the road into the trees on the other side. There, we split into two groups. I was with Paddy, and we went for the bombers lying under the cover of the trees. We just walked down the line of aircraft lobbing Lewis bombs onto their wings. When the job was finished, Paddy and I sped out of the place.

'When we halted for a break, the bombers started to go up – it must have been about two hours as we were using time pencils of that duration. The Germans didn't seem to know what had happened: they were firing into the air or out to sea. In fact, it took them a heck of a long time to get wise.

'After the raid we made our way to the RV (rendezvous) with the LRDG on the escarpment. We walked all day, and it was still light when we spotted an enemy road party to our left. Paddy told me to act like a native, and we managed to get away with it. Unfortunately, we got lost on the way back, but we ran into a Bedouin camp at the top of the escarpment and they looked after us.

'Our luck didn't end there. The LRDG was nearby, in another camp, and one of them came over looking for food. Paddy, Johnny Rose and myself managed to get back to base, but Johnny Byrne was captured. I found out that we had destroyed 15 aircraft at Berca.'

Below left: The legendary Paddy Mayne, successor to Stirling's command, whose leadership and daring earned him the undying respect of those who served with him.

Lieutenant, SAS, Western Desert, 1942

Lieutenant Edward McDonald is dressed in KD shorts, a KD bush jacket and Arab head gear – a *shemagh* held in place by a black woollen *agal*. The tie thongs attached to the hem of the *shemagh* enable the wearer to close the cloth over the face for protection during a desert sand storm. Arab sandals and leather gauntlets are worn, and armament consists of a hand gun and a Sykes-Fairbairn commando dagger.

seek cover in the Jebel Akhdar. In spite of their apparent failure, however, it transpired later that the operations had diverted large enemy ground and air forces from the front line, and therefore could be judged strategically valuable. But David Stirling's doubts had been fully justified.

After Montgomery's victory at El Alamein, the Eighth Army advanced somewhat ponderously towards Tripoli, and the SAS was given a number of tasks to accelerate the end in Africa. These missions included giving assistance to the Eighth Army in capturing Tripoli, reconnoitring the Mareth Line and harassing supply lines. Stirling himself went on an expedition to northern Tunisia, not only to make contact with the First Army, but, 'to bring in my brother Bill's 2nd SAS Regiment.' With 2 SAS, and by dividing his own regiment into two, Stirling could then maintain three regiments in all: 'one in each of the three main theatres, the eastern Mediterranean, the central Mediterranean-Italy area, and the future Second Front.' Thus he gave an indication of the breadth of his strategic vision and, although it was not left to him to organise this deployment, for David Stirling was captured in Tunisia during this patrol, his ideas were put into practice. After his capture, Paddy Mayne and George Jellicoe between them ensured that there was plenty of SAS activity in the eastern and central Mediterranean, while during the battles for France and Germany, the SAS were more active and more numerous than ever before.

Rommel's railway line bringing up petrol and ammunition was cut time and time again

What had David Stirling's idea amounted to during the 18 months that he had directed SAS operations, from July 1941 until January 1943 when he was captured? We may perhaps turn to the evidence of two men who were closely connected with it all. The SAS doctor, Pleydell, pointed out that for those who were fond of statistics the figure of some 400 aircraft destroyed on the ground could not be ignored; that during the crucial autumn of 1942, before the decisive battle of El Alamein, Rommel's railway line bringing up petrol and ammunition was cut time and time again; that nearly 50 attacks were made on German key positions; that they caused the diversion of air and ground forces from the main battle.

As Montgomery put it: the SAS was worth a division to him on the southern flank. The second man is Sandy Scratchley, who had been so active in the desert and who early in 1944 wrote a letter about previous SAS operations in order to help those trying to decide how to employ them in the Second Front. Scratchley, in pointing out that they had to be used strategically, working in small parties, sabotaging communications and generally disrupting the enemy's transport, supplies and aircraft, showed what huge dividends their desert activities had yielded – in the enemy guarding of airfields alone, to say nothing of the 300 or 400 aircraft destroyed, and the endless time wasted by enemy aircraft searching for SAS parties. Happily his advice was heeded, and the SAS in Italy, France and Germany made a huge contribution to the final victory in World War II.

THE AUTHOR Major-General John Strawson served with the 4th Hussars during World War II and was Chief of Staff, United Kingdom Land Forces before retiring. He has written several books including *A History of the Special Air Service Regiment*.

BOB BENNETT, BEM, MM

An original member of 'L' Detachment, Bob Bennett was with 1 SAS for most of World War II. At the outbreak of the conflict, he was in the Brigade of Guards, but soon joined No. 8 Commando. In mid-1941 Bennett transferred to the SAS and fought throughout the desert campaign. During the latter stages of the war he served in Italy, northwest Germany, and Norway. After the SAS was disbanded in 1945, he joined the Allied Screening

Commission and was a military advisor to the Greeks during the Greek Civil War until 1949. After a spell in civvies and a time with the Royal Artillery, he began training men of K Squadron, earmarked for the Korean War. In January 1951 he was sent to Malaya where he served with B Squadron, Malayan Scouts (SAS) until 1953.

Returning to the UK he was put in charge of the tough selection programme for men wanting to join the SAS. Between 1955 and 1962, when he left the army, Bennett was the regimental sergeant-major of 21 SAS.

SAS

Moving into Sicily and Italy in 1943, SAS men showed that their skills in raiding and demolition were as sharp as ever

BY EARLY May 1943 Axis ambitions in North Africa lay in ruins, crushed between the mighty hammer blows of the British and US armies. As the long, weary lines of Italian and German prisoners marched into bitter captivity, Allied commanders planned their next move: the invasion of Sicily and Italy. Churchill's 'soft underbelly of Europe' seemed ripe for the taking.

The course of the war was also of intense interest to the men of 1 SAS as they lazed in the baking heat of the Middle East sun, at their base near Azib, in northern Palestine. Despite the triumphs of the last two years in the desert, their future seemed in doubt. David Stirling had been captured in Tunisia and was heading for Colditz, and it seemed that the SAS had enemies in high places. Even the redoubtable Major Paddy Mayne, Stirling's

ITALIAN ADVENTURES

Bren LMG

Calibre .303in
Length 115.6cm
Weight 10.2kg
Feed 30-round box magazine
System of operation gas
Rate of fire (cyclic) 500rpm
Muzzle velocity 744mps

fore sight assembly
flash hider
barrel

bipod

gas regulator
gas port

forward mounting pin (for tripod)

gas cylinder

carrying handle

energetic replacement, was missing, following a non-operational rumpus in Cairo.

Sergeant Bob Bennett, one of the original members of David Stirling's 'L' Detachment, later remembered the air of uncertainty in the SAS base:

'David Stirling was in the bag. Paddy Mayne wasn't with us and we heard that he was facing a court martial. On parade one day, we were told that, as the Desert War was over, our role was finished and that the SAS was going to be disbanded.

'Fortunately, the brasshats must have had second thoughts. We were given a new name, the Special Raiding Squadron (SRS), and a new role – more like commandos. They must have decided that Paddy was the only man capable of leading us and the whole thing (the court-martial charge) was dropped.'

With Mayne in command, the immediate future of the SRS was assured, and the 250 men gathered together in Northern Palestine began training for Operation Husky, the invasion of Sicily. Time was precious and the SRS buckled down to train for the coming beach assaults. Nothing was left to chance: the men had to be in tip-top condition, they had to learn to work as a single unit, and to be briefed exhaustively on their new objective.

A short time before the Allied invasion of the Italian mainland, as the SRS was undergoing ski training, the veil of secrecy surrounding the SRS's mission was lifted; the target was revealed as a six-gun battery on the southeast coast of Sicily, just south of Syracuse, on the Capo Murro di Porco. Unless the guns were spiked, the Allied invasion fleet could be blasted out of the water.

With the dawn of the invasion drawing closer, the SRS linked up with their landing ship, the *Ulster Monarch*, and sailed down to the Gulf of Aqaba to practise rock climbing and amphibious assaults. Although most men were trained commandos with a wealth of combat experience, Mayne imposed a strength-sapping daily routine: from dawn to dusk the men jumped from LCAs (Landing Craft, Assault) into the warm waters of the gulf and then stormed ashore to climb the precipitous cliffs beyond the beach.

At the end of the Aqaba exercises, the SRS returned to the shores of the Mediterranean. Shortly before the invasion, sche-

After North Africa and the capture of David Stirling, 1 SAS was renamed the Special Raiding Squadron (SRS) and command was handed over to Lieutenant-Colonel Paddy Mayne. After intensive training in amphibious assault techniques, the SRS spearheaded the Allied invasion of Italy. The toughest fight took place at Termoli in October 1943 when the SRS and a squadron from 2 SAS battled against the Germans holding the town. Left: Major Scratchley (front row, left) with men of 2 SAS after the battle.

magazine
piston post
magazine catch
trigger
return spring rod
change lever
trigger spring
sear
return spring
rear sight assembly
pistol grip
stock
rear mounting pin (for tripod)

INFANTRY SUPPORT

The Bren was undoubtedly the finest mass-produced light machine gun to see service during World War II, and became one of the favourite weapons of the SAS.

The gun's origins date back to the early 1930s when the British Army was looking to replace the out-dated Lewis gun. One of the weapons under scrutiny was the ZB26, a 7.92mm light machine gun developed by the Czech State Armament Works in Brno. After competitive trials lasting some two years, the ZB26 was accepted by the War Office with the proviso that its calibre was changed to take the standard British .303in rimmed round.

The production of the Bren began in 1937 at the Royal Small Arms Factory, Enfield and output quickly reached nearly 400 per month. The gun entered service in early August of the next year and was an instant success with the troops. The Mark 1 model of the Bren, a gas-operated weapon fitted with an easily replaceable barrel, was mechanically an extremely simple weapon.

The gun's only weakness was the 30-round curved magazine which was prone to stoppages. However, because of its simple design, the Bren was a remarkably durable weapon capable of taking a lot of punishment and rough handling.

Although the Bren underwent a series of modifications during the war, primarily to reduce its weight, the basic design remained unaltered. Later models stayed in service until the late 1950s.

Above: The Bren was one of the finest support weapons of the war.

duled for 10 July, the SRS embarked on the *Ulster Monarch* and sailed from Suez for Sicily. As the ship ploughed through the roughening sea, the men checked their weapons and gear. From the outset, the SAS had been allowed a wide degree of choice in their selection of personal weaponry and each man was equipped with his favourite smallarm. Bob Bennett was carrying an enemy machine pistol:

'I had a 9mm Schmeisser I'd picked up from a mined German armoured car in the desert. The British Tommy-guns were no use to us because of the weight of the ammo – you just couldn't carry enough. We carried all sorts of equipment. The grenade discharger cup which fitted onto our rifles was very effective.'

As the *Ulster Monarch* hoved into sight of the Sicilian coastline, the night air was rent by the wail of the ship's tannoy as the captain gave the order for the SRS to embark on the assault vessels. This manoeuvre, which had been so simple on the still waters around Aqaba, proved a nightmare. Bennett saw the first men trying to clamber into the bucking craft tethered to the side of the *Ulster Monarch:*

'The sea was roaring away and the ship was heaving from side to side. As each man tried to get into the landing craft, the boats would swing away from the ship, leaving a yawning gap. We eventually got into the craft and headed for the shore. It was about 0200 hours.

'On the way in, we saw a smashed glider and bodies bobbing up and down in the sea. We couldn't do anything about it, but the bosun returned and picked them up.'

The seven-man assault teams raced for the battery, silhouetted against the moonlight

After hitting the beaches, the assault teams threw themselves against the cliff and began to claw their way to the summit. They were surprised by the apparent lack of opposition. Most had been expecting a rough ride. Yet the beach was not mined; there was no sudden cutting burst of machine-gun fire; nor the ear-splitting explosion of grenades. All was quiet, except for the steady drone of Allied bombers returning to their bases, having given the coastal defences a good stonking.

Once on top of the cliff, the seven-man teams moved in on the battery, silhouetted against the moonlight. The Italian garrison, about 700 strong, was still underground and it was just a matter of winkling them out. Most were too shell-shocked to put up much of a fight; others were just too scared to stick their noses above ground. As the assault teams began rounding up prisoners, demolition squads went into action to spike the guns.

Heavy fighting continued throughout the night with the SRS attacking command posts, bunkers and barracks. The assaults, often carried out at bayonet point, were successful and the enemy positions were destroyed. As dawn broke on 10 July, the SRS men were able to see the scale of their success. For the loss of one man killed and six injured, they had put six heavy guns out of commission, killed around 100 Italians and captured some 2-300 more. Indeed, the 'bag' of prisoners became so unmanageable that Paddy Mayne ordered the Italians into a convenient field, stripped them of their belongings and told them to wait for the main invasion force.

Mayne had more urgent matters on his mind than the policing of a few hundred prisoners and, gather-

ing his scattered teams, he pushed on towards Syracuse, some five miles to the north of Capo Murro di Porco. The journey involved considerable fighting, but finally the SRS reached the town on the 12th. Relieved by the leading elements of the British 5th Division, the weary SRS teams re-embarked on the third afternoon onto *Ulster Monarch* for a much-needed rest.

Bob Bennett was one of the men enjoying this break and later remembered the sudden and unexpected call-to-arms:

'We were all pretty much knackered after the

march into Syracuse and everyone started relaxing. Some time in the afternoon it came over the blower that we were going to do another landing, but not to worry because the place had already been taken. We were just going in to secure the place, and we were told to take half our normal supply of ammunition. We all started to treat it as a day out, rather than an operation.'

The SRS were in for a nasty surprise. Their objective, Augusta, a town a few miles north of Syracuse, was held by elite troops from the Hermann Göring Panzer Division. Manning machine-gun nests and gun positions in the hills around the harbour, they were determined to prevent the SRS from leap-frogging further up the coast of Sicily.

As the *Ulster Monarch* steamed gracefully into the quiet waters of Augusta harbour, the SRS assault teams searched for their landing points. As the time for embarkation into the ship's six landing craft drew nearer, it seemed as if the town really was deserted and that the operation was going to be a picnic after all. Suddenly, a blistering barrage shattered the

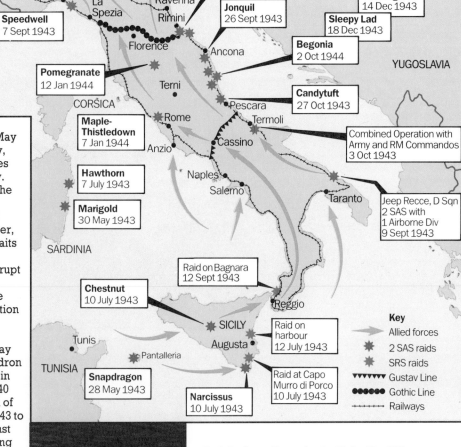

Italian Campaign
2 SAS and SRS, 1943 - 1944

Maple-Driftwood 7 Jan 1944
Boabab 27 Jan 1944
Saxifrage 14 Dec 1943
Jonquil 26 Sept 1943
Sleepy Lad 18 Dec 1943
Begonia 2 Oct 1944
Speedwell 7 Sept 1943
Pomegranate 12 Jan 1944
Candytuft 27 Oct 1943
Maple-Thistledown 7 Jan 1944
Combined Operation with Army and RM Commandos 3 Oct 1943
Hawthorn 7 July 1943
Marigold 30 May 1943
Jeep Recce, D Sqn 2 SAS with 1 Airborne Div 9 Sept 1943
Raid on Bagnara 12 Sept 1943
Chestnut 10 July 1943
Raid on harbour 12 July 1943
Snapdragon 28 May 1943
Raid at Capo Murro di Porco 10 July 1943
Narcissus 10 July 1943

ITALY · Milan · Turin · Venice · Genoa · La Spezia · Ravenna · Rimini · Florence · Ancona · Terni · Pescara · Termoli · Rome · Cassino · Anzio · Naples · Salerno · Taranto · Reggio · Augusta · Tunis · Pantelleria

FRANCE · CORSICA · SARDINIA · SICILY · TUNISIA · YUGOSLAVIA

Key
→ Allied forces
✳ 2 SAS raids
✳ SRS raids
▼▼▼ Gustav Line
●●● Gothic Line
++++ Railways

Following the Axis surrender in Tunisia in May 1943, the Allies turned their attention to Italy, and the US Seventh and British Eighth Armies landed on the south coast of Sicily on 10 July. The SRS and 2 SAS operated in advance of the main invasion forces, the SRS launching raids against the batteries at Capo Murro di Porco, the town of Augusta and, in September, Bagnara as the Eighth Army crossed the Straits of Messina to mainland Italy. Meanwhile, detachments of 2 SAS were deployed to disrupt enemy rear areas in Sicily in support of the invasion, while other groups operated in the north of Italy, harassing lines of communication to slow down German reinforcement of southern Italy.

On 3 October, as the Allies fought their way up the Italian peninsula, the SRS and a squadron of 2 SAS carried out a major assault landing in conjunction with No. 3 Commando and No. 40 Commando, RM, at Termoli in the vanguard of the Eighth Army advance. From October 1943 to January 1944, 2 SAS continued the war against enemy supply lines in central Italy. Deploying by parachute and landing craft, they launched raids against airfields, destroyed railway bridges, ambushed road columns and interdicted rail communications.

Far left, above: Preparing for Sicily. The SRS was sent to the Gulf of Aqaba to practise amphibious assaults and rock climbing. Far left, below: Loading weapons and ammunition. Left: The objective, a large Italian battery at Capo Murro di Porco, had to be destroyed before the main Allied landings could take place.

illusion – the town was occupied. Fortunately, the *Ulster Monarch* was so close to the shore that the shells, fired from guns sited in the hills around the harbour, whistled over the ship and plunged harmlessly into the sea.

Then, the assault boats struck out for the harbour. Bob Bennett was in one of the leading craft and later recalled the fury of the fire directed at the incoming vessels:

'Some British ships in the area started bombarding the defences around the harbour. By the time we reached dry land, we had suffered eight or nine casualties – the area was well-covered by machine guns. But we did manage to get into the town, despite the unexpected opposition.'

The fighting for the rubble-strewn streets and shell-blasted houses of Augusta was a messy affair in which sudden death lurked at every corner. Houses had to be cleared one at a time, and enemy snipers had to be rooted out from their camouflaged hides. Moving as sections or troop-sized detachments, the SRS used classic street-fighting tactics to secure the town. Bob Bennett's troop was involved in the house-to-house battle:

'You just went down both sides of the street with each group covering the buildings on the opposite side. Of course, you had the 'Back Charlie' of each section walking backwards to cover the rear. When we found an occupied building, grenades were the weapon. You just threw a few in and then smashed through the door, spraying the room with fire as you went. We killed quite a few this way, and there weren't many prisoners.'

By late evening, the SRS had cleared the town and its men were holding positions around Augusta in anticipation of an enemy counter-attack. The night was tense as men cradled their weapons, their ears strained for the slightest sound that might herald the expected assault. Yet by the early morning of the 13th, the 5th Division was on the outskirts of the town – the Germans had pulled back to the north.

After completing four major landings within the space of three months, the SRS was withdrawn from Italy. However, 2 SAS stayed on to wreak havoc behind enemy lines. Main picture: A fighting patrol from 3 Squadron, 2 SAS during Operation Tombola. Between March and April 1945 they caused 1000 enemy losses and destroyed the HQ of a German army corps. Below left: An SAS team in action with a 3in mortar. Below right: Two SAS men, festooned with belts of .303in ammunition for their Vickers machine gun, move up to engage the Germans near Castino.

The action at Augusta proved to be the last sea-borne landing by the SRS during the Sicilian campaign, and the men returned to Augusta for a spot of leave. Despite heavy resistance, Sicily had fallen to the Allies by 19 August and the focus of the campaign then switched to the Italian mainland, which was invaded in early September. On 3 September, the British Eighth Army crossed the Straits of Messina and landed near the town of Reggio. The Germans began a fighting withdrawal and the SRS was ordered to capture the port of Bagnara, a few miles to the north of the main British positions around Reggio.

For the Bagnara operation, the SRS had swapped the *Ulster Monarch's* landing craft for a much larger US landing ship. After sailing from Messina, the ship despatched the assault teams in landing craft onto the mainland at 0400 hours on 12 September. Bob Bennett later remembered the fierce resistance the SRS encountered when it got light:

'The two gangways crashed down and we went ashore. A party had already scoured the beach for mines – there weren't any. As soon as it got light everything opened up and we suffered quite a few casualties before getting into the town. I remember that as we reached the main street, the

Germans started shelling. They flattened the place – we lost two chaps straight away – and then we pulled back to try to outflank the German positions on the hills above the town.'

'We used the local vineyards as cover. You were taught to reserve your ammunition, and we never used a grenade, or fired, unless we knew there was going to be something on the other end of it. The Brens and Vickers were the best weapons out there and did quite a lot of damage to the enemy.'

Despite spirited attacks on the Germans, the SRS were unable to clear the hills around the town and had to beat off a series of counter-attacks over the next two days while guarding a key bridge, until relieved by more British troops. The SRS lost five men killed during the fight for Bagnara, but their determined resistance and holding of the bridge enabled the Eighth Army to advance deeper into the toe of Italy. Exhausted by their efforts, the SRS men were withdrawn to Sicily to rest and prepare for their next mission: the capture of Termoli on the Adriatic coast.

The Termoli operation took place in the early morning of 4 October and the SRS used the larger US landing craft for the assault. They landed north of Termoli, along with two Commandos, No. 3 and No. 40 Commando, RM, and fanned out through the town, setting about their assigned tasks. Bob Bennett's troop was to secure a bridge to stop any German attempts to blow it before the arrival of the British Eighth Army, advancing northwards from Foggia.

'Eventually we got to the bridge after meeting opposition en route. It was quite heavy and everyone was getting it. Spasmodic, and often heavy, fighting continued until the next day when the Germans retreated and pulled right out of Termoli town.'

Slowly but surely, the SRS detachments worked their way round the town, ending up in a monastery. The Germans appeared to have retreated but, in fact, had only pulled back to organise a counter-blast. The monastery came under heavy artillery fire as the enemy launched their first attack, and Sergeant Reg Seekings saw the effect of one shell:

'We were just dismounting when a shell landed in the centre of the truck. Some of the men were carrying grenades that exploded as well, making a terrible mess. I was blown clear of the truck with another man, but was smothered from head to foot with blood and flesh. They were all killed.

'I went to find Paddy Mayne to report what had happened. We stayed awake for the rest of the day and the following night getting drunk. We had lost 22 men in one go; they had been blown to pieces and their bodies were scattered all over the place.'

Despite the losses, the SRS raced to the perimeter and established positions along a railway embankment with men from the two Commandos, also involved in the operation. The fighting was bitter and prolonged, but the German assaults over the next three days were finally beaten back.

Termoli marked the end of the SRS's contribution to the Italian campaign. In just three months, Mayne's warriors had carried out four successful amphibious assaults behind enemy lines and fought with remarkable spirit against an often numerically superior foe holding strong defensive positions. However, while the SRS returned to the UK, 2 SAS continued the fight for Italy. Led by David Stirling's brother, William, 2 SAS were given a roving commission to cripple the enemy's supply lines. His men struck at vulnerable points behind the front line, destroying bridges, hitting airfields and co-ordinating the efforts of partisan groups. In many cases, small teams were inserted by parachute and then harried the Germans for several weeks before returning to Allied lines. Living in constant fear of betrayal, the men fought with the courage and tenacity that had carried the SAS through the North African campaign.

Although David Stirling was not on hand to witness these triumphs, the SRS and 2 SAS had lived up to the standard of excellence he had demanded in the desert. The SRS were now to turn their attention to a new theatre: the Allied invasion of France.

THE AUTHOR Ian Westwell would like to extend his grateful thanks to Bob Bennett and Reg Seekings, two of the original members of 'L' Detachment, for their extensive help in the production of this article.

SAS

OPERATION KIPLING

Dropping into occupied France, the SAS disrupted Nazi communication systems to spread havoc behind German lines in August 1944

IN EARLY AUGUST 1944, two months after the successful Allied lodgement in Normandy, General Patton's US Third Army was pushing eastwards from Le Mans towards Orleans and Fontainebleau. Well in the fore of the advancing Allied forces, a small section of C Squadron, 1 SAS, was tasked with Operation Kipling, a typical, dangerous behind-the-lines mission, perfectly suited to the fighting skills and operational flexibility of the SAS.

Kipling was the code name for an SAS parachute infiltration, some 150 miles behind German lines. The initial phase was carried out by six men of 1 SAS: Sergeant McDiarmid, Corporal Payne, Lance Corporals Hall and Myler, Trooper Weymouth and myself. For me, the operation began in the 'cage' at Fairford in Gloucestershire, a small, barbed-wire enclosed camp just outside the airfield. Since the early hours of D-day small groups of men had been 'disappearing' from the cage, to drop silently into occupied France. Some were never heard of again. Now, it was my turn.

I was to drop with my troop headquarters into an area to the west of Auxerre. My mission to reconnoitre the area in order to assess its suitability for the deployment of C Squadron, 1 SAS. If it looked good, they were to come in by glider and my job was to find a suitable landing ground and set up petrol and ammunition dumps at strategic jumping-off points.

As team leader, total responsibility for the planning and successful completion of the operation was now mine. First, there were large-scale maps of the vicinity to be studied, then an aerial reconnaissance of the area I had chosen would be carried out. The resulting aerial stereos (stereoscopic photographs) were examined in minute detail for signs of unexpected hazards, a final choice of base, and routes to the base from the dropping zone (DZ). It was essential that every detail and nuance of the immediate area be studied and committed to memory by each man in the party. None of us knew if the night would be dark or moonlit, fine or stormy, or where the Germans might be. I hoped to get more information on these crucial factors from a visit to Special Forces headquarters and SOE (Special Operations Executive) in London.

On the afternoon of 13 August I was told, 'The drop is tonight.' Up to that time I had expected to drop 'blind'. Now I learned that I was to be received by Major Bob Melot, our intelligence officer, who had

Below left: August 1944. Patton's Third Army fights its way east towards Fontainebleau. To aid the Allied offensive, SAS detachments were dropped behind German lines where they worked closely with the French maquis (left, a maquis Bren gunner) and executed many daring operations against the retreating Germans.

DERRICK HARRISON

Captain Derrick Harrison volunteered for the army on the day Germany marched into Poland. In 1940 he was commissioned into the Cheshire Regiment and served in England with the 4th Battalion. He then transferred and went to the Middle East with the 6th Battalion as part of the 44th (Home Counties) Division for the Alamein offensive and later became 2 IC, Mobile Troops, Base Camp, Geneifa on the Suez Canal. To escape this task he volunteered, unsuccessfully, for both the Sudan Defence Force and the British-officered Jebel Druze in Lebanon.

Eventually, hearing of 'a mysterious, secret unit', he walked into the SAS camp at Kabrit, was interviewed by the legendary Paddy Mayne, and was accepted. He took part in the SRS actions in Sicily and Italy, parachuted into France in August 1944 (Kipling and Houndsworth operations), operated in support of Corps Field Security, Holland, in the winter of 1944-45, and operated with the SAS ahead of the Canadian armour in Germany. He was awarded the Military Cross for his part in the Les Ormes action.

Above: The author (third from right, standing) with members of C Squadron in the 'cage' at Fairford before the launch of Operation Kipling.

been with A Squadron in the Morvan, and by the local maquis resistance groups. I also learned that my mission had been changed! I was to lie-up: it was to be reconnaissance only until I received a signal from London of the launching of a large airborne operation in the Paris-Orleans gap. My group was then to make the 100-mile dash to link up with the airborne forces and report with details of German troop strengths and dispositions. If necessary, I could send for more men.

There was no flying from Fairford that night, so we were driven to another airfield where a large black Stirling bomber sat waiting on the dispersal point. Shortly after 2200 hours the Stirling's engines awoke with a roar and the great plane lumbered across the field and into the night. We slept fitfully until wakened by the thump of German flak and the glare of searchlights. We were crossing the French coast. When next I woke, we were approaching our dropping zone. As we struggled to fasten our leg-bags, the RAF despatcher and flight engineer flung open the folding doors above the jumping hole. I moved to the edge of the hole and looked down at the moonlit French countryside moving slowly past. The other five men moved up close behind me. 'Red light on'... 'Go!' As the light flashed green I vanished into the night.

Chute open. Release leg-bag. It had jammed. As I tugged at it, the rope came free and, snaking wildly, wrapped itself round my hand. I felt a finger break.

As I landed, men from Maquis Chevrier moved forward to pick up my chute and lead me to where Bob Melot was waiting. A young French woman splinted my broken finger with my escape file while

SAS training emphasised the handling of foreign weapons (below, stripping down captured German smallarms). Below left: A typical SAS jeep, with its Vickers K twin-barrelled guns and armoured shield.

SAS IN EUROPE

In the four months following D-day in June 1944, some 2000 SAS men were deployed across the length and breadth of occupied France and the Low Countries. They operated, in uniform, from more than 40 secret bases up to 250 miles behind the German lines.

Their successes included 43 railway lines blown up, 17 trains derailed or disabled and 40 railway trucks destroyed. Bridges were blown, vital telephone lines cut and 118 military vehicles destroyed or captured. Enemy killed, wounded or taken prisoner by the SAS numbered nearly 1000. In addition, the capture of a further 3000 prisoners was negotiated.

Further successes included a synthetic oil refinery which was mortared and set alight twice, a goods yard and railway turntable destroyed, and a gasoline factory demolished. The SAS also armed and helped train between 2000 and 3000 maquisards.

On the intelligence side, 12 enemy airfields were reconnoitred, and Field Marshal Rommel's tactical headquarters was twice located and reported. Enemy troop movements and dispositions were reported. as well as targets for the RAF, leading to the destruction of 11 petrol trains, 12 ammunition dumps, one flying-bomb site, one German division on the move, two enemy airfields, one radio station, and one SS barracks.

Bottom: 23 August 1944. The author with his driver 'Curly' Hall (jeep on the left), half an hour before the Les Ormes action. Right, top to bottom: C Squadron in Courtenay after their meeting with the Americans; the house near Sommecaise where the author met the US Special Forces; the village of Les Ormes, just after the battle.

the rest of the men collected our equipment containers and loaded them onto a gasogene truck before leading the way to the maquis camp, deep in the Forêt de Merry Vaux. As we moved into the forest more men appeared and, with leafy branches, quickly erased our tracks. Commandant Chevrier had a well-organised maquis – drill, weapon training, Bren-gun outposts, and an ordered routine.

After breakfast and a chat about the local situation with Bob, I decided to send for more men. Accordingly, a signal was sent to London asking for Lieutenant Stewart Richardson and his section to be dropped the following night, with one jeep. We would use the same DZ as before.

At around midnight we rendezvoused with the maquis at the DZ and three piles of brushwood, with a small tin of petrol by each, were set out about 80yds apart, along the line of the wind. By each fire stood a maquisard, ready to dash the petrol on and drop a match at a given signal. Some 30yds at right angles to the last fire stood Bob Melot's sergeant, Duncan Ridler, ready to flash the recognition signal with his torch when the planes arrived.

The planes were expected at about 0200 and, as we waited, the cold and the tension increased. It was not unknown for a German plane, spotting fires prematurely lit, to swoop down and strafe a DZ. At that time we had to rely on the expected time of arrival, the expected direction of flight, the engine

sound and the plane's silhouette to distinguish friend from enemy.

Almost on time, the silhouette of a Halifax appeared over the trees. 'Fires.' On the shout, the piles of brushwood flared up. Ridler flashed 'F' with his torch and the plane began its run-in. Out of the Halifax came the jeep, suspended below four large chutes, then the containers and finally the men. There was a crash, and our precious jeep landed among the trees. When at last we retrieved it, it was twisted 20 degrees out of true. The second plane failed to arrive.

The following night there was another parachutage. We had chosen a new DZ some three or four miles away, just in case the Germans were on to us. We were expecting the rest of Stewart Richardson's men and two more jeeps. Shortly after 0230, the first Halifax started its run-in. Away went the first jeep from the open bomb-bay, straight into the trees! Then the containers, followed by the men. We were

still frantically collecting men and containers when the second Halifax arrived. Away went the jeep, not into the trees but straight into one of the fires. Happily the jeep's crating smothered the flames.

We were just congratulating ourselves when a cry went up from one of the maquis outposts that White Russians were coming. Used by the Germans in repressive measures against the French, tales of their brutality were legion. The maquisards had spotted a coach full of armed men winding its way towards the DZ. Quickly, we manoeuvred the one jeep fitted with machine-guns into ambush position and disposed ourselves in whatever cover we could find. As we prepared to open fire there came another cry, 'Don't shoot. Don't shoot. They're French.' They were indeed French, members of the FFI (French Forces of the Interior), the military arm of the Resistance. They, in turn, thought that they had run into a German ambush!

This confusion, however, was typical of the situation in the Kipling area. The very next day, Bob Melot brought me news that two American Special Forces officers had arrived in my area, advisers to the force we had nearly ambushed the night before. This force was now based in the nearby village of Sommecaise, and was about to start operations. They agreed to meet us to discuss our conflicting roles, in the

overgrown garden of a ruined house at the crossroads between Sommecaise and Les Ormes. We arrived first and, to protect ourselves, placed an armed jeep in ambush position. The Americans and the French commandant arrived on foot, having left their black Citroen under cover. Bob Melot and the Frenchman started at once to tangle in very fast French which I could not follow. The senior American interrupted, 'Seems we've got conflicting instructions. We're to start operations. You're to lie low. Why?' That was the crunch question, and one I was not prepared to answer. Happily the American accepted that they too should lie low until I gave the word.

Our difficulties were further exacerbated by the fact that on the previous day, Chevrier's camp had suddenly been flooded by some 300 deserting French gendarmes, who had taken to the maquis to avoid forced service in the Waffen SS. And they had come up in broad daylight. So, in the midst of our other problems we had to find ourselves a more secure base. And that night we had another para-

Operation Kipling
C Squadron, 1 SAS, August 1944

On 14 August 1944, as the US Third Army under General Patton pushed towards the Loire at Orleans, an advance party of C Squadron, 1 SAS, under Captain Derrick Harrison, landed by parachute near Auxerre, 150 miles behind German lines and commenced reconnaissance operations. As the Allies drew nearer, the SAS went on the offensive.

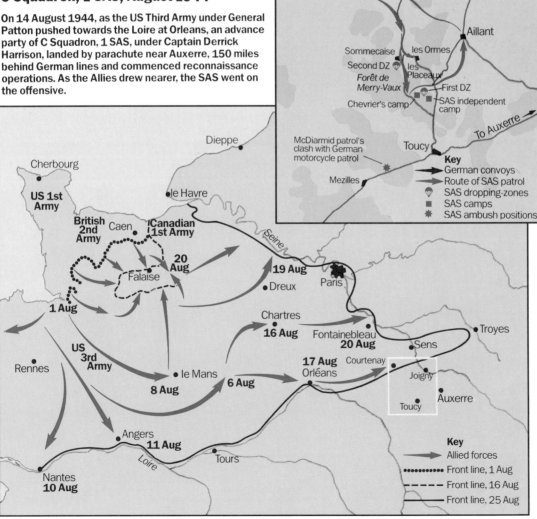

chutage – Captain David Barnaby and 10 men.

There were now 27 of us, and five armed jeeps. All I needed was the signal from London. It came the following afternoon, just five hectic days after the first drop. Each leader had his own code name and code pad. I was 'Sabu 66'. The code was supposed to be foolproof. Need I say more. One incorrect group that came in had two possible meanings and because of heavy static, we were unable to get a re-coding until the following morning. It then read 'Operation cancelled' – the Paris-Orleans gap airborne op was off.

We were now able to start operations on our own account. First blood went to McDiarmid's patrol which clashed with a German cycle patrol on the Mezilles-Toucy road. Eight prisoners were handed over to a nearby maquis group. Resistance intelligence was nothing if not enthusiastic, and armoured convoys could turn out to be horses and carts. One convoy, in fact, turned out to be a lone, middle-aged and footsore German. He fell asleep by one of our ambush positions and thought he had been captured by the maquis. His relief when he found we were British knew no bounds.

But it would be less than fair to blame the Resistance for inaccurate reporting. The situation was, by this time, very fluid and could change within a day or even a matter of hours. One such occasion was the ambush of the Courtenay-Sens road. We had received reports that there was very heavy German traffic using this route, 40 or 50 miles to the north. I decided to have a go at it and set out at first light with my own and Stewart Richardson's jeep, having checked the vehicles and cleaned the guns.

Our only hope was a surprise attack: drive through the village at speed and trust to our firepower

On discovering that the Germans were concentrating at Joigny, we skirted just south of the town and took to the woods. We had not yet managed to get our hands on any local Michelin maps and had to rely on the less detailed, and less accurate, British military maps, which is probably why we got lost. It was with some surprise that in the middle of the afternoon we found ourselves driving right across the road we had come to strafe.

We had been observing for perhaps half-an-hour, when two men in civilian clothes strolled by our ambush hide-out. Taking no chances, we grabbed the surprised men. It was now our turn to be surprised. The Americans, they said, were just down the road at Courtenay. If the men had not happened by, we had stood a very good chance of shooting up the American army. Instead we drove slowly, and very carefully, down the road and into General Patton's headquarters. From there, we were sent down to Combat B to tell my story to a US colonel who steadfastly refused to believe a word I said. But they did treat us very well, and when we left in the morning we were loaded up with K rations.

Despite this débâcle, our spirits quickly rose again when, a couple of hours later, we came across a man who had just arrived with the news that a German convoy of 50 trucks had passed through the

Left: An SAS jeep in France. On the left is Corporal Duffy who was captured in August, and then escaped from a hospital near Fontainebleau, dressed as a German medical officer. Top: Members of 1 SAS. Three of Harrison's Kipling team are shown: Lance-Corporal Myler (extreme right), Sergeant McDiarmid (second right) and Corporal Payne (second left).

next village, not half-an-hour before, headed for Joigny. In hot pursuit, we set off but to no avail. Yet another convoy had vanished. Or had it?

We returned to the Kipling area at about 1400. When I told Bob Melot about our bumping Patton's armour he could scarcely believe it. It was then that I noticed Richardson's jeep moving off. Apparently, in the dash to overtake the convoy, one of his gun-mountings had fractured and he was going over to Aillant to have it re-welded. 'Not by yourself, you're not,' I said, 'I'll go with you.' Together we moved out.

As we reached the road we saw an ominous pillar of smoke rising into the air over in the direction of Les Ormes. We headed towards it at speed. As we got nearer we could see that it was indeed Les Ormes that was burning. Arriving at the cross-roads, we saw a woman on a bicycle pedalling shakily towards us. 'Quick, messieurs. The Boches.' From behind her came the sound of firing.

In such situations plans are made at great speed, but they are, nonetheless, plans. It was clear that quick action was essential. Equally, the five of us were certainly outnumbered, but by how many? Was this our vanishing convoy of the morning?

Our only hope was a surprise attack: drive through the village at speed and trust to our firepower. The Union Jacks on our jeeps jerked into life as we accelerated into the village square. In the road stood a large German truck and two staff cars, blocking the way through. A crowd of SS men in front of the church dashed for cover as I opened up with my machine-guns, and as the vehicles burst into flames, I saw some of the Germans fall. But now I was in trouble. My jeep had come to a sudden halt, my Vickers K jammed and the Germans were firing back.

I yelled to my driver, 'Curly' Hall, to reverse. Getting no reply I glanced across. He had taken a burst of machine-gun fire and was slumped over the wheel. Now, distantly it seemed, I heard the other jeep's guns coming into action behind me. But my own predicament was demanding all my attention.

I had grabbed my carbine and was now standing in the middle of the road firing at everything that moved. Germans seemed to be firing from every

During the autumn of 1944, the SAS continued operations in northeast France. Here, on the main axis of the German retreat, the SAS came up against formidable opposition in areas crawling with enemy troops. In Operation Loyton (August/September), for example, teams from 2 SAS were constantly under attack and many captured SAS men were shot by the Gestapo. By the spring of 1945, the SAS were operating in Holland and northwest Germany. While squadrons from 1 and 2 SAS crossed the Rhine, pushing northeastwards towards Hamburg (Operation Archway), other SAS teams operated in conjunction with the Canadian Army advance in Holland. Below: Three jeeps on patrol in Holland. Note the heavy jeep coats issued to the SAS to combat the harsh and icy conditions encountered in northern Europe in the winter of 1944/45.

doorway. I felt my reactions speed up to an incredible level. It was almost as if I could see individual bullets coming towards me as I ducked and weaved to avoid them. And all the time I was shooting from the hip, and shooting accurately.

Suddenly, my right hand was warm, wet and slippery – blood. I had been hit. This posed another difficulty: how to change magazines. Somehow, in a fumbling manner, I managed. Then I heard Stewart Richardson shout a warning: 'To your left! The orchard.' I moved to the left and saw some 20 men moving through the small walled orchard towards me. Fire! Change mag. Fire! Slowly they fell back, leaving some of their number dead or wounded.

Now I saw that Fauchois, one of Richardson's crew, had dashed forward in an attempt to retrieve Hall's body. I yelled to him to get back, as the Germans concentrated their fire on him. Brearton, Richardson's driver, was now turning his jeep round, to bring the rear Vickers into action. As I sprinted for the jeep, a head appeared at a window in the house above. Without hesitation, Richardson raised his Colt 45 and dropped the German with one shot. With a scream of tyres and a final burst from the Vickers, we left.

Later that night, Stewart Richardson took a foot patrol into the village. We had, apparently, interrupted the execution of some 20 hostages, most of whom had made their escape in the confusion of our attack. The Germans had lost some 60 dead and wounded, one truck and two staff cars. We had lost one man killed, one wounded, and one jeep.

Today, in Les Ormes there stands at the corner of the square a white monument to Lance Corporal Jimmy Hall and a maquisard.

This was the end of Operation Kipling. Four days later I was leading a column of six armed jeeps into the mountains of the Morvan to continue the fight.

THE AUTHOR Captain Derrick Harrison served with the Special Air Service on operations in Europe 1943-45.

In April 1945 the French contingent of the SAS Brigade parachuted into Holland. Their mission was crucial – to disrupt German efforts to mount a line of defence in the face of the oncoming Allied armies

Below: A French para draws in his 'chute on a landing zone. The two French units that made up 3 and 4 SAS were experienced parachutists, ideally suited to the behind-the-lines strategic operations that were the hallmark of the SAS.

SAS

THE FRENCH CONNECTION

JACQUES PÂRIS DE BOLLARDIÈRE

Jacques Pâris de Bollardière was born on 16 December 1907 in Chateaubriand, France. After completing a course of studies at the Prytanée Militaire de la Flêche, he went on to St Cyr and the Centre d'Hautes Etudes Militaires. Bollardière then served with the French Foreign Legion in Algeria and Morocco. After fighting with distinction in the 13e Demi-Brigade de la Légion Etrangère (13 DBLE) at Narvik during the Norwegian campaign of 1940, Bollardière joined up with de Gaulle's Free French Forces in June 1940. With the 13e DBLE he served in Senegal, Gabon, Eritrea, Syria – where he was wounded – and Libya. In 1944 he came to the United Kingdom and then parachuted into France on 11 April and fought with the *Maquis* (French Resistance) in the Ardennes from June to September.

In April 1945, Bollardière was commander of the 3e Régiment des Chasseurs Parachutistes (3 SAS) and parachuted into Holland as part of Operation Amherst.

After World War II he served in Indochina and Algeria. It was in Algeria that Bollardière became a controversial figure through his outspoken criticism of the brutal methods used by the French during the Battle of Algiers.

He decided to leave the regular army in 1960, becoming involved in various projects for the redevelopment of Brittany. He also became an active member of the pacifist movement and president of the anti-nuclear group 'Les Francais contre la Bombe'.

Bollardière was highly decorated and was a Grand Officier de la Légion d'Honneur, Compagnon de la Libération and also a recipient of the DSO. He died on 22 February 1986.

THE FRENCH SAS

In 1945 the SAS Brigade consisted of 1 and 2 SAS (British and Commonwealth), 3 and 4 SAS (French), an Independent Belgian Squadron, and 'F' Squadron – a reconnaissance, intelligence and signals unit. The two French SAS units were designated by the French 2^e and 3^e Regiments des Chasseurs Parachutistes (2 and 3 RCP – 2nd and 3rd Chasseur Parachute Regiments). These two units trace their origins back to September 1940 when the 1ere Compagnie d'Infanterie de l'Air (1st Air Infantry Company) was formed. In April 1941 the unit was renamed the 1ere Compagnie Parachutiste (1st Parachute Company) and a large contingent was sent to the Middle East. Between 1941 and 1944 the French paras were expanded and redesignated on a number of occasions while operations were mounted in North Africa and the Mediterranean.

In January 1944 the SAS Brigade was formed in Ayrshire but was not committed to action until after D-day. From June 1944 the French SAS took part in a great many operations, parachuting in behind enemy lines in France to harass and disrupt German troop and supply movements, to organise and arm the French Resistance and to attack and cut rail links. One of their most successful early operations, launched on the night of 5/6 June, was Operation Dingson/Grog. Under the command of Major Bourgoin, 4 SAS (2 RCP) parachuted into Brittany and their operations resulted in 2000 enemy casualties and the arming and organising of 25,000 Resistance fighters.

The French SAS played a very considerable role in the liberation of France and the Low Countries and were to remain within the Brigade until 1 October 1945 when they returned to the French Army.

Henry Crerar of the First Canadian Army, offering the services of the 2e and 3e Régiments des Chasseurs Parachutistes, SAS, for the forthcoming drive into northeast Holland. At this stage in the war, the advancing Allied armies were spearheaded by massive aerial and artillery bombardments, designed to blast the German forces into submission and keep casualties among the Allied formations to a minimum. The Dutch, however, were far from happy about their country being turned into a formal battlefield or shattered by such a tactic.

A further problem was the terrain. The area east of the Zuider Zee, like much of the country, was crisscrossed with canals and waterways. Any Allied advance would be severely bogged down by a resolute German defence, structured around command of the many key bridges in the area. It would also cost a great many lives.

With Crerar's First Canadian Army poised in the Apeldoorn-Deventer area, an operation was planned that would overcome both these obstacles. Working in conjunction with Lieutenant General Guy G. Simonds of the 2nd Canadian Corps, Calvert arranged the details of a plan in which the French SAS would be dropped ahead of the advancing infantry, while his second-in-command, Colonel Guy Prendergast, organised the finer points of the fly-in. On 3 April the two French parachute units,

Left: Colonel Bourgoin (standing seventh from the right) pictured with his French SAS. Bourgoin's men achieved considerable success during operations behind German lines in the months after D-day. Far left below: Kitted out and ready to go, the French SAS pose for the camera before setting out on Operation Amherst. Left below: Major Puech-Samson, who commanded 4 SAS in Holland, receives the DSO from General Browning in 1944. Below: Operation Amherst gets under way – Lieutenant-Colonel Jacques Bollardière and his stick, on board the Stirling that took them to Holland.

ON THE NIGHT of 7/8 April 1945, the men of the two battalions of French SAS gathered for their final briefing from Brigadier Michael Calvert, commanding officer of the Special Air Service Brigade. The atmosphere on the airfield at Earls Colne in Essex was tense as the men received their final instructions. Morale was terrific, for they had been longing to get into action and now their time had come. They hated the Germans with the intensity that only the people of a conquered country can feel for the nation that has overwhelmed them, and Calvert remembered feeling almost sorry for the enemy troops who were going to meet these tough Frenchmen in the not too distant future. The briefing over, the SAS paras boarded the armada of 47 Stirling transports that stood ready and waiting out on the airfield and took off. Operation Amherst was under way.

From conception to jump-off, Amherst had been planned in record time. Only nine days before, after discussions in Brussels with Brigadier Calvert on his troops' readiness for a major operation, Major General Sir Francis W. De Guingand, Montgomery's Chief of Staff, had sent a signal to Lieutenant General

designated 3 SAS and 4 SAS, were ordered to move to the Mushroom Farm Transit Camp in Essex. There, the two French commanders Lieutenant-Colonel Jacques Pâris de Bollardière (3 SAS) and Major Puech-Samson (4 SAS) and their men were briefed on the objects of their mission by Brigadier Calvert:

'Your regiments will be dropped into the Groningen-Coevorden-Zwolle triangle, 48 hours ahead of the leading infantry on the ground. Your objectives will be fourfold: to create maximum confusion in the area and prevent the enemy from establishing defensive lines; to prevent the enemy destroying the bridges leading north in order to allow the Canadian forces to advance rapidly; to prevent the destruction of the aerodrome at Steenwijk; and to raise the local Resistance in the region. You will have to hold out for 72 hours of intense activity, which will be followed by a long leave. I am proud of the honour of commanding you and wish you the best of luck in accomplishing this mission.'

In conjunction with the French landings, Calvert had also arranged for his Belgian SAS, under the command of Major Edouard Blondeel, to move up to

Above: French SAS during operations in a forest in Holland.

Below: A column of German prisoners is led away.

Coevorden in their armoured jeeps on 6 April, to provide support for the French paras should the Canadians fail to relieve them within 72 hours of their landing. The stage was set.

The drop on the night of 7/8 April was far from easy. The 684 paras left the Stirlings at 1500ft in sticks of 15, dropping down through 10/10ths cloud towards the enemy below.

For the German troops stationed in the area, the

French SAS in Holland
8-16 April 1945

The forces of Montgomery's 21 Army Group were poised on the borders of Germany and Holland in April 1945 for the final offensive against the Nazi troops. The Canadian 1st Army, which included Polish troops, were faced with the difficult task of the liberation of Holland. They were up against tough opposition: the 3rd Fallschirmjäger Division was a highly experienced group of fighting men and the 34th SS Division was largely composed of Dutch Nazis, men who had everything to lose if the Allies won the war. Furthermore, the countryside which the Canadians had to cross was broken up by numerous canals and small rivers. It would be easy for the enemy forces to blow up the bridges across these and delay the advance of the Allied troops. To deny this advantage to the Axis forces, the men of the French SAS were assigned to support the Canadians. They would be parachuted behind the lines along the main routes of advance to seize the vital water-crossings.

Advance of 21 Army Group
8-18 April 1945

Key
Allied forces
Front line
7 April 1945

Key
SAS Parachute drops
Advance of Canadian First Army

Night drops

7/8 April 684 members of 3 and 4 SAS — the French squadrons — are dropped at night by RAF Stirlings into drop zones in central Holland, mainly along the road to Groningen. The German occupation forces are confused into thinking that a major airborne landing is underway, which enables the SAS troopers to regroup and to attack their objectives.

Drive to Winschoten

12 April Thirty armoured jeeps reach the French SAS at Coevorden. They provide an element of manoeuvrability which had been missed in the operations of the first four days. The French are reinforced by the activities of the Belgian SAS squadron which drives up the road to Groningen in advance of the Canadian troops.
13 April Winschoten falls to the SAS and the last German escape route out of Holland was closed.

In the vanguard

8 April The troops of the Canadian 1st Army begin their advance into central Holland on two axes.
11 April The valuable support provided by the French SAS enables the Canadians to advance as far as Emmen and Assen. Particularly important is the capture of two bridges over the Oranje canal.

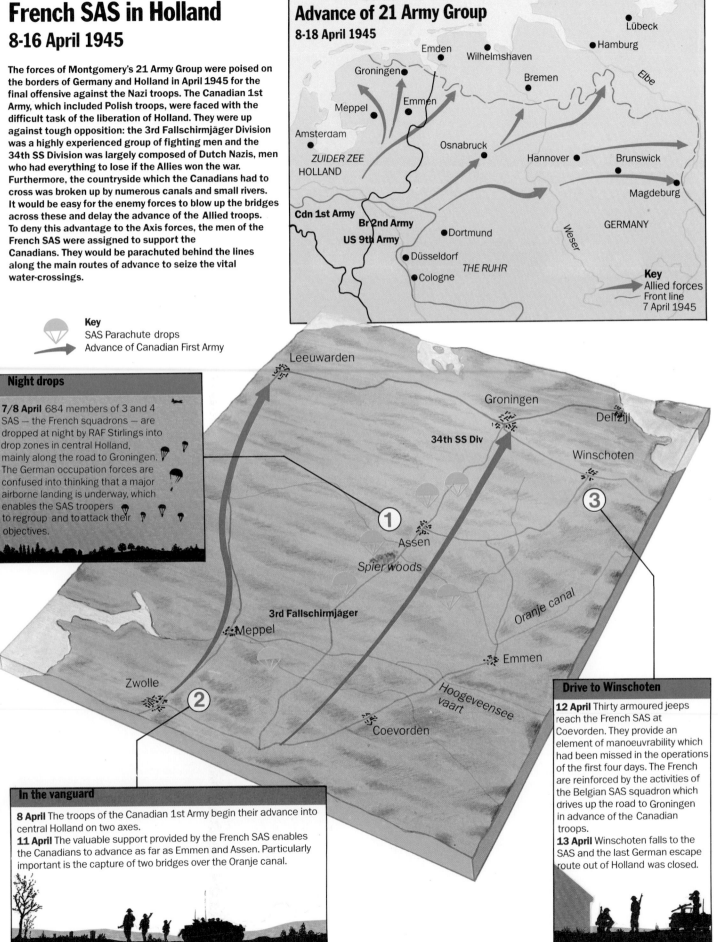

incursion came as a complete surprise. Reports of the landing of a large force of parachutists and of heavy fighting in all sectors poured in while the Germans tried to get a grip on the situation amid the reigning chaos. The Germans' perception of what was happening was further distorted by the dropping of 140 battle-simulators, immediately after the paras, that produced a convincing chorus of bangs and crashes, easily mistaken for the sound of mortar fire and the crackle of rifles and automatic weapons.

But while the Germans were confused, the French SAS also had their problems. In many cases, the 'G' radar-fix navigational system being used did not prove to be accurate and the sticks were dropped a good way from their intended dropping zone. It is to the great credit of the French stick leaders that they took this initial setback in their stride. Without exception, they either managed to locate their original objectives or moved forward to attack the nearest German garrison in the area.

Lieutenant-Colonel Bollardière came down in open country near the village of Spier, in the centre of the Amherst triangle of drop zones. Seeking cover, he moved into an area of woodland directly to the west of the village, where he assembled a force of more than 100 men from the various sticks that had dropped in the vicinity. Now that he was organised and ready for action, Bollardière decided to launch an attack against the defended village, which he regarded as a worthwhile and prestigious target for his men to take.

To support him in this assault, he contacted the Canadian HQ with a request for air support, but this was denied on the grounds that it was against policy to 'shoot up Dutch villages' unless absolutely necessary. Undeterred, Bollardière decided to press on with the attack plan but to delay it for 48 hours until the Canadian forces had got a bit nearer. In the interim, however, his paras were far from idle. Bollardière divided them into separate forces and they launched numerous attacks against German troop movements along the main road between Hoogeveen and Assen, and sabotaged a railway line.

On the night of 10/11 April Bollardière and about 40 of his men moved on Spier. In the ensuing fracas they expelled the company of German troops occupying the village, killing or wounding some 20 enemy soldiers, while only two of their number were wounded. But there was more to come. The Germans deployed a force of 200 paratroopers south from Assen to retake the village and a fierce battle broke out during the morning of the 11th. Lightly armed with Stens, carbines and with only one Bren gun at their disposal, the French SAS had a tough time beating back the German counter-attack. After an hour and a half, with the Germans only 40yds away from the French defensive positions, the situation had become critical. Suddenly, a force of Canadian armoured cars from the 8th Recce Regiment, 12th Canadian Hussars, arrived on the scene and the Germans were forced to retreat. Casualties in this second engagement were considerably heavier, the French losing seven men, including Bollardière's second-in-command Major Simon, and the

Right: A French SAS soldier, wearing the coveted red beret of the British airborne forces, prepares to move out to lay an ambush against German troop movements in the Amherst area of operations. Below and below left: The cutting edge of the SAS, the armoured jeep. These vehicles mounted a considerable weight of firepower and their speed and rugged construction were perfectly suited to small-unit raiding. Much to the annoyance of the French SAS, it was impossible to drop their jeeps with them and for most of the operation in Holland they were forced to operate on foot. Thirty jeeps, however, did get through. The Belgians, who supported the paras, used these vehicles to great effect, especially in the storming of the German positions at the village of Winschoten. Bottom left: Members of Lieutenant Legrand's stick. Third from the right is Sergeant Boutinot, one of the veterans of the fighting in North Africa.

Germans a further 40.

Elsewhere in the area of operations, the SAS sticks were chalking up further victories. In the southernmost area, around Meppel, some of the French paras made contact with two squadrons from the 18th Canadian Armored Car Regiment, 12th Manitoba Dragoons, and over the next few days mounted a number of road ambushes against German forces.

Major Puech-Samson, commanding 4 SAS, dropped in the Westerbork area to the north of Coevorden and regrouped his sticks. After a meeting with the local Dutch Resistance, Puech-Samson decided to deploy his men against the Police HQ for East Holland, situated in Westerbork. With the Resistance to guide him, Puech-Samson and his men attacked the building and fatally wounded the Chief of Police. His next action was to lay an ambush on a bridge over the Oranje Canal. The German garrison then evacuated Westerbork, but returned in strength when they had ascertained the size of the French force. Puech-Samson withdrew his men but held on to two bridges over the Oranje which would later prove useful to the infantry advance.

Throughout the Amherst area of operations, the SAS operated along similar lines – capturing villages and bridges, laying ambushes, and harassing the German forces as they tried to organise an effective defence. But, while they achieved some notable successes, they were hampered in their tasks by the lack of one vital ingredient to their operational style – their armoured jeeps. Without these vehicles, the SAS felt impotent, for the jeeps possessed the speed and weight of firepower ideally suited to their raiding tactics. When Amherst was planned it was intended that the jeeps should be dropped into Holland after the paras, but the RAF objected to dropping the vehicles at night onto landing zones shrouded in mist. Prendergast argued that, even if they lost 50 per cent of the vehicles, the SAS's job would still be made much easier, but the RAF refused to be swayed. Eventually, 30 jeeps did get through to the French, brought up to Coevorden by British drivers from the Brigade HQ, and delivered to the paras as the advance pressed northwards.

Under a barrage of shells from the Polish gunners, the Belgian SAS stormed the German positions

The area in the north between Assen and Groningen was the most problematic. The Dutch SS brigade was stationed in and around Groningen and, realising that they would be shot by the Dutch Resistance if they gave in before the arrival of the regular Allied armies, put up a fierce fight. A further problem was that the Canadian advance was held up by administrative delays and a last-minute change of deployment of the Canadian armour. The Canadians were part of the main Allied front line and had to work in conjunction with the rest of the front and, as luck would have it, their armour was called upon to advance eastwards in support of a similar thrust by other units to the south of them. This still left the Canadian infantry in position for the northward thrust but the French paras, whom Calvert had promised would be overrun within 72 hours, were now likely to have to hold out for a week or more.

Calvert decided to support them with the 400 Belgian SAS, and a daring bluff he had devised to turn the odds in his favour. Travelling in a large staff car flying a Union Jack, Calvert and a French-speaking officer named Potter Miller Mundy advanced in front

BATTLE HONOURS

During World War II the 2ᵉ Régiment de Chasseurs Parachutistes (2 RCP) – designated 4 SAS in the SAS Brigade – was awarded the Legion d'Honneur, the Croix de la Libération and the Croix de Guerre avec 7 palmes. These awards were made for their actions in North Africa in 1942 and 1943, in France and Belgium in 1944 and in Holland in 1945.

On 11 November 1944, at a ceremony in Paris, General de Gaulle, President of the Provisional Government of the French Republic, awarded 2 RCP the Croix de la Libération (below inset) and cited the following commendation for their courage and outstanding achievements: '2 RCP, under the command of Lieutenant-Colonel Bourgoin, is an elite formation with the singular honour of being the first French unit to fight again on the soil of the fatherland. They were parachuted into Brittany in June (1944) and then proceeded to regroup and organise over 10,000 members of the Resistance. With their aid, and in spite of heavy losses, they successfully attacked enemy formations and struck at the German telephone network, munitions depots and road communications. They also played a major part in the success of the Allied breakout from the Normandy bridgehead, and were in the vanguard of the liberation of Brittany.'

of the Belgian SAS with their jeeps to give the impression that the fighting was all over. As they arrived at a Dutch village, the local population would rush out to greet them and the Dutch Resistance would deal with any Germans who looked as though they might put up a fight. The French paras they met en route were extremely pleased to see them and the column soon arrived at Assen. There they encountered fairly stiff opposition, but the Polish battery of self-propelled guns that the SAS had managed to take with them proved invaluable in the battle.

Their toughest fight, however, came right at the end, when they had almost completed their relief task. Some 200 men from a German parachute battalion had dug themselves in around a crossroads at Winschoten, a village just outside Groningen. With Canadian air support and a barrage of shells from the Polish gunners, the Belgian SAS stormed the German positions with all guns blazing.

Apart from mopping-up operations, the whole region was now under French and Belgian control, and the road to Emden clear, with the Canadians following up rapidly. For several days after the Groningen engagement, the French SAS remained scattered all over northeast Holland, and at one stage Brigadier Calvert began to fear that the French casualties had been very high. But gradually the men trickled back into the re-forming area.

Of the original 684 paras who had jumped on the

night of 7/8 April and who were joined the following night by a further stick of 12 men, 31 were killed, 35 wounded and 15 were listed missing (later recovered). French estimates of enemy losses during the operation counted 260 killed, 220 wounded and 186 taken prisoner.

Operation Amherst had been a complete success. The Canadian and Polish forces had overrun the area with very little fighting and the minimum of damage to the Dutch civilians and their property. The French had fought magnificently and in their honour Brigadier Calvert managed to arrange, at a very high level, for them to be allowed to wear the British parachutists' red beret when they originally formed the nucleus of a new French Parachute division at Pau. This they wore with a great deal of pride during their actions abroad after the war. Lieutenant General Sir Richard Gale congratulated them on the swiftness of the operation and for carrying out what he considered to be the finest and most valuable airborne operation of the war.

THE AUTHOR Brigadier Michael Calvert commanded the SAS Brigade in Europe during World War II and was awarded both the French and Belgian Croix de Guerre avec palmes, the French Legion d'Honneur (Officier) and the Belgian Ordre de Leopold II (Commandante).

Above: Brigadier Calvert presents Bollardière with the SAS flag. Bottom: Victory in France – the SAS on parade in Paris.

The SAS spearheaded the Allied offensive into Germany in 1945

BY THE SPRING of 1945, Hitler's Third Reich was crumbling under the crushing onslaught of Allied armies advancing from both the east and west. France had been all but cleared, the Battle of the Bulge was over and only one final barrier stood between the Western Allies and the final push into the German homeland: the mighty river Rhine that flowed down Germany's western border from Switzerland to the North Sea. On the night of 23/24 March, the British and Americans launched waterborne assault teams across the Rhine. Advancing under the protection of a massive aerial and artillery bombardment, the landing forces clawed their way ashore and estab-

Below: Snapping at the heels of a demoralised enemy, the men of A Squadron, 1 SAS, prepare to thrust deeper into northwestern Germany in the final weeks of the war. Right: Taking a well-earned rest, SAS men pose for the camera. Their jeeps, mounting a potent combination of Vickers K and Browning machine guns, were capable of generating an awesome display of lethal firepower. Below right: Johnny Cooper (centre left) and Reg Seekings (centre right), two of the most experienced members of A Squadron, had been with the SAS since the Desert. Bottom right: Reg Seekings at ease.

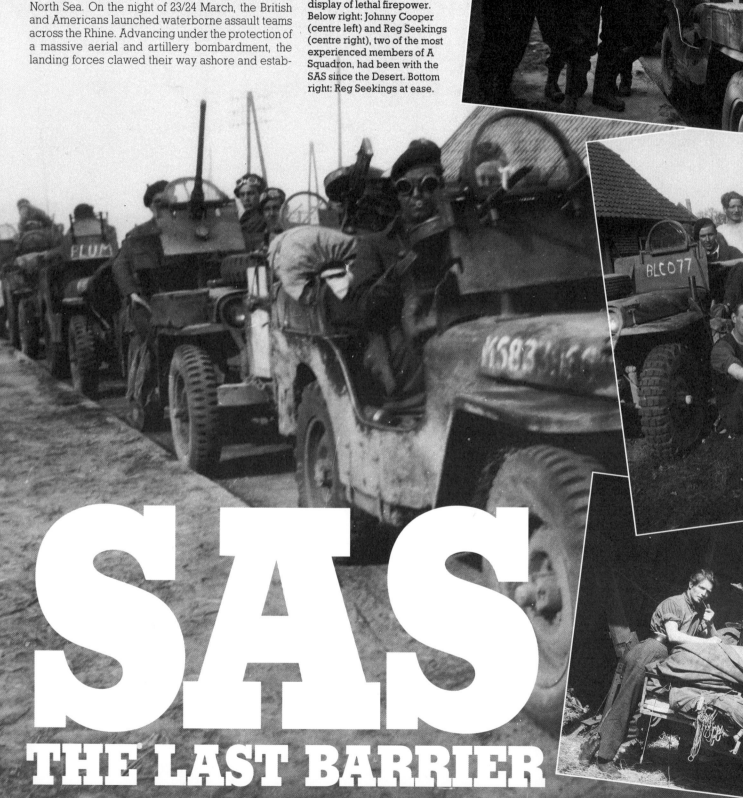

SAS
THE LAST BARRIER

lished the first bridgeheads on German soil. It was time for the SAS to launch their final offensive of World War II.

Sergeant-Major Bob Bennett was with D Squadron, 1 SAS, during the drive into northwestern Germany and later recalled their hectic dash to reach the crossing point opposite the town of Wesel:

'We crossed the Channel in a tank landing craft and docked at Ostend. From there we drove eastwards through Belgium, and then raced through southern Holland near the city of Venlo. We eventually reached the Rhine where we met up with the Buffaloes [amphibious assault craft] that were going to get us across the river on the 25th.

'In fact, the Rhine was no obstacle at all; XXX Corps had pretty nearly flattened everything on the other side. They had put up one of the biggest barrages of the war just before the main assaults. On the other side, the first people I saw were some US paras and our commandos. We were prevented from advancing for a time as the fighting was still going on, but we were let through when our mission was explained.'

After reaching Wesel, 1 SAS divided into its four component squadrons in preparation for the operation, code-named Archway. The mission was in two parts: first, the squadrons were to carry out reconnaissance duties for the Allied airborne divisions east of the Rhine, and secondly, they were to undertake long-range raids deep into Germany to identify pockets of resistance for Montgomery's 21st Army Group to neutralise, accept the surrender of enemy units, and disarm the local population.

Each SAS squadron was a self-contained unit, able to operate independently for weeks on end – hitting hard and moving fast. Bob Bennett later remembered the organisation of a squadron that was ideally suited to the campaign ahead:

'I should say that there were about 100 men in each squadron. D Squadron was made up of tough Irishmen, a good bunch of soldiers but a bit mad. A typical squadron had about 26 armoured jeeps, with three or four men to a jeep, and there were two troops with three sections per troop.'

The jeeps used by the SAS in Germany were the perfect means of carrying out these deep thrusts into enemy territory: rugged and reliable, they packed a fearsome punch. Bennett later recalled their weapons and customised design:

'The whole front of each jeep was covered in armoured plate, with semi-circles of bullet-proof glass to protect the driver and front-gunner. Some vehicles were also fitted with a wire-cutting device above the front bumper.

'Armament consisted of a twin Vickers for the front-gunner, another pair for the rear-gunner and every third or fourth jeep carried one 0.5in Browning heavy machine gun. The driver had a Bren gun. We'd first used the Vickers in the desert, and they fired 500 rounds a minute, which was pretty demoralising to the men on the receiving end. Each gun had a 100-round magazine filled with a mixture of tracer, armour-piercing, incendiary and ball. It was a lethal weapon. Each crew also had a 2in mortar, grenades and plenty of ammunition for their sidearms.

'With 50 gallons of fuel, each jeep had a range of around 500 miles. There was a petrol tank under the passenger seat and two others in the back, which made it a bit cramped for the rear-gunner. They made it difficult for him to bring his gun to bear on a target.'

Advancing towards Hanover, D Squadron quickly settled into a routine: moving by day, sorting out any opposition, and resting up by night. It was a gruelling and often dangerous regime, with the squadron operating anything up to 70 miles in advance of the Allied armies. Bob Bennett later recalled the procedure for a night stop:

'At night we'd put up in farms, hide the jeeps and sleep in the barn. We always looked for places out in the open to give a clear view of the area and prevent the enemy from mounting a surprise attack. Usually, there would be three or four sentries on guard all night.

'The jeeps always came first. Whenever we halted for the night, each crew checked the tyres, gave the engine the once over and sorted out any faults. Everyone was mechanically minded and many men had been with jeeps since the desert days.

'After a few days our rations ran out, so we had to live off the land. We always kept a look out for large country houses. Once inside, we headed for the kitchen as there were usually great big hams hanging over the fireplace. But this was only in a few places, and most Germans were short of food.'

'We halted, gathered in a bunch, and as predicted the whole hillside opened up with enemy fire'

Although there was a lack of opposition in some areas, other squadrons were called on to deal with enemy units holding carefully sited ambush positions. Reg Seekings and A Squadron had to clear out one particularly troublesome pocket of resistance that was holding up an armoured unit:

'The target was a railway embankment. Our tanks had been repulsed by 88s and they had called in Typhoons. I was asked to advance under their cover across a plain devoid of cover and draw the enemy's fire.

'We didn't get any response from the enemy so the Typhoon leader asked if I would stop in the middle of the open as a target. He promised that the Germans would only fire one salvo before he dealt with them.

'We halted, gathered in a bunch, and as predicted the whole hillside opened up with enemy fire. The first shot went over our heads. I heard shouts of "Tally ho" over the radio, and the Typhoons fired their rockets, completely obliterating the guns.

'We then carried on and a farmhouse went up in flames. We came across heavy resistance from units of the Volksturm, but we inflicted heavy casualties on them. However, I had my jeep knocked out and broke off to get my crew some medical aid. We captured the embankment.'

Despite meeting the odd pocket of resistance, the men of D Squadron kept up the momentum of their advance and reached Hanover in the second week of April. For the first time Bob Bennett saw the scale of destruction wrought by the Allied bomber offensive on German cities:

'We went through Hanover and it really shook me up. I don't think there was a building left standing after the bombers had been over. By this stage, we could tell that the German army was totally demoralised and falling apart. The only pockets of resistance we met were from fanatical SS.

'They were very good with their 88s. Several times we had a smoke shell exploding directly

THE LAST CAMPAIGN

During the final months of World War II the SAS were closely involved in the Allied drive into northern Europe. Although part of 2 SAS fought in Italy, the bulk of the brigade saw service in Holland, Germany and Norway.

Working independently or with armoured units, individual squadrons were used to protect the flanks of friendly units, to prevent the enemy from organising solid defences, and to drive wedges through pockets of resistance. Missions could last up to a couple of months.

Between early April and May 1945, the Belgian SAS were involved in Operation Larkswood, a fighting reconnaissance in northeast Holland to protect the left flank of an armoured thrust. During the same period, 2 SAS took part in a mission, code-named Keystone, to disrupt enemy forces opposing the Allied advance north from Arnhem. The third operation of this period, Amherst, took the French SAS to the northeastern corner of Holland where they helped regular troops to seal off the enemy's rearguard.

Once the Allies had crossed the Rhine, the SAS were embroiled in the headlong pursuit of the shattered enemy. During Operation Howard, Paddy Mayne's 1 SAS spearheaded the advance of the 4th Canadian Armoured Division into Wilhelmshaven. The final SAS mission in northwestern Germany, known as Archway, involved a deep thrust up to the Baltic coast and the port of Kiel.

The entry into Kiel marked the end of the war with Germany, but the SAS had one last task to perform: the occupation of Norway. Arriving in mid-May, the SAS were involved in gathering up Nazi sympathisers and helping to repatriate German troops. The operation, code-named Apostle, ended in late August and the SAS then returned to England, their wartime career over.

Officer, 1 SAS, Germany 1945

This officer wears the paratrooper's red beret with the SAS badge and a 'Denison' smock. Other items of clothing include despatch rider's breeches and motorcycle boots. The 1937-pattern webbing pouches hold a compass and ammunition for the revolver.

Above: The Willys jeeps used by the SAS in Europe were fitted with armoured plate and bullet-proof glass to protect the driver and front-gunner. Armament usually consisted of a combination of Vickers K, often mounted in pairs, and Browning machine guns. Extra fuel tanks gave the jeeps a range of over 500 miles.

Above right: Pushing far ahead of the main Allied units, the SAS were ordered to arrest high-ranking Nazis before they could flee the country. Here, two suspects are on their way to the rear for interrogation. Right: During their mopping-up operations, A Squadron worked with Captain Hunter of the Field Security Police (left). An ex-hunter from Kenya, his task was to check detainees' stories.

guns harmless or confiscate them. At one point, I had 12 shotguns. We also found hundreds of a new type of anti-tank weapon, the Panzerfaust.

'There were very few men in the villages, mostly women and kids. On one occasion, we were told that the SS were holding a village. We did a dawn attack but the place was deserted except for very hungry women and children. As tough as D Squadron were, they were soon getting rations off the jeeps and giving them to the villagers.

'Occasionally, we'd run into groups of German soldiers who were just waiting to be taken prisoner. One day, Lofty Collier and myself walked into a big restaurant to get a drink. The bar was at the other end of the room. The place was full of German officers sitting around the tables with their wives. As we walked in, they pulled out their pistols and put them on the tables. We walked down to the far end, expecting to be shot in the back at any moment, but nothing happened. We finished our drink and strolled out of the building. They must have been waiting to be taken prisoner.'

Although the SAS were in contact with the Allied armies during the race to Lubeck, they operated with almost complete freedom. Once they had started the headlong rush to the Baltic, there was little point in issuing orders or holding briefings. However, Lieutenant-Colonel Paddy Mayne was co-ordinating the squadrons in the field and would dash from unit to unit giving advice, assessing progress, getting involved in the action and joining in any festivities that were taking place. Bob Bennett remembers one binge in particular:

'We got word that Colonel Paddy was planning to visit D Squadron and our commander, Major Tompkins, suggested that we should lay on a bit of a celebration. We went into a village to look for some drink. I went into a house to see what I could find. There wasn't much about except for several bottles of coloured liqueurs and some wood alcohol. We got a great big bath tub and filled it up with all the spirits. The drink was terrible stuff, but we had a good old time and everyone got very merry.'

After dealing with the enemy near Lubeck, 1 SAS struck out for the port of Kiel

On the way to Lubeck, D Squadron picked up members of T Force, a unit of top scientists whose job was to beat the Russians to the Baltic ports and gather as much information as possible on German weapons and military hardware. Racing against time, the SAS ranged far ahead of the advancing Allied armies, moving deeper into enemy territory. Although the war was all but over, the Germans were still killing prisoners. Bob Bennett later recalled one particular incident near the Baltic coast:

'A senior German naval officer came up to me, and started gibbering away. I sent for Sergeant Ridler who could speak German, and we all went into this office. I sat down and watched, but didn't have a clue about what was being said.

'Later, I discovered that the officer was complaining about some prisoners who had escaped from two sinking ships. He was worried about them spreading disease and had ordered his men to shoot them. Of course, we put a stop to that straight away. Sergeant Ridler got really annoyed when the officer started grinning and he pulled the Iron Cross from the chap's throat in disgust.'

above our heads. They were using them to find the range. We got the message loud and clear, and you never saw jeeps move so fast. If an 88 opened up, the driver would throw the jeep into reverse and go like the clappers to get out of range or under cover.'

The horrors of Hanover, however, did little to prepare D Squadron for what lay ahead. Travelling to the northeast in the direction of the Bay of Lubeck, they discovered Belsen, one of the most notorious concentration camps in the Third Reich, on 15 April. Bob Bennett was one of the first men to enter the camp and the memory of what he saw has remained with him to this day:

'Most of the guards were Hungarian and seemed to be on drugs. When we got there, they were still shooting some of the inmates, but the camp was so large we just couldn't do anything about it. Obviously, I'd never been in a concentration camp before. It made you feel ill; those poor people were just skin and bone. We were in Belsen for about an hour before the army arrived and took charge.'

After leaving the grim scenes of Belsen behind, D Squadron resumed their drive towards the Bay of Lubeck. Resistance was virtually non-existent and the men concentrated on disarming German civilians and accepting the surrender of enemy troops. Bob Bennett later remembered the routine:

'Every place we went into we'd get hold of the mayor and tell him to order the locals to bring their weapons to the town square. We'd make all the

EXPANSION

At the close of 1943 the Special Raiding Squadron reverted to the original title of 1 SAS, and with 2 SAS was placed under the control of the 1st Airborne Division. In January 1944 the British military authorised the creation of an SAS Brigade for operations in Europe. Later in the year, 1 and 2 SAS assembled in Ayrshire to form the nucleus of the new unit. Aside from the original regiments, the new commander, Brigadier Roderick McLeod, had charge of 3 and 4 SAS, consisting of French troops, a Belgian Squadron (later 5 SAS), and 'F' Squadron. Total strength was around 2000 men.

'F' Squadron came from the GHQ Liaison Regiment or 'Phantom', and was led by Major Hopkinson. The squadron's task was to gather intelligence behind enemy lines and report back to base. Two patrols from the unit were assigned to 1 and 2 SAS, while the French and Belgians had their own signallers.

The brigade HQ worked with several non-SAS units: 46 or 38 Groups RAF, used to insert men and equipment, the Special Operations Executive, and the 1st Airborne Division. In February 1945 McLeod left the brigade and his position was taken by Brigadier Mike Calvert, an ex-Chindit with great experience of unconventional warfare. Calvert led the SAS until the end of the war in Europe. After the German surrender in May 1945, the brigade was quickly disbanded: 5 SAS was returned to the Belgian Army on 21 September; and 3 and 4 SAS were handed back to the French Army on 1 October. A week later, 1 and 2 SAS were disbanded. During SAS operations in Europe, the brigade killed or wounded some 8000 enemy troops and captured another 23,000. Some 350 SAS men became casualties during the campaign.

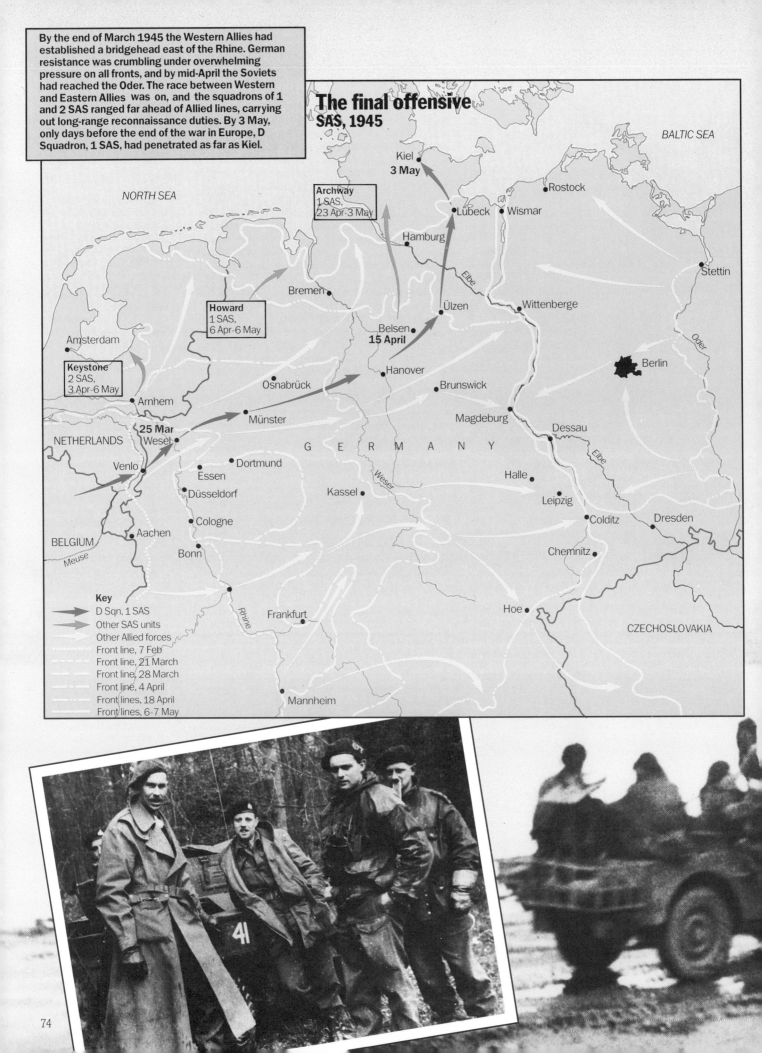

By the end of March 1945 the Western Allies had established a bridgehead east of the Rhine. German resistance was crumbling under overwhelming pressure on all fronts, and by mid-April the Soviets had reached the Oder. The race between Western and Eastern Allies was on, and the squadrons of 1 and 2 SAS ranged far ahead of Allied lines, carrying out long-range reconnaissance duties. By 3 May, only days before the end of the war in Europe, D Squadron, 1 SAS, had penetrated as far as Kiel.

The final offensive
SAS, 1945

BALTIC SEA

NORTH SEA

Kiel
3 May

Rostock

Archway
1 SAS,
23 Apr-3 May

Lübeck   Wismar

Hamburg

Stettin

Bremen

Elbe

Ülzen

Wittenberge

Howard
1 SAS,
6 Apr-6 May

Belsen
15 April

Amsterdam

Hanover

Berlin

Oder

Keystone
2 SAS,
3 Apr-6 May

Osnabrück

Brunswick

Arnhem

Münster

Magdeburg

Dessau

25 Mar

NETHERLANDS   Wesel

G E R M A N Y

Elbe

Venlo

Dortmund

Essen

Kassel

Halle

Düsseldorf

Weser

Leipzig

Colditz

Dresden

BELGIUM

Cologne

Chemnitz

Aachen

Bonn

Meuse

Rhine

Key

⮕ D Sqn, 1 SAS
⮕ Other SAS units
⮕ Other Allied forces
Front line, 7 Feb
Front line, 21 March
Front line, 28 March
Front line, 4 April
Front lines, 18 April
Front lines, 6-7 May

Frankfurt

Hoe

CZECHOSLOVAKIA

Mannheim

Main picture: A jeep from D Squadron races into Kiel in early May 1945, on the last leg of an epic trek that had taken the SAS from the blistering heat of the Western Desert to the fertile plains of northern Germany. Accompanied by top scientists from T Force, the squadron was searching for details of German secret weapons. On the journey to the Baltic, D Squadron captured a train-load of V2 rockets (below right). However, the Inns of Court Regiment gained the credit (below). Bottom left: A bunch of SAS officers hold an open-air conference in front of a Daimler Dingo scout car. Bottom right: Men of D Squadron take a break outside a German farmhouse. During rest periods, the SAS took advantage of the food and shelter provided by the farms. Bottom, far right: The SAS celebrated VE-night in Brussels in their own distinctive style.

After dealing with the enemy near Lubeck at the end of April, 1 SAS was ordered to strike out for the port of Kiel. D Squadron was split into different groups to take the members of T Force to their objectives, the U-boat pens and the Walther armaments factory. To Bob Bennett, it seemed to be the most hazardous drive of the operation:

'I went off with Major Tompkins and eight jeeps and we drove straight into Kiel, which was a hell of a run. I thought we had done some crazy things in the past, but this time we were really putting ourselves out on a limb – 60 or 70 miles in front of the nearest support. On the way in, we came up against a pill-box. I thought we were in for a bit of action, but to our amazement the Germans manning the position just came out with their hands in the air.

'Kiel was almost empty. It was a strange feeling. There we were in the middle of the place, expecting the Germans to open fire at any moment, yet there wasn't a soul about. Unlike Hanover, Kiel had survived the worst of the Allied bombing.

'We went for the naval headquarters in Kiel. I sat outside the building while Major Tompkins and one of the T Force chaps went in for a look around. Apparently, they were trying to persuade a senior German officer to surrender. After a little time, they came out and said that he had agreed to cease all further resistance.

'From there we went up to the canal and saw a ship trying to get away. We lined our jeeps up along the banks and belted it with fire from the Vickers. The boat came back and two Norwegians told us what had been going on. The Germans had been taking prisoners out into the canal, shackling them together and throwing them overboard.'

Kiel marked the end of D Squadron's part in the fight for northwestern Germany and the whole of 1 SAS was ordered back to Ostend prior to embarking for England. The men of D Squadron left Kiel on 3 May and raced back to Belgium. Bob Bennett later recalled the journey:

'I was about a dozen miles from Brussels having a coffee when the German surrender came over the radio. We did some celebrating in Brussels. I remember somebody drove one of our jeeps into a bar to order a drink. It was a tremendous relief to us all that the war was finally over.'

The SAS, however, had one last task to perform. Norway was still occupied by German troops who had to be disarmed and repatriated. After returning to England, the SAS was flown to Stavanger, and then began the mopping-up operation. The job lasted some four months and the SAS returned to England. In October 1945, 1 and 2 SAS were disbanded.

The SAS had been in action for just four years. In that time they had played a major role in North Africa, Italy, France and Germany, taking the war to the enemy whatever the odds, and displaying the utmost professionalism. David Stirling's great vision had been realised to the full and, despite the temporary disbandment of the regiment, the SAS was destined to return to the field of battle.

THE AUTHOR Ian Westwell would like to extend his grateful thanks to Bob Bennett, BEM, MM, and Reg Seekings, DCM, MM, for their extensive help in the production of this article.

New style V-ramp

Big V-bomb haul

MUSEUM OF SECRETS

Alexander Clifford tells below how a British regiment captured a huge mass of German secret weapons, including V2s, on their way to the Hague, and fantastic apparatus for handling the rockets.

STEYERBERG, GERMANY, Monday.

THIS tiny country railway station is a museum of V-weapons. The Inns of Court armoured cars captured the place in time to check whole train-loads of V1s and V2s that were on their way to England via Holland.

I counted 51 V1s packed in one train. There was a fantastically complicated crane affair for lifting V2s around. There was what looked like a launching apparatus for V2s. There was a train which had contained V2s.

The only things that weren't there were the V2s themselves. The Nazis got them away by the skin of their teeth.

The V2s had been on their way to The Hague when suddenly the

EXPERTS probe a queer type V-ramp, captured near Zutphen.

V cargo goes

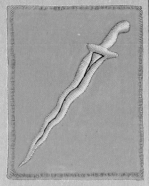

To take on communist insurgents, at their own game, Michael Calvert set up a new version of the famed World War II SAS

LIEUTENANT GRENFELL turned his body slightly to rest his arms. He and Trooper Costello had been lying in ambush all night on a jungle track at a junction where various animal paths met to cross the narrowest part of a swamp. The ambush consisted of a string of Mills grenades at 10yd intervals, interspersed with two 3in mortar bombs, all connected up with cordtex instantaneous fuze to a fuzebox and plunger lying in front of Grenfell's face. The four-man SAS patrol was trying out their colonel's idea to catch more than just one or two of the Malayan Chinese guerrillas who occasionally ventured down the track. As the bandits usually moved at least 10yds apart, a weapons-only ambush usually killed only one or two of a party, the remainder being protected by the thick jungle. With a string of grenades placed to the side of the track and stretching 150 yds along it, the SAS hoped to kill more men at one go, especially the more important ones in the centre of the column. This type of ambush could only be done by highly skilled and determined men who understood explosives – men of the SAS.

The SAS colonel's precept was, 'The fewer you are, the more frightened you are, therefore, the more cautious you are and, therefore, the more silent you are. You are more likely to see the enemy before he

Grenfell and Costello, the various implements of their ambush were marked out by translucent pieces of fungus cut into different shapes. One denoted the key to detonate the grenades. Others indicated an M1 carbine, a waterbottle, a Mills grenade and the end of the communicating cord. The two men wore mosquito veils and gloves. Anti-mosquito cream was not used in case it was smelt by the guerrillas' scout.

Grenfell and Costello took it in turns to watch the path. Movement of guerrillas by night in the deep jungle was not common, and the remainder of the SAS squadron which was not spread out in similar ambushes on other possible tracks was moving to attack a reported occupied camp in the Korbu Forest Reserve, 15 miles from the roadhead at the Kunchong Jalong tin mines and 35 miles from the railway town of Sungei Siput in Perak. The area consisted of dense primary rainforest interspersed with small clearings (called kampongs) made by the Sakai, most of which had been left to deteriorate into secondary jungle when they moved, usually after a death. The immediate surrounding hills rose up to over 4000ft, but where Grenfell lay, there was swamp-land along the Sungei Plus.

It was nearing dawn. The cicadas' and frogs' chorus was being silenced by the squawks of the occasional bird. Grenfell shook Costello. As the darkness cleared, they heard a noise foreign to the jungle – a clink of metal. They had placed themselves in this ambush position (which was now on its seventh day) so that there was a faint skyline where the track

will be able to see you.' Also, over the years, since the time the Japanese had occupied Malaya in World War II, the communist guerrillas had made it their business to look after, make friends with and dominate the Sakai tribes who lived in the deep jungle, so that they became the 'ears and nose' of the bandits.

The SAS party consisted of an officer and three men. Two men lay in ambush next to each other so that they could communicate by touch; the other two rested and slept under a camouflaged mosquito net about 100yds away from the track. Communication between the two parties was by a cord tied to the ankle of one of them. They also had a small radio transmitter to maintain contact with base.

It was pitch dark under the jungle canopy. Around

curled over a slope. Costello, who had been both a gamekeeper and poacher before he joined the army (and was one of the few soldiers allowed to wear an earring before he joined the SAS, as he said that he was a gypsy), nudged Grenfell, who pulled back the mosquito veil from his face. Sure enough, there was movement. It was not an animal. They heard some whispering. They saw a near-naked Sakai tribesman moving slowly from side to side down the track with his head bent low and feeling the ground with his hands and feet, then waving a uniformed figure on.

They were obviously suspicious. It may have been the smell of the metal of the bombs, or the residue of oil on them, or the cordtex. The SAS had learnt to eat the same sort of food as the guerrillas so that their sweat and dung smelt the same. They were not allowed to smoke or drink alcohol for some days before an operation for the same reason. Their latrine was over 100yds away, but it was difficult to conceal an alien smell from Sakai tribesmen.

Grenfell remembered to jerk the line to warn the other two SAS men. He wanted to be certain that there were more than just two guerrillas, so as not to waste the explosives which had been carried there with great effort and care. But the guerrillas were now only 15yds away, and might turn tail at any moment. He decided to fire the charges. He

Below: An innovative leader of unconventional forces, Mike Calvert, the founder of the Malayan Scouts, set up a thorough and rigorous jungle training programme. Here, a recruit, wearing a fencing mask and armed with an air rifle, stalks a similarly armed opponent. Bottom: A quartet of Calvert's ragged irregulars poses for the camera. Below left: Calling down a Sycamore helicopter. The use of choppers enabled the Scouts to respond to enemy activity at a moment's notice.

BACKGROUND TO EMERGENCY

Prior to the Japanese invasion of Malaya in 1941, the Malay peninsula was attached to Britain by treaty.

Its population in 1940 consisted of 2,600,000 Malays, 2,100,000 Chinese, 602,000 Indians, plus a few thousand whites. The deep jungle was inhabited by indigenous aborigines. The Malayan Communist Party was formed in the 1920s. In 1942, after the Japanese conquest, it organised itself into a resistance army of about 5000 men. Assisted by specialised British agents it fought a guerrilla campaign against the Japanese, while a Japanese-sponsored Malay police force tried to hunt it down.

Soon after VJ (Victory over Japan) Day the British Army returned to Malaya in force, but not before the Malayan People's Anti-Japanese Army (MPAJA) had obtained great kudos by taking the surrender of most of the Japanese forces: Chin Peng, then military leader of the MPAJA, attended the Commonwealth Victory Parade in London and was awarded the OBE. Between 1945 and 1948, the situation in Malaya began to deteriorate. The communists increased their influence in organisations such as trade unions, while the Malay sultans demonstrated no wish to come to an accord with the substantial Chinese minority that was becoming increasingly disaffected.

In June 1948, three rubber planters in Surgei Siput were murdered, and from this time on, the crescendo of terror began to mount, until by the early 1950s, five British, six Gurkha and two Malay battalions were only just holding their own against a communist guerrilla movement. In this situation a new approach was needed, and the wartime SAS was to be reborn.

pressed Costello's head down with one hand and with the other pushed down the plunger, burying his own face into the ground at the same time. There was an almighty explosion and bits of metal whined overhead. The two SAS men lay there for a while to see if anything moved. Nothing stirred except the acrid smoke from the explosives. A few sticks and leaves fluttered to the ground. The cord on Grenfell's arm was tugging, showing that Johnson and Free-body, the other two SAS men, were moving up.

Once Johnson and Freebody had arrived and taken up a covering position, Grenfell crept forward cautiously to see the result of his ambush. He found the aborigine and one uniformed Chinese guerrilla dead on the forward slope of the hill. Further along the track, he saw three more bodies, but nothing more. It presumably had been only a reconnaiss-ance party. His job now was to report the result in a few words to his squadron commander and wait for orders.

This done, he and Costello searched the dead for documents (the Sakai wore only a loincloth and a bandolier so there was little trouble there), before the bodies started to putrefy in the heat. They then collected their arms and ammunition and withdrew to their second rendezvous (RV). They still tried carefully to avoid leaving obvious imprints on the track, although the afternoon rains, which usually started at 1600 hours, would soon clear any traces.

The explosion, which had echoed right across the valley, had fully alerted the remainder of Grenfell's

Sungei Chinak guerrilla camp
Malayan Scouts 22 SAS, April 1952

On 13 April 1952 one squadron of 22 SAS took the jungle war against the communist insurgents in Malaya's Perak state to one of the enemy's 'safe' camps, forty miles east of the town of Sungei Siput. After this 'Silent Raid', the guerrilla camps were no longer safe havens.

Camp entrance

Dam

Water pipe

Cookhouse

Water point

Parade ground

Tall tree

Washing area

Rubbish dump

Bashas

Latrines

Sungei Chinak

Dense primary jungle

THAILAND

GULF OF THAILAND

Location of guerrilla camp

Taiping

Kunchong
Jalong

Ipoh

Sungei Siput

MALAYA

STRAITS OF MALACCA

Kuala Lumpur

SUMATRA

SINGAPORE

troop of 14 men, who had been manning two similar ambushes on likely tracks. As previously arranged, they connected their explosive ambush both to a trip-wire and a pressure switch across the track, as well as a time charge set to go off after four days, thereby rendering the area safe if nothing had been caught by then. Often, in traps of this nature, the only casualties were wild pigs.

The troop withdrew to the RV for a supply drop, as they were out of food. There, they prepared a helicopter patch, which entailed blowing down two trees near the swamp. The helicopter brought in the squadron commander, Major Durrell, a police officer and the intelligence corporal. The crew took away the documents and weapons for investigation.

The SAS colonel and Major Durrell were dis-appointed at the meagre results of weeks of prepara-tion and operations. It was still early days in the employment of the SAS in Malaya, and the officers and men were still not fully trained or inured to living for long periods in the jungle. However, the SAS colonel, who had fought with the Chindits in Burma, believed that the guerrillas could only be overcome by a small, well-trained, highly-motivated, special-ly-equipped force which lived and operated in the

same environment as the guerrilla. Already, in training, the SAS had practised such operations, remaining in the jungle for 100 days at a time without ill-effects.

The SAS colonel also believed in the use of brains to beat the enemy. As he said to Major Durrell:

'The bandits will obviously always avoid pitched battles and will only fight when everything is to their advantage. We must try to use wile and guile to turn the advantages against them. We need more knowledge and intelligence. It seems to me that the key lies with the aborigines who live in the jungle. The bandits have made friends with them, protect them, respect them and reward them. What do we do? We bomb them and their miserable huts in the deep jungle where they fled from the invading Malays centuries ago. We must change this. We must now compete for their friendship and loyalty. We also now have some of the bandits' own weapons and we can at least turn these against them.'

So, at the SAS colonel's behest, the chief-of-staff called a conference, which an assistant commissioner of police, a top Special Branch officer, a senior medical officer, who was an expert on tropical medicine, an RAF photography expert, the Protector of Aborigines and the Chief Curator of Forests attended, as well as the local Area Commander. After a fruitful discussion, the SAS colonel was sufficiently satisfied with the result to begin planning the next SAS operation – the 'silent raid'.

It was clearly out of the question to use helicopters for the initial insertion. One disadvantage of using helicopters (and there were only three Sycamores at that time available in Malaya), was that they gave away the position of the patrols in deep jungle. Yet resupply and liaison were essential. There was no animal transport available, as in Burma, and no organised native carriers, as in New Guinea. So there was no alternative but to arrange concealed dumps of food in the vicinity of an operation, or, if a navigable river was available, to use boats. The Sungei Siput area was mountainous with fast streams. So, before the operation, strategic dumps of food were set up well beyond the roadhead.

Meanwhile, every effort, including medical aid, was made to win over the friendship of the Sakai and wean them away from their allegiance to the guerrillas. Besides the sterling efforts of the Department of Aborigines with their colourful representative, 'Jungle Jim', who worked wonders with the Semelai and the Temers who inhabited that area, the police also had Sakai patrols whom they had trained and lent to the SAS. The RAF also agreed not to bomb kampongs in the jungle.

Five weeks after the ambush affair, the SAS squadron was ready to operate again in the Sungei Siput area. The weapons, ammunition and grenades that Lieutenant Grenfell had collected had been 'recy-

After months of harrying the bandits, the Scouts were short of men, and in early 1951 Calvert called for replacements. In response, 'M' Squadron, 21 SAS, a territorial unit, was sent to Malaya. Above left: The squadron's CO, Major Tony Greville-Bell (second from right) confers with his officers: Lieutenant Jeff Douglas, Captain Alastair MacGregor and Captain Jock Easton. Above: A typical landing zone.

cled' in the SAS workshop. The fuze of the grenades had been replaced with special instantaneous fuze so that, on release, the grenade would blow up the thrower. Similarly, the cordite propellant charge in the ammunition had been replaced with a cut-down detonator over the cap, which was plugged into place with plastic explosive sufficient to blow the firer's face in. The weapons collected were Lee-Enfield .303in rifles. The wooden butts were hollowed out, and explosive with a detonator and trigger mechanism which worked on a ratchet placed inside. This device was set so that after the bolt action had been used a number of times, the whole thing exploded.

The job now was to get the weapons and ammunition to the guerrillas. Lieutenant Durrell's troop was entrusted with this mission. Two specially picked and trained Sakai of the local Temer tribe and one Special Branch Hong Kong Chinese sapper, who had fought with the SAS colonel in Burma, went with him. The squadron, under a deception plan which included passing themselves off as part of a Royal Marine Commando which was stationed nearby, infiltrated the jungle through the rubber plantations at night. With dumps of food and signal batteries already installed, they could operate for at least three weeks in the jungle without resupply.

The guerrilla base camp was on the Sungei Chinak, a small tributary of the Sungei Mu, 40 miles east of Sungei Siput and just below the 7110ft mountain, Bukit Yong Yap. It took the squadron a week to get into position, which included the irksome task of covering their tracks. The heavy afternoon rain assisted in this. The bare minimum of cooked meals was allowed over this period and the troops lived mainly on rice, dehydrated fish, green vegetables and vitamin tablets so that their dung resembled that of the Chinese and Sakai. They also used leaves instead of paper.

Grenfell pitched his operational bivouac within 500yds of the camp. He had left one section at an RV on the Sungei Mu, so that any members of the troop, lost or dispersed, could fall back on it. This section had a brilliantly coloured balloon which they could inflate with hydrogen through an acetylene burner and put up through the top canopy of the trees, as an

Above: Major Mike Calvert was the ideal choice to form and lead the Malayan Scouts. He had experience of jungle warfare, having fought with the Chindits against the Japanese in Burma during World War II. He had also gone on to lead the SAS Brigade in the final stages of the war in Germany. Called to Malaya in early 1950, Calvert came up with a two-part plan to defeat the guerrillas: the creation of a deep-penetration unit and the relocation of the populations of outlying villages into protected encampments, where they could no longer provide food and shelter for the guerrillas. Below: A jungle insertion by helicopter.

SOS signal to light aircraft or helicopters, if they had wounded to evacuate. But as the area might be overlooked from Bukit Yong Yap, the balloon was not to be hoisted until after the operation.

On 12 April, Grenfell advanced under cover of the usual afternoon rainstorm to within 100yds of the camp. There was much bamboo about, and the dead bamboo made a noise like a rifle shot if trodden on. Progress was slow. Leaving the four other SAS men in a fallback position, Grenfell crept forward behind the two Temers and Sapper Charlie Fung, as a thunderstorm flashed and rumbled overhead. Through the rain and trees, they at last saw the outline of the huts. Chinese recruits and some convalescents were sheltering in the huts, chattering away. There appeared to be no obvious guards. As it grew dark, the two Temers and Charlie Fung crept foward on their separate tasks – to deposit the ammunition clips amongst those in reserve, the grenades in a box and the rifles in racks made for that purpose.

Their work done, they crept back to Grenfell. Then, Grenfell and Charlie Fung went foward and upward to a slope just above the camp, where they placed a Battle Simulator in the dense jungle. This simulator had an added attachment that would pump a jet of red smoke upward through the trees when the device was activated. The simulator was set to go off at dawn. Grenfell withdrew his party to the RV and signalled squadron HQ that the Silent Raid had taken place and that the fireworks would start at dawn.

At 0600 hours sharp, on 13 April, an almighty noise racketed through the valley as the Battle Simulator cracked and boomed, and discharged smoke through the trees; answered by the recruits and staff firing off their guns and throwing grenades. Three Typhoons, laid on for the purpose, lined themselves up on the brilliant balloon above the RV and bombed and strafed the area around the red smoke.

The various squadron ambushes just waited, each with its 100yd-string of grenades and bombs. By the evening of 13 April, success stories started to come into headquarters. First, 20 men were caught in an ambush – 10 were reported killed. Another small party was wiped out. Some 30 men were caught and put up a fight, three of them being killed by their own grenades. Further fights took place with casualties. Stragglers were killed and two valuable prisoners were taken.

At Kampong Gulang, where Grenfell had prepared a helicopter strip, the SAS colonel, the squadron commander, plus some police officers and an intelligence team, were relayed in and moved to the guerrilla camp, which was now deserted. The camp was occupied by the police and SAS, and given a detailed search.

At a winding-up conference at Ipoh, the commander was congratulated on the success of his operation, but was told that no public announcement could be made. Any success would be attributed to other units so that the SAS presence could be concealed. Two SAS men were slightly wounded and one stung badly by wild bees. After the conference, the colonel was admonished privately by the GOC, for employing methods that could be used with devastating effectiveness by the guerrillas against our own troops. The details of the silent raid remained silent.

THE AUTHOR Brigadier Michael Calvert, DSO commanded the 77th Indian Infantry Brigade, the Chindits, in Burma in 1944. Later, he led the SAS Brigade during the final months of World War II.

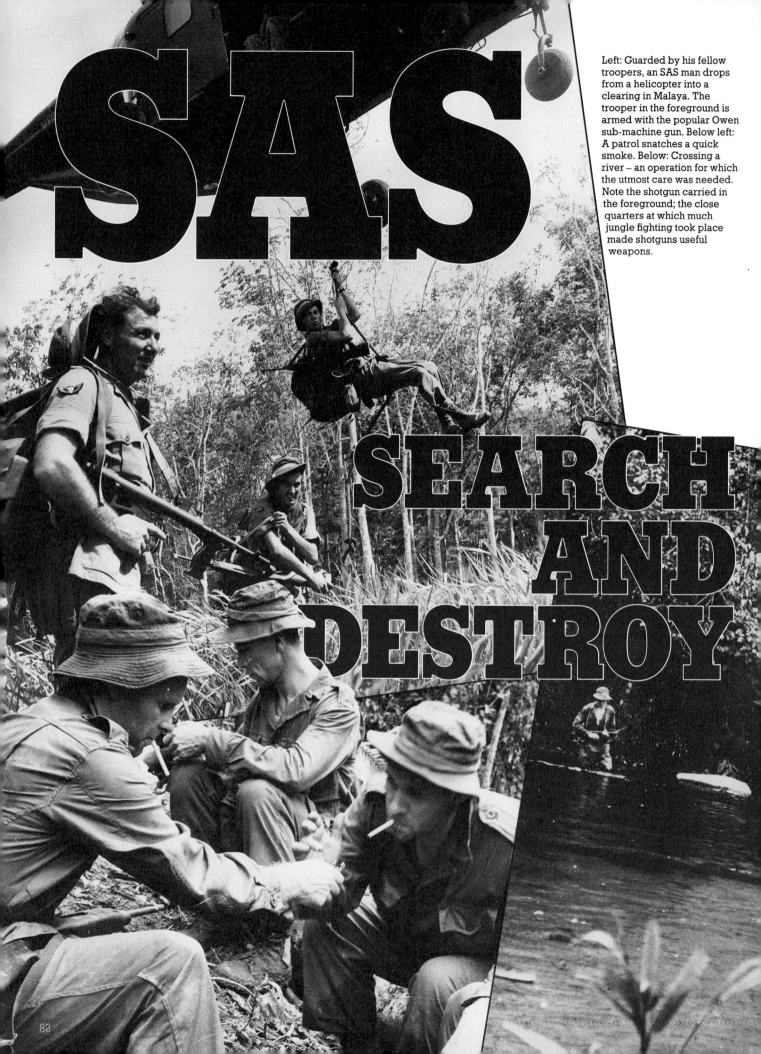

SAS

SEARCH AND DESTROY

Left: Guarded by his fellow troopers, an SAS man drops from a helicopter into a clearing in Malaya. The trooper in the foreground is armed with the popular Owen sub-machine gun. Below left: A patrol snatches a quick smoke. Below: Crossing a river – an operation for which the utmost care was needed. Note the shotgun carried in the foreground; the close quarters at which much jungle fighting took place made shotguns useful weapons.

In the unglamorous war against communist terrorists in Malaya the squadrons of 22 SAS employed tough and effective tactics to track down and eliminate their adversaries

IN 1953, the commanding officer of 22 SAS, Lieutenant-Colonel Oliver Brooke, arranged a meeting with Captain Johnny Cooper of B Squadron. Cooper, an SAS stalwart from the old days and David Stirling's navigator in the Desert, was instructed to raise a new squadron to fill the gap created by the recent departure of the Rhodesian Squadron. The sudden loss of a third of the regiment's operational strength in Malaya would, unless replacements could be found, compromise the SAS's ability to carry out long-term deep-penetration missions against the communist terrorists (CTs) holed up in the peninsula's mountainous and jungle-covered interior.

After a few weeks of intensive activity, Cooper had gathered together about 100 men to form C Squadron. Only one officer, Lieutenant Bruce-Murray, and 20 men, including Sergeant-Major 'Black Jake' Matthews of Oman Police fame, had had any jungle experience; the rest were fitters from the workshops and medical staff – completely and utterly untried against the CTs. However, Cooper had every faith in his men; a faith that was soon justified:

'On one occasion, a man came staggering into our camp and reported that two of my boys, Corporal "Digger" Bancroft and Trooper Wilkins, had been killed by bandits on the other side of a nearby mountain. Bill Speakman, a Korean VC, was with me. He had passed his selection in Malaya and was on his jungle training course before going to Changi for his initial parachute course.

'We contacted No. 848 Squadron, Royal Navy Fleet Air Arm, the naval unit that had done our parachute drops, and they said that a chopper would be sent to bring out our dead. It was about 1000 hours. I organised a 10-man party, including Bill, to bring the casualties out.

'At about last light, I saw the huge figure of Bill moving down the lower slope of the mountain. He came down and dropped the body of Bancroft at the side of the helicopter. Bill's feet were cut to ribbons but he just turned round and said, "Sir, I'm going straight back." At about 1100 hours on the following morning he returned with the other body. His feet were worse, but he refused to be casevac'd. He was typical of the sort of chaps I had in the squadron.'

By the mid-1950s, the British strategy in Malaya of harassing the bandits in the jungle fringes, denying the CTs the food and intelligence that up until then been provided by the Chinese squatters in the villages, was beginning to pay dividends. The guerrillas had been forced onto the defensive and many groups had retired to the relative safety of the deep

LIEUTENANT-COLONEL JOHN COOPER

John Murdoch Cooper, MBE, DCM, (shown below left in Malaya) joined the Scots Guards in April 1940. He was one of the original members of 'L' Detachment and served with the SAS in the desert until the end of the North African campaign, winning a DCM and a Mention in Despatches. Commissioned into the Green Howards in September 1943, Cooper was soon posted back to 1 SAS. He parachuted into France in 1944, fought with the maquis and was again mentioned in despatches for his part in the northwest Europe campaign. Demobilised in 1947, he joined 21 SAS, TA, in 1948 as a lieutenant; in 1953 he was promoted to captain, and formed C Squadron in Malaya.

Promoted to major, Cooper led A Squadron from 1958, and was awarded the MBE for his services during the Emergency.

From Malaya, Cooper turned his attention to South Arabia. He led A Squadron in the Jebel Akhdar campaign of 1958/59 and then stayed on in Oman, joining the Sultan's Armed Forces.

During the mid-1960s he took part in Anglo-French participation in the Yemen, and during the Dhofar insurgency commanded the Sultan's Armed Forces Training Regiment, until 1974. Lieutenant-Colonel Cooper continued serving in Oman in a security role until 1980.

A SECURE FUTURE

By 1952 the successes of the Malayan Scouts had opened the way for the creation of 22 SAS. The only regiment of the regular army to be spawned by a unit of the Territorial Army, 22 SAS initially consisted of an HQ and four squadrons. In the autumn of that year, Major John Woodhouse, one of the Scouts' original officers, went back to England and set up a base at the Airborne Forces Depot, Aldershot, to train replacements for 22 SAS. In 1955 he returned to Malaya with a new squadron. Led by Major Dudley Coventry, it consisted of men drawn from the three regular battalions of The Parachute Regiment. During this period, the Rhodesians of C Squadron returned to their homeland and were replaced by the 170 men of the Independent New Zealand Squadron. By 1956, 22 SAS had a full strength of 560, divided between A, B, D, NZ and Para Squadrons and a regimental HQ.

In 1957 the organisation of 22 SAS was hit by the reform of the British Army. In July the regiment's establishment was reduced to two squadrons and an HQ. The SAS's connection with the airborne forces was finally severed: the Parachute Squadron returned home and the traditional beige beret replaced the maroon beret worn since 1944.

At the close of the year, the New Zealanders returned home and one of the British squadrons was broken up and its personnel allocated to the two remaining squadrons. Although the cuts were savage, it was significant that 22 SAS was not totally disbanded and its future seemed assured.

**Trooper, SAS
Malaya 1960**

Armed with an Owen sub-machine gun, this trooper has jungle-green drill uniform with a canvas bergen rucksack and canvas and rubber boots. The Malayan Command formation sign (a yellow kris on a green background) is worn on the left shoulder.

jungle. However, if the Emergency was to be brought to a successful conclusion, it was vital that the security forces carry out deep raids against the enemy's bases and deny them the succour they extracted from the indigenous tribes, the Aborigines.

The men of 22 SAS worked in conjunction with the civil and military authorities, but the scale and scope of their operations were entirely different. The SAS penetrated deep into the primary jungle on assignments that could last up to three months. Regular units usually operated in groups of platoon strength whereas four-man patrols were the norm for the SAS. After a stint in the jungle, the men would have a month off: two weeks leave and two weeks retraining to keep them in shape.

As the threat of guerrilla attacks in southern Malaya gradually receded, the SAS was increasingly involved in the pacification of the region around the Cameron Highlands, primarily in a large area of Pahang bordering on the state of Kelantan, and along the frontier with Thailand. The local CTs maintained their headquarters in the highlands and were forcing the Aborigines to provide them with food and information regarding the security forces. The SAS role was to gather the natives in protected villages and carry the war to the enemy.

The decision to deploy the SAS in a particular area was taken at the very highest level, during the regular meetings of a joint civil, military and police body known as Paragon Control. Representatives of each state would 'bid' for the services of a squadron, basing their request on available intelligence. Once general agreement was reached, the commanding officer of the SAS and his operations officer would give a full briefing to the relevant squadron commander. Cooper attended many pre-deployment meetings and was well aware of the SAS's role:

'The CO would explain the area of operation and provide details of CT activity. The idea was that we would harass the CTs, and establish protected settlements for the Aborigines. As part of the overall "hearts and minds" programme, we had to wean the natives away from the bandits by providing food, accommodation and medical assistance. By building jungle forts, we could protect the natives from CT intimidation. Our first area of deployment was on the Sungai Brok; the camp was known as Fort Brook.'

'He killed three guerrillas in a very successful two-man operation...'

As the fort was being built and the adjacent areas cleared for cultivation, more and more natives began to leave their villages for the shelter of the encampment. Many were so terrified of CT reprisals that they refused to divulge any information to the security forces, but a few were willing to guide SAS patrols. With the aid of their local knowledge and the invaluable help of Sarawak trackers attached to the squadron, Cooper was soon able to report a successful brush with a group of guerrillas:

'We went in on 22 October and stayed for 122 days. During that time we managed to contact members of the Senai tribe but were being continually harassed by the CTs. I sent Bruce-Murray out to patrol the upper reaches of the Sungai Brok. He was a first-rate jungle operator and managed to suss out a bandit camp. He killed three guerrillas in a very successful two-man operation that got the area started up.'

Once the construction of a fort was nearing completion and the natives had been gathered in, the responsibility for protecting the Aborigines passed to the paramilitary forces, often the Police Field Force, and the SAS teams would then carry out long-term deep-penetration raids in pursuit of their elusive enemy. Apart from the odd piece of 'hot' intelligence provided by the locals or the security forces, each squadron was left to its own devices, acting on the initiative of patrol leaders in the field.

Working from the forts, each of a squadron's troops would be allocated an area of jungle to patrol. To prevent friendly forces from firing on each other, the squadron commander made use of easily identifiable landmarks, such as rivers or ridge lines. In the early stages of the Emergency, teams jumped into the jungle, but as the landings in the trees were often dangerous and produced a crop of injuries, later patrols would walk to their objective or be inserted by helicopter. Each troop remained in direct contact with the squadron HQ and provided a SITREP (situation report) every night. As troops radioed in, their reports were collated and then despatched to the regimental HQ at Kuala Lumpur for further analysis.

The troops would usually operate within an area for up to 14 days – the maximum length of time between airdrops. As each man carried rations for

The Malayan Emergency
22 SAS, 1952-1958

During their campaign against the communist terrorists (CTs) in Malaya, the SAS undertook a series of small-scale operations in the jungle. These patrols denied the bandits vital supplies and intelligence, and made a major contribution to victory. On several occasions the SAS worked with regular troops, carrying out large-scale sweeps in areas of enemy activity. One such operation in late 1952, code-named Termite, saw the SAS working for two months with Gurkha and Fijian units in the state of Negri Sembilan. Some 16 CTs were accounted for.

The SAS spent some nine years in Malaya, and killed or captured about 100 bandits. By taking the war to the enemy, the SAS seriously undermined their will to continue the fight.

Map labels:
THAILAND
Alor Star
KEDAH
Kota Bahru
Tanach Merah
SOUTH CHINA SEA
1952
Anak Reng
PERAK
Belum Valley
Kelantan
KELANTAN
TRENGGANU
Ipoh
Beehive (1955)
Termite (1954)
Cameron Highlands
1958
Telok Anson
Benta
Kuala Lipis
Bagan Datoh
Cato (1953)
Raub
MALAYA
Kuantan
SELANGOR
PAHANG
Kuala Lumpur
NEGRI SEMBILAN
Seremban
Hive (1952)
STRAITS OF MALACCA
MALACCA
Labis
Eagle (1953)
JOHORE
Changi
Johore Bahru
Singapore

Key
* Major SAS operations
▢ Swamp

Left, main picture: Aerial resupply was a crucial part of SAS strategy in Malaya. Left, inset above: An SAS jungle fort, Fort Brooke, here shown after it had been handed over to the civil authorities. Left, inset below: 'Speakman's Hill', from which Bill Speakman, VC, carried back the bodies of two SAS men killed by communist guerrillas.

two weeks, resupply was vital after this length of time. However, the approach of an aircraft, circling over the pre-arranged drop zone, and the sight of several billowing para- chute canopies would alert any bandits in the area and compromise the mission. Troops very rarely stayed in one area after receiving supplies, preferring to head im- mediately for a new operational base.

After a process of trial and error, the SAS troops settled into a routine that combined caution with aggression. The troop leader would establish a secure base camp from where three or four-man patrols would be despatched to cover the jungle within a four-mile radius. Camps were set up near a fresh water supply with easily defended approaches. Trip flares and bamboo booby-traps were placed to cover the perimeter. The camp itself was never left; while two patrols were scouring the area, another group would remain behind to protect the troops' food and ammunition, and above all, their only means of com- municating with the outside world, the radio.

In the eerie, twilight world of the Malayan jungle, patrols had to move with great cau- tion, ever wary of sudden ambush, through some of the most unforgiving and treacher- ous terrain in the world. Cooper recalled that even nature seemed to conspire against the men:

'In secondary jungle, often areas of dense bamboo, we had to do a lot of cutting with our machetes and didn't move very quickly. Worse, the noise we made carried for miles if it wasn't masked by the screams of monkeys. When we moved through swamps, the noise was terrible and, covered in leeches, we were lucky to cover 200yds in an hour.

'Moving through primary jungle was much easier as there was little ground vegetation, but we had to watch out for snakes. We tried to avoid well-used tracks as the CTs often set up ambushes or pig traps of sharpened bamboo along the way.'

The patrol attacked, and in a brief firefight killed the guerrillas

The perseverance of the SAS teams in the endless round of patrolling did pay dividends on several occasions. In August 1956 Sergeant Turnbull and three troopers tracked four CTs for five days until the enemy reached their base. Waiting until a rainstorm forced a sentry into the group's basha (a grass and thatch hut), the patrol attacked and in a brief firefight killed the guerrillas. Towards the end of the Emergency, in February 1958, 37 men of D Squadron led by Major Thompson parachuted into the Telok Anson swamp in Selangor and after 14 weeks forced two bands of guerrillas to surrender.

Constant action placed great strains on the squad- rons and many were well below strength through illness and injury, but those men who remained continued to pursue the enemy with dogged deter- mination. One of the most spectacular and important successes was the ambush of Ar Poy, one of the CT district officials, by Captain Muir Walker and some

Left: All sorts of transport was used by the SAS in Malaya. Elephants might seem ideally suited to the conditions, but, unfortunately, these beasts from Thailand proved a positive hindrance. Panicking in thick jungle, they lay down and rolled onto their loads, crushing the precious rations. Below: from left, Corporal Lyle, Lieutenant Bruce-Murray and Trooper Downing, after a 122-day patrol for which they become famous within the SAS. Far right, above: Major Douglas of B Squadron, wearing the 'tree-jumping' kit used at Belum Valley. Far left, below: Sergeant Hanah, after a successful jump into the forest.

men from A Squadron. On a routine patrol, the team found a well-built basha and packed the bamboo supports with plastic explosive. Signs of recent use suggested that a party of CTs was still in the area, so the patrol settled down to wait for the enemy. As Cooper recalled, it was to be two weeks before the ambush was sprung:

'There were two men in the ambush party at any one time. They were relieved every 24 hours and went back to a camp, 2200yds deeper in the jungle. We had a set routine: no smoking, no cooking, no talking, and a crawl-line running out for 300 yards to the "toilet". Our body odours were completely different from the CTs' because of our different diets.

'After 14 days of watching, the enemy finally turned up. Trooper O'Brien was on duty at the time, and when the four Chinese entered the basha he pushed the plunger – nothing happened. After so much rain, the explosive was useless. O'Brien was alone and couldn't signal back for fear of alerting the enemy. He waited until they came out onto the balcony and then opened fire with his Belgian FN FAL rifle. He killed Ar Poy, who was the District Committee Secretary.'

The removal of a high-ranking official was a major blow to both the organisation and prestige of the CT units working in the area. Denied leadership, short of food, and bombarded by propaganda from 'voice' aircraft and pamphlets urging them to surrender,

many left the jungle and gave themselves up to the authorities.

Faced by the growing success of the British counter-insurgency effort, several of the leading figures in the CT movement fled to the relative security of Thailand. Here, untroubled by the in-effectual Thai Army, they were able to direct the activities of bandit groups by radio. The military authorities were quick to recognise that the closure of infiltration routes across the border and the destruction of the enemy's transmitter would severely hamper their ability to wage a guerrilla campaign.

On one occasion, an SAS radio picked up wireless transmissions; the station appeared to be located somewhere between Kota Bharu and Alor Star,

Below: Frank Williams, SAS, (wearing headband) brings back a captured bandit. Bottom: A patrol returns from the jungle. The packs weighed 60-70lbs. The men shaved and cleaned up as soon as they reached a road or rail link – beards were not tolerated once off patrol.

possibly in the Valley of No Return. B Squadron, led by Johnny Cooper, was given the task of finding and destroying the radio. Flown to Kota Bharu by the RAF, the squadron then sailed down the Kelantan river to Tanach Merah, the starting point for the mission.

During the slow, tortuous march to the valley, Cooper became acutely aware that the squadron had a maximum of 14 days to find the station:

'First, we had to go over the Anak Reng, a 6000ft ridge. It took 12 days of hard slogging to reach the summit and by that time most men had lost a lot of weight. There was no sign of CT activity so I split the squadron into troops to cover more ground. Our rations were running out and, once we had taken an airdrop, our cover would have been blown.'

'On the 13th day, Lieutenant Punchy McNeil and his troop were working their way down a very narrow defile and heard the sound of gushing water. McNeil went forward to carry out a recce and discovered a waterwheel. The CTs had blocked the river channel and the waterwheel was connected to three Bedford generators, producing enough power to run the wireless.

'McNeil and his men got into position, went in and clobbered everybody in the station. The destruction of a vital link between the local CTs and their leaders in Thailand helped to undermine bandit activity in the border region.'

In various guises, the SAS fought throughout the critical years of the Malayan Emergency. The counter-insurgency war was always unglamorous and often unrewarding, yet the SAS squadrons, by sticking to the task, had found a niche in unconventional warfare that they alone were able to fill. In helping to defeat the CTs in Malaya, the SAS had also assured their own future; a future that would next take them to the scorching heat of Oman and the battle for the Jebel Akhdar.

THE AUTHOR Ian Westwell and the publishers would like to extend their grateful thanks to Lieutenant-Colonel Johnny Cooper, MBE, DCM for his invaluable and extensive help in the production of this article.

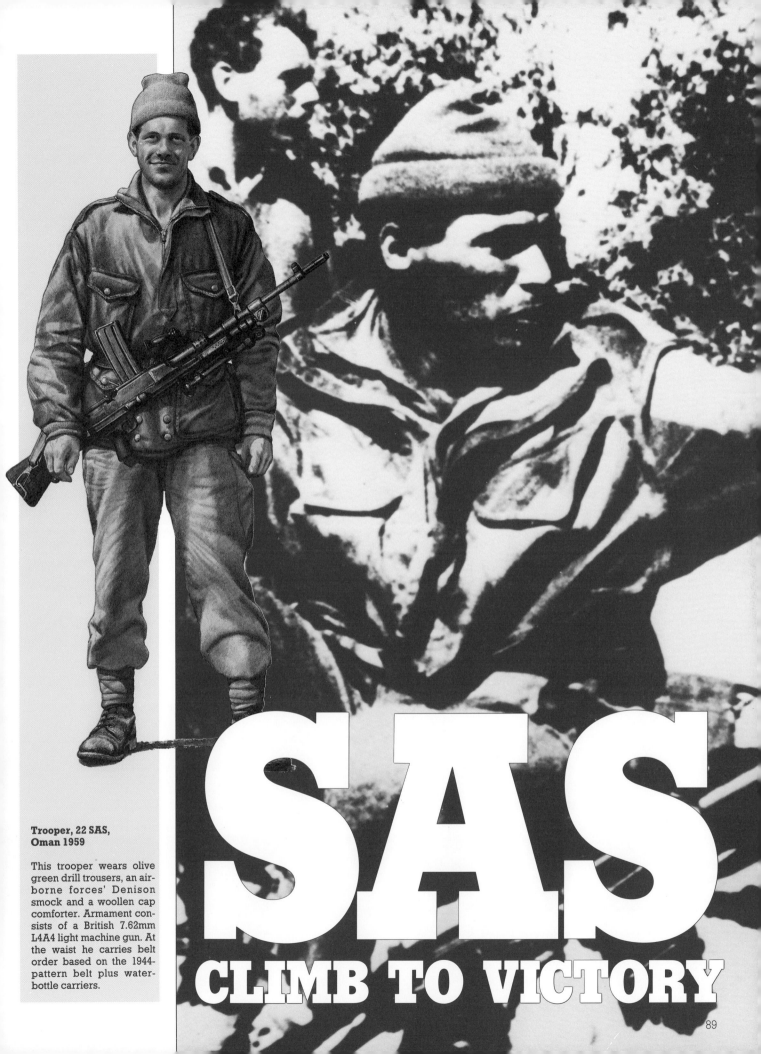

Trooper, 22 SAS, Oman 1959

This trooper wears olive green drill trousers, an airborne forces' Denison smock and a woollen cap comforter. Armament consists of a British 7.62mm L4A4 light machine gun. At the waist he carries belt order based on the 1944-pattern belt plus water-bottle carriers.

SAS
CLIMB TO VICTORY

In 1958 22 SAS was called to Oman to spearhead an assault against the rebel stronghold on the Jebel Akhdar, a near-impregnable mountain plateau

ON A HOT and humid day in mid-November 1958, several transport aircraft lumbered down the runway of an airfield in Malaya and took to the air on a northwesterly heading. On board were the 80 or so men of D Squadron, 22 SAS, a beefed-up squadron, fully equipped and ready for operations, but with little idea of where they were going. As the aircraft left the Malayan peninsula behind, the men speculated on their final destination. The clue lay in the hectic days of preparations they had recently made.

Several weeks earlier, out of the blue, the squadron had been pulled out of the jungle only to be told that their services were required in an entirely different country. Without delay, training exercises began for their new deployment – training that had little to do with jungle fighting. A corporal serving with the squadron remembered the routine:

'Everything was done in the full heat of the day. We set up a series of hard marches with bergens, weapons and ammunition, and at the end of each march there was more and more range work, more and more open work, as opposed to work which we'd always done in jungle, and longer range marksmanship, well over the 25 or 30yds which we had previously engaged in.'

Throughout this period, the secret had been well-kept. Only the CO, Lieutenant-Colonel Tony Deane-Drummond, the ops officer and the squadron commander, Major John Watts, were party to it, but the shrewder members of the squadron had a pretty

good idea it was to be somewhere in the Middle East. As the aircraft pulled up on the airstrip on the island of Masirah and the squadron was finally briefed, their suspicions were confirmed – they were in Oman and their target was the Jebel Akhdar.

The Jebel Akhdar (Green Mountain) rises precipitously from the Omani desert to form a sheer and formidable massif, topped by a plateau and surrounded by jagged peaks rising to 10,000ft. For over two years this mountain stronghold had been the domain of rebel forces opposed to the regime of Sultan Said bin Taimur. The rebels were well armed with mortars, light machine guns and rifles and had dug themselves in with prepared fortifications and a system of deep caves for protection from aerial harassment. Although mainly contained within the confines of the Jebel, the rebels had successfully resisted any attempts by the Sultan's Armed Forces (SAF), assisted by detachments of British Life Guards, Trucial Oman Scouts and Aden-based RAF units, to take the Jebel. Frustrated by the stalemate, specialist help was requested and on 18 November the SAS arrived on mainland Oman.

D Squadron quickly set out for the area of operations in a column of one-tonners under Captain Peter de la Billière, but soon ran into trouble. A member of the squadron recalls the perilous trek along the road to Nizwa which was strewn with rebel mines:

'That was a journey and a half. I myself was blown up twice in two different trucks. The mines they were using were both Soviet and American but luckily they were anti-vehicle mines, mainly concerned with knocking the vehicle off, so you tended to find yourself driving along at one moment and then sitting on your arse in the desert the next after a spectacular explosion and all sorts of

of the squadron's troops arrived in Nizwa while the other two split off to the north side of the Jebel, to a place known as the Persian Steps. From the village of Tanuf on the south side and the Persian Steps on the north, D Squadron began operations on the Jebel.

It was tough acclimatising to their new conditions. Malaya had been hot, wet and humid, but on the Jebel it was scorching by day and bitterly cold at night. There was little vegetation and precious little water. They were also up against a very different enemy. One of the participants on the first OP patrol (24-hour reconnaissance) recounts his troop's first contact on the Tanuf Slab:

'We got to the top and we found positions that the enemy had obviously occupied, so we decided to get into their positions rather than make new ones of our own, because we knew enough about them to realise that they would spot a new position on the skyline the same as we would if it was our area. At about 0630 the sun came up and we fried and fried and fried. We had two extremes. At night it was cold enough on top of the mountain to freeze the water bottle, and we weren't as well equipped then as we are today. All we had were OG trousers and jacket and a very thin standard issue pullover. We didn't take sleeping-bags on a 24-hour recce since all they did was slow you down, and anyway, we didn't intend to sleep, not knowing whether they had established night picquets.

'Around about 1400 hours I had another three men with me in my patrol and we were looking down and covering an area when, lo and behold, I saw this Arab start making his way up. He got up to within about 300yds of us when he must have spotted some sort of movement because he shouted up at me, obviously thinking I was one of them. So we shouted down, but then he decided, having had his rifle on his shoulder in the sling position, that something wasn't quite right here, so he took it off whereupon I shot him. My mate alongside me shot him as well and we just blew him away. Within 30 seconds we were under fire from numerous places. They were hyperactive and their reaction was perfect and they started shooting from all areas and concentrating on us. Further along the ridge, the other half of our troop was trapped and one of them, Corporal 'Duke' Swindells, was shot.'

Cool in the face of the rebel onslaught, the men held their fire until the enemy were almost upon them

With the aid of RAF Venoms blasting the rebel positions with rockets, the troop managed to extract itself and thereafter the SAS confined its reconnaissance to night patrolling, out of the fiery heat of the day and with less chance of being spotted and overwhelmed by numerically superior rebel forces. They also developed a keen respect for their opponents, who were trained and highly professional.

Meanwhile, the two troops under Captain Rory Walker, deployed on the northern side of the Jebel, had met with some success and had managed to gain a foothold on the mountain. Guided by local tribesmen, Walker's force scaled the Jebel and set up in sangars on the heights of Aquabat al Dhafar (nicknamed Sabrina on account of its twin summits) only 300yds from rebel positions. They were soon spotted and came under fierce attack. Cool in the face of the rebel onslaught, a detachment of men under

Page 89: Captain Peter de la Billière (left) and Major John Watts, OC D Squadron, on the Jebel. Far left: Sergeant 'Tanky' Smith mans a Browning during the raid on the rebel cave. Left: The remains of the rebel fort at Tanuf which was blown up by the SAS. Top: Sergeant medic Bill Evans who survived the explosions of four rebel mines on the gruelling journey to Nizwa. Above: Sergeant 'Herbie' Hawkins, whose coolness in the face of a rebel onslaught secured an early success for the SAS.

bits of metal flying around. I remember there was one really unfortunate guy, Bill Evans, who was the sergeant medic, who got blown up on four separate occasions. Every truck he climbed onto got blown up. By the end he was thoroughly shell-shocked and a bit ga-ga.'

Battered and bruised, caked with dust and dirt, two

Sergeant Hawkins held their fire until the enemy were almost upon them, then they opened up, killing nine rebels and putting the rest to flight.

The patrolling continued as the squadron got the hang of the terrain and the rebel tactics and positions. On one patrol, carried out by de la Billière's troop, Arabs were observed disappearing into a large cave and, in a war that so far had presented the SAS with little in the way of specific targets to hit, it was decided to follow up the recce with a strike on the hideout. A machine gunner who went up the Jebel that night remembers the action:

'As de la Billière's troop had done the recce, they would do the nearest bit and would put a 66mm rocket or Carl Gustav rocket into the cave – several in fact. Our troop was designed to cover them and we were on a slightly higher ridge about two or three hundred yards above them. We climbed up that night, early morning came and I was behind the Browning. I had persuaded John Watts that the ideal weapon for Oman was the .30 Browning where you had the range you didn't have with the LMG, but, like all machine guns, it attracts a lot of attention. We set the gun up overlooking the cave and then, first thing in the morning, several men came to the entrance of the cave and were about to start leading the donkeys out. Whereupon, three rounds rapid from the Carl Gustav went straight in the middle and *whoof*, they blew the cave in and a fair number of them to pieces. Once again, within a minute and a half, we were all under attack. They were amazing in their reactions plus their knowledge of the ground. They were born for it and their reactions were fast. We were under attack from their mortars. We were under attack from their LMGs and from individual tribesmen who were all spoiling for a fight. So, with the help of my machine gun and the RAF who arrived – we had them on a sort of taxi-cab system – we extracted ourselves without loss.'

A great firefight started and we were in a position where we couldn't move out of the rocks

But not everything was going D Squadron's way and there were several sticky moments that could have had disastrous consequences were it not for the men's superb fitness and cool headedness when in a tight corner. One of the problems was the lack of good maps and detailed information on the inhospitable terrain on the heights of the Jebel. On one occasion, acting on information provided by a British seconded officer to the SAF, a half troop found itself on the razor-edged Muti ridge on the eastern side of the Jebel shortly before sunrise. Their NCO recounts how they nearly got wiped out:

'We got to a certain point and above us, some 250ft away, was the summit. As always, we got ourselves into fighting positions and were about to send out a patrol. In the usual SAS manner we sat about for 10 minutes in absolute silence when, lo and behold, we heard these two Arabs talking to each other above us. There we were in a position where you couldn't go backwards, you couldn't go forwards and we were totally exposed. We couldn't get to them so we made ourselves comfortable and hoped against hope that we could spend the day

Above: Members of 22 SAS are briefed prior to the main assault. Planning for the operation had to be very thorough since SAS strategy involved both the leaking of false information to the rebels and a diversionary attack to distract the enemy's attention from the main assault route. Below: Sabrina, the rebel-held position where Tony Jeapes' spirited attack won him the MC. Far right: The village of Saiq, deep in the heart of the rebel-held plateau.

Jebel Akhdar
22 SAS, January 1959

When D Squadron, 22 SAS, was first deployed in Oman in November 1958, the mountain stronghold of the Jebel Akhdar was held by well-armed and entrenched rebel forces. Early in January A Squadron arrived, and 22 SAS started preparations for a decisive assault on the Jebel. At 0300 on 26 January the first phase of the operation began with A Squadron's attack on the Aquabat al Dhafar.

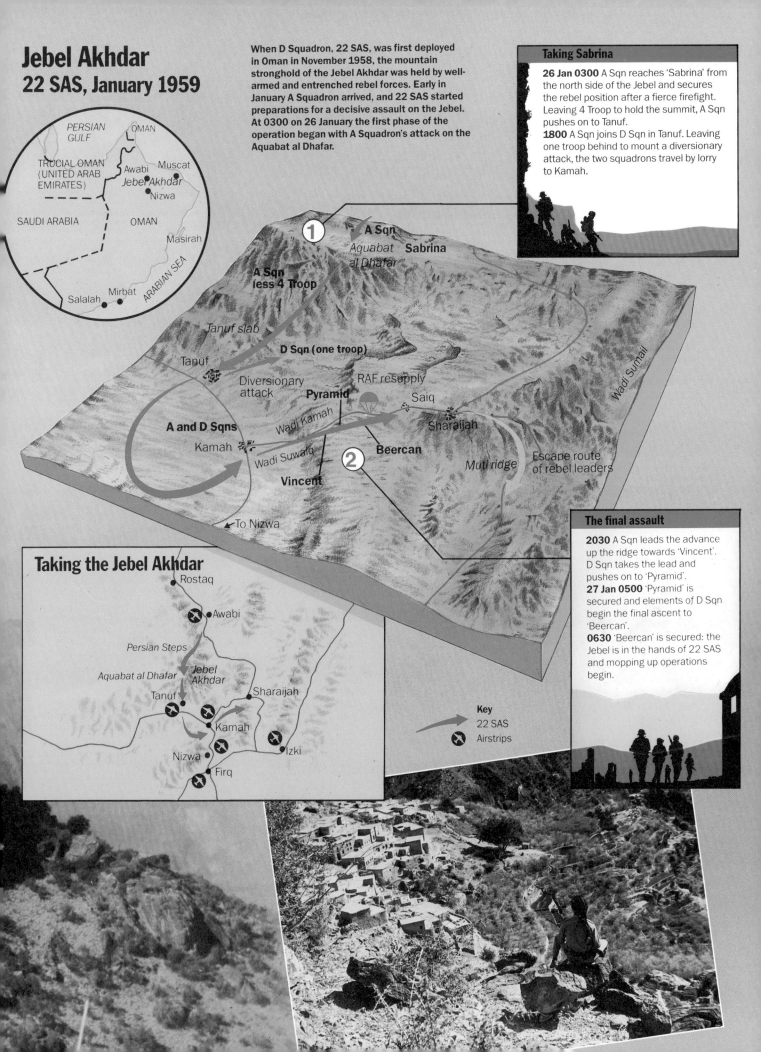

Taking Sabrina

26 Jan 0300 A Sqn reaches 'Sabrina' from the north side of the Jebel and secures the rebel position after a fierce firefight. Leaving 4 Troop to hold the summit, A Sqn pushes on to Tanuf.

1800 A Sqn joins D Sqn in Tanuf. Leaving one troop behind to mount a diversionary attack, the two squadrons travel by lorry to Kamah.

The final assault

2030 A Sqn leads the advance up the ridge towards 'Vincent'. D Sqn takes the lead and pushes on to 'Pyramid'.

27 Jan 0500 'Pyramid' is secured and elements of D Sqn begin the final ascent to 'Beercan'.

0630 'Beercan' is secured: the Jebel is in the hands of 22 SAS and mopping up operations begin.

Map labels (main relief map)

PERSIAN GULF
TRUCIAL OMAN (UNITED ARAB EMIRATES)
OMAN
Awabi
Muscat
Jebel Akhdar
Nizwa
SAUDI ARABIA
OMAN
Masirah
ARABIAN SEA
Salalah
Mirbat

1
A Sqn
Aquabat al Dhafar
Sabrina
A Sqn less 4 Troop
Tanuf slab
D Sqn (one troop)
Tanuf
Diversionary attack
RAF resupply
Pyramid
Saiq
Wadi Sumail
A and D Sqns
Kamah
Wadi Kamah
Sharaijah
Wadi Suwaiq
Beercan
2
Vincent
Muti ridge
Escape route of rebel leaders
→ To Nizwa

Taking the Jebel Akhdar

Rostaq
Awabi
Persian Steps
Aquabat al Dhafar
Jebel Akhdar
Tanuf
Sharaijah
Kamah
Nizwa
Izki
Firq

Key
22 SAS
Airstrips

FIGHTING ON THE JEBEL

For the troops of D Squadron the climate and terrain of the Jebel Akhdar came as a sharp shock. A few weeks previously, they had been engaged in counter-insurgency operations against small bands of communist terrorists in the jungles of Malaya. The Malayan campaign had demanded entirely different survival techniques and engagements had been fought over a distance of a few metres in the dense foliage of the tropical terrain.

On the Jebel conditions were entirely different. The rock of the Jebel is hard and metallic and silent movement was extremely difficult. SAS troopers wore nail-shod boots that not only generated a lot of noise but soon came apart on the rough and abrasive surface. Deep-sided ravines slice their way through the plateau and, to cover a short distance over the Jebel, SAS patrols had to spend many hours climbing and descending the sheer, rocky faces. Sounds, echoing through the ravines, played strange tricks on the troopers – a sudden noise from several hundred metres away could seem to come from behind a nearby rock.

Living off the land was well nigh impossible, so the SAS patrols had to carry all rations and equipment with them. Since patrolling required the use of climbing ropes to negotiate particularly difficult terrain, the troopers were well laden when they set out. Donkeys were used on occasion to hump their gear but the small Somali donkeys, imported for the task, proved worse than useless on the alien Jebel terrain. To make matters worse, the climate on the Jebel alternated between sub-zero conditions at night and scorching, white heat during the day. And, not to be forgotten, the enemy knew the country intimately.

there without them seeing us and then move on the next night. It got daylight and by that time we felt there were between six and 10 up there. As dawn light came they had a good look around and spotted the two SAF blokes who had come with us and that was enough. They thought we'll have these no bother at all. Then a great firefight started and we were in a position where we couldn't move out of the rocks otherwise we'd have been dead. In the SAS you always have to see the humour in things. They knew we were there and they were sending exploratory shots pinging all over the place, and we wanted to draw their fire to see if we could knock off a couple. So I took an empty soup tin and said to the guy who was with me, "OK, put the can on the end of your rifle and poke it up and see if that'll draw their fire and I'll engage them." That didn't work, so then we put a cap comforter on the end of the rifle and poked it out. That drew an immediate response of shots but they weren't going to show themselves because they'd read the same cowboy books as we had. We then realised, through a lot of shouting and hoo-ha, that they were going to bring up reinforcements and have our scalps so we called John Watts up and explained the situation. Everyone was roundly cursed.

'To deal with the situation, mortars were brought up and the RAF called in. Whilst this mortaring was going on we decided that we had to extract, so, by a series of leap frogs, we went past each other and got off the ridge and lower down. They pursued us all the way.'

By this time, the Life Guards' Ferret armoured cars had come up to spray the rebels with Browning machine-gun fire and, finally the pursuing rebels were driven off, back into the haven of the Jebel. Miraculously, the SAS had escaped unscathed, the only casualty being one of the SAF Baluchis who had received a bullet in the backside. Everyone else had extracted with only cuts and bruises.

By Christmas, despite some SAS operational successes, the rebels were still firmly entrenched on the Jebel and the stalemate continued. It was clear that to gain control of the plateau, the SAS would require more manpower and that the Jebel would have to be stormed in force. To this end, A Squadron, under the command of Major John Cooper, was brought in from Malaya to join D Squadron for the final push. Cooper's reinforcements flew out in four aircraft to Awabi on the northern side of the Jebel, and from there they motored down to the Persian Steps and climbed up to the positions held by Rory Walker's two troops from D Squadron.

Major Cooper's newly arrived squadron was soon in action against rebel positions on Sabrina. Unlike D Squadron, they were not acclimatised to the wintry conditions and their commanding officer remembers the hardships they encountered:

'It was the coldest winter for God knows how long. We had arctic sleeping-bags, cold and wet weather equipment – it was really freezing. We had a lot of parachute drops up there, especially of mortar bombs, and we had to use the parachutes to keep warm. There was rain, freezing sleet, snow – it was horrible. And we'd come straight from Malaya.'

In mid-January 1959, several attacks were launched on Sabrina and around Tanuf on the south side to tie down the main rebel forces. These, however, served a dual purpose, in that they were also part of a simple, yet cunning, deception that was crucial to the whole operation. The two squadrons of 22 SAS were massively outnumbered by their rebel opponents and if their main assault was to succeed, the element of surprise would have to be exploited to the full.

The key decision was where to attack. A full frontal assault into well-defended positions would be suicidal, so any of the known approach routes was out. In a twin-engined Pioneer, Tony Deane-Drummond and his two squadron commanders, John Watts and John Cooper, reconnoitred the area, looking for a possible way up the Jebel to take its defenders unawares. After scouring the terrain they decided upon a strenuous but climbable route, not even a track, running from the village of Kamah up between the Wadi Kamah and the Wadi Suwaiq. An on-the-ground recce by members of de la Billière's troop revealed the presence of a 0.5in Browning machine-gun post, but no in-depth defence. This would be their point of entry.

To reinforce the deception, the Arab donkey handlers were told that the attack was to go in from Tanuf. They were instructed, on pain of death, to tell no-one of the plan. Within nine hours the rebels on the mountain were preparing to take on the SAS in the heights above Tanuf.

With the whole of D Squadron in Tanuf, the first phase of the operation was launched by Cooper's A Squadron on Sabrina at 0300hrs. Cooper describes the attack:

'I attacked Aquabat al Dhafar with three troops while one, with all the machine guns from the others, laid a barrage on Sabrina. Tony Jeapes' troop was the one that scaled the pinnacle on the high side and got over the top and killed three or four. When Tony got on the top and scarpered these boys, he poured fire down on the other side and won the firefight. He had Corporal Wright shot up in the groin. Wright was the only casualty that Tony had, but Tony himself was very lucky. A chap had a misfire at point-blank range as Tony went over the top of a sangar. By morning my three troops had Sabrina and the enemy retreated.'

For his part in the action, Jeapes was awarded the Military Cross.

The two squadrons were heavily loaded with weapons and ammunition as they began the slog up the Jebel

The attack on Sabrina held the enemy's attention and reinforcements were despatched from the village of Saiq on the plateau to retake the position. Meanwhile, A Squadron left Sabrina and headed down to Tanuf to join D Squadron for the final push. The operation was going according to plan.

By 1800 hours on 26 January, A Squadron was in Tanuf catching a couple of hours' sleep. Both squadrons were then loaded into trucks and they set off by a roundabout route to the assembly area at Kamah, where they arrived after dark. At 2030, at the same time as a diversionary attack was mounted up the Wadi Tanuf by a troop left behind to further the deception, they crossed their start line.

The two squadrons, despite the favourable reconnaissance regarding enemy strength in the area, were heavily loaded with weapons and ammunition as they began the back-breaking slog up the Jebel. John Cooper recalled the first moves as they worked

Top: Captain Rory Walker (standing) after the assault on Suleiman's cave (circled). Above: Major John Cooper, OC A Squadron, with an Omani tribesman on the Jebel, some years after the conclusion of the SAS campaign. Left above: Lieutenant-Colonel Tony Deane-Drummond surveys captured rebel weapons during the mopping up operations after the main assault. Left: Members of 16 and 17 Troops, D Squadron, on Sabrina in December 1958.

OMAN AT WAR

When D Squadron, 22 SAS, arrived in Oman in November 1958, the country had been in the throes of civil war for some 16 months. Rebel forces, intent upon overthrowing the ultra-conservative regime of Sultan Said bin Taimur and establishing a republic under the religious leader, the Imam of Oman, Ghalib bin Ali, were well ensconced on the mountainous plateau of the Jebel Akhdar in the north of the country.

In June 1958 Ghalib's brother, Talib, had landed in Oman with some 80 armed men and moved onto the Jebel. The sultan reacted by deploying his Oman Regiment against the rebels but Sheikh Suleiman bin Himyar, the powerful leader of the Beni Riyain Jebel tribe, who was already at odds with the sultan over the right to grant oil-exploration licences, rose up in support of the imam and the Sultan's Armed Forces (SAF) were forced to withdraw.

In desperation, the sultan requested aid from Britain and a small force was despatched to Oman where, in conjunction with the SAF, it contained the rebels on the Jebel Akhdar. Throughout 1958, however, rebel attacks in the area undermined the SAF and further help was sought from Britain to resolve the stalemate. To expand and increase the effectiveness of the SAF, Colonel David Smiley, a regular British officer, was appointed Chief of Staff to the forces. Despite some successes in the area, Smiley did not have the resources to secure a convincing defeat over the rebels and he realised the necessity for further reinforcement. Britain's delicate political footing in the Middle East ruled out the extensive deployment of British armed forces in Oman and so, with the back-up of a detachment of Life Guards equipped with Ferret armoured cars, elements of the Trucial Oman Scouts, and RAF units based in Aden, a small SAS force was committed to flush out the rebels.

their way up towards the three objectives, code-named Vincent, Pyramid, and the summit, Beercan: 'We went up, my squadron (A) leading, and we got to Vincent. John Watts' D Squadron went through me and then, going along towards the ridgeline that went up to Pyramid, we had to drop down. We lost about 1500ft. There was no time for reconnaissance and it was dark. It was bloody difficult and we were carrying a hell of a lot of weight.'

By 0500 the following morning D Squadron held Pyramid and was poised to advance on Beercan. It was essential to secure the commanding position above, at Beercan, by daybreak, so Deane-Drummond and John Watts decided to lighten the men's loads down to essential weapons and ammunition and make a dash for the summit. An hour-and-a-half later, exhausted from 10 hours of solid climbing, two troops from D Squadron held Beercan. The Browning, discovered by de la Billière's preliminary recce, was seized and the SAS took a parachute resupply.

So successful was the ruse that the two squadrons encountered minimal opposition. To many it seemed an anti-climax, but, as they consolidated their positions on the top of the Jebel, all were thankful that casualties had been so light. Tragically though, a sniper's bullet had struck a grenade in one of the

Below: Sergeants 'Tanky' Smith and Pete Harding study a map of Oman at the base camp at Ibri a year after the taking of the Jebel. The SAS returned to Oman a year or so after the campaign to check that the situation was still stable and to carry out various 'hearts and minds' programmes, and one-tonner patrols in the desert wastes of the 'Empty Quarter'.

men's rucksacks, seriously wounding Troopers Carter, Bembridge and Hamer. Carter and Bembridge later died of their wounds.

In the wake of the SAS spearhead came the Life Guards and troops of the SAF. The SAS moved on into the rebel villages of Saiq and Sharaijah, where tribesmen were disarmed and caches of weapons and documents unearthed. The rebel leaders, Suleiman, Ghalib and Talib, were nowhere to be found. They had escaped down the Jebel and had disappeared into Saudi Arabia. Leaderless, the rebels surrendered easily, although none were happy about handing over their arms. A few isolated pockets of resistance were dealt with over the next few days and by 5 February the Jebel was firmly in SAS hands.

The Jebel operation was a classic example of SAS intervention, where a small force of highly skilled troops and imaginative planning, coupled with solid air support, can achieve results far beyond the scale of a more conventional military strategy. Major (now Lieutenant-Colonel) John Cooper is, however, more modest and pragmatic in his appraisal:

'It had to be done quickly. If you'd sent in a battalion of infantry it would have cost a lot of money. Here you were sending only a small gang. It was an SAS job because we had the ability to carry pack-mule loads and we were all very fit.'

THE AUTHOR Jonathan Reed and the publishers would like to thank the SAS Regimental Association and Lieutenant-Colonel John Cooper for their invaluable assistance in the production of this article.

SAS
ASSIGNMENT YEMEN

Lieutenant-Colonel John Cooper tells the story of a secret, undercover SAS expedition into Yemen in 1963

Below: In the desert of southeast Yemen. The Anglo-French expedition went in with a Yemeni royalist camel caravan, carrying arms northwards to the tribesmen in the Khowlan.

CIVIL WAR IN YEMEN

On 26 September 1962 the ruler of North Yemen, the Imam Mohammed al-Badr (shown below), was overthrown by a military coup led by Colonel Abdullah al-Sallal, chief of staff to the Yemeni Army. Mohammed al-Badr escaped from the capital, Sana, to refuge in the mountains where he organised a royalist army of Zeidi tribesmen which received support from neighbouring Saudi Arabia. Sallal proclaimed the Yemen Arab Republic and the new republican government received substantial military support from Egypt's President Gamal Abdel Nasser who was promoting left-wing Arab nationalism in the Middle East, directly hostile to conservative religious rulers like the Imams. Britain and France were both concerned at the turn of events in Yemen and the spread of Nasser's influence in the Middle East. In June 1963, John Cooper's eight-man Anglo-French party was despatched to report on the situation and to ascertain whether Sallal's government depended on continued Egyptian military support. The civil war in Yemen was to continue for nearly seven years of hard and bloody fighting, resulting in the Imam going into exile in England and a coalition government of royalists and republicans being formed.

IN EARLY June 1963 I was stationed in Muscat on the Arabian peninsula and was then second-in-command, under Colonel Clive Chettle, of the Muscat Regiment of the Sultan of Oman's armed forces (SAF). One day, out of the blue, I received a telegram from my old CO in the wartime SAS, Colonel David Stirling, asking me to join him in Aden for a meeting. The message was brief and gave no indication as to what he wanted. Now, to fly from Muscat to Aden in those days was a no-go – there was no air transport available and commercial airlines didn't fly that route – so I answered his cable saying that it was impossible. A further cable from David then arrived, asking me to meet him in Bahrain instead.

I realised from the veiled contents of his cables that there had to be a lot of security behind these requests, so I went to see Colonel Hugh Oldman, who commanded the SAF, and told him, in confidence, what was required of me. Oldman then brought in Captain (later Brigadier) Malcolm Dennison, who was one of the top security men in Oman, and it was decided, as a ploy to cover my rather hasty departure from Oman, that my mother was to be dying. Colonel Oldman sent a telegram to this effect and I was given two weeks' leave to join an aircraft in Bahrain and fly to the UK to visit my 'dying' mother.

On arrival at Bahrain I was met by a Doctor Phillip Horniblower from 21 SAS TA, who, incidentally, was later to be the medical officer on the SAS Everest expedition in 1976. Horniblower took me to the Speedbird Hotel where he briefed me: I was to lead a joint Anglo-French operation 'somewhere in the Middle East'. The reason I had been selected, it materialised, was the fact that I had been out in Oman for quite some time – I had commanded A Squadron 22 SAS in the Jebel Akhdar campaign of 1958-59 and

was now a seconded officer to the SAF – and thus had a good working knowledge of conditions and the people in that part of the world. Details of the operation would have to wait until later. David himself came into Bahrain at midnight, having flown around the clock, and told me that the next day (5 June), we would be flying out to the UK.

On arrival at London on the evening of the 5th, we immediately transferred to a flight to Paris, where we found the city alive with D-day anniversary celebrations. It was also my birthday! From the airport we went to a meeting in a flat belonging to a French government aide, Peter de Bourbon Palmer, just off the Champs Elysées. There, David Stirling, Phillip

Hornblower, myself and Colonel Jim Johnson, who had just finished commanding 21 SAS, sat around a table with a party of very high-ranking officials from both the British and French governments and, at last, a clear picture of what I was going to do emerged.

I was to lead a mixed party of British and French regulars into North Yemen to ascertain whether the republican government, established by Colonel Sallal of the Yemeni Army in a coup the year before, was being supported as a puppet regime by massive Egyptian military backing from President Nasser, which was now believed to be pouring into the country. Neither the British nor the French government was prepared to recognise the new regime if their suspicions were proved correct.

So that was the task – to reconnoitre and join up with the royalist forces who were fighting a guerrilla war against the republicans and their Egyptian supporters, and look at the problem from the other side of the fence. I was then informed by Ahmed Hammed Shami, the royalist Yemeni ambassador to London, that we would be going in via Aden and that all arrangements had been made. In Aden we would meet up with Squadron Leader Tony Boyle, who was then secretary to the Governor of Aden.

Well, we returned to London and I was asked to put in a list of weapons that I would need. I was told that the French would be pro-

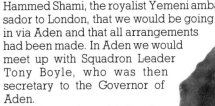

viding two men from the Deuxième Bureau and two French colonial officers, while the British contingent would consist of three regular SAS personnel, specially selected by Colonel John Woodhouse who was then CO of 22 SAS at Hereford. I duly produced my list: plastic explosives, sidearms, Schmeissers – the lightest weapons possible since we would have to collapse them and carry them in our suitcases on the journey to Aden.

I then received notification from Colonel Woodhouse of the men I would be taking with me: Sergeant Dorman, a mortar expert with whom I had served in Malaya, Corporal Chigey who was a very experienced medical man, and Trooper Richardson, an all-round arms expert and an old hand at SAS operations.

My next task was to assemble the team. Officially, since this was a clandestine mission, the men were on leave, but each was assigned a pick-up point in the Hereford area where they were to wait for me. In a hire-car, procured for me by Jim Johnson, I motored up to Hereford at night and collected the men from their various rendezvous points in the depths of the countryside.

All of us then turned up at Johnson's London

Below left: The author, Lieutenant-Colonel John Cooper, perched confidently aboard his camel. Cooper's association with the Arab way of life provided him with a good deal of experience with camels, but the other members of his party were not so fortunate: raw backsides from several days in the saddle inclined them to walk for much of the three-week trek to their destination in the mountains east of Sana. **Left:** Fresh from Hereford, the three regular SAS men of the party pose for a photo with the Sherif of Beihan's right-hand man at the Sherif's house at Nakoub. From left to right are Dorman, Chigey and Richardson. **Below:** Cradling a Schmeisser, Sergeant Dorman keeps a watchful eye open as the expedition picks its way up a steep and rocky wadi.

And, lo and behold, after about 20 minutes, a DC-3 of Aden Airways taxied alongside with its props going. We rushed down the steps from the Comet, crossed the tarmac, and boarded the DC-3.

Taking off again, we were told that we would be landing at the town of Beihan, very close to the Yemeni border, which the Egyptians had started to bomb in raids against settlements in the frontier area. Stationed around the Beihan airstrip was a British ack-ack regiment, and as we climbed out of the aircraft I turned to the Frenchmen and said, 'I am not going to speak English, you must speak French'. There was no point in giving the game away at this stage, British regiment or not. So, we all chatted away – well they did and I did the best I could with my French – and we were immediately picked up by a truck. We motored off straight away through the British camp where a lot of officers from the ack-ack unit were trying to find out who we were, but since they didn't speak French we got away with it. From Beihan, we drove up to Nakoub, only 15 miles from the border with Yemen.

Silently, as darkness fell, we padded our way over the border into North Yemen

That afternoon we stayed at a house belonging to the Sherif of Beihan and were issued with Arab-type clothing. We were then told that we would be going in very, very early the next morning and so we settled down to prepare for the journey ahead.

Preparations completed, we were taken to a lying-up area near to the border. There were all the camels, crouched down, and after loading the beasts, the eight of us set out with a huge caravan of about 150 camels carrying weapons and supplies northwards to the royalists. Silently, as darkness fell, we padded our way over the border into North Yemen. It was the

flat, and down in the basement, we prepared our weapons. The next day, however, the Profumo affair broke and that evening David Stirling was told over the telephone that the operation would have to be cancelled. The British government was obviously not prepared to risk another political embarrassment should our clandestine mission come to light. But David was adamant that we should go ahead, especially since he had received a sizeable amount of capital from the Yemeni royalists to finance the operation.

We split up. I went one way, via Italy, while the other boys took an aircraft to Tripoli in Libya, where we all met up in the passenger lounge to wait for the Comet to take us on to Aden. There was an amusing incident in the departure lounge that nearly blew the whole mission: we had just collected our baggage from the flights that had brought us into Tripoli, when one of the cases broke open, spilling out, of all things, rolls and rolls of plastic explosive. Some of the Libyan airport security guards helped us to pack the stuff away, not realising what it was they were handling!

We then sat tight and waited for the Comet. When it arrived, we climbed aboard and met up with the four Frenchmen who were already on the flight. Finally, we landed at Aden where a gentleman from the British governor's office, under instructions from Tony Boyle, came aboard and told us to stay where we were.

The skipper of the Comet had obviously been briefed that we were special people and that we would be collected by the British authorities in Aden.

Above: Journey's end. Abdullah bin Hassan, commander of the Fifth Royal Army, rides forward at the head of his tribesmen to greet the expedition. Right: In conference with the royalists at their base in the Khowlan. John Cooper (left) discusses forthcoming operations with Abdullah bin Hassan (centre) and his lieutenant, Mohammed. The Yemeni tribesmen were a tough and hardy bunch, and often what they lacked in knowledge of modern weapon systems and tactics was compensated for by their understanding of the ways of the mountains and their fighting spirit.

Left: Members of the Fifth Royal Army display a large fragment of an Egyptian gas-bomb canister. The Egyptian forces in Yemen were extremely reluctant to take the war into the mountains and preferred to remain within the confines of their own enclaves. Total air superiority, however, allowed them to launch air strikes against settlements in the royalist-held areas.
Below: Dorman looks over the rubble of a recently bombed village. Apart from high explosive and chemical-gas weapons, the Egyptians also dropped napalm. Below inset: A survivor of a napalm attack shows the burns received to his face and neck.

start of a very long and strenuous penetration march.

Because of Egyptian air activity, it was necessary to travel at night, and during the day we camouflaged ourselves and holed up in the camel scrub. Camels were cut loose and sent off to graze and all the kit was stored away out of sight of any prying Egyptian reconnaissance. It took almost three weeks to reach the Khowlan, the mountainous region around the capital, Sana, which averaged a height of around 8000ft.

Our biggest obstacle on the trek in was a place called Sirwah, where there was a large Egyptian garrison whose job it was to stop the camel supply caravans getting through. We had very tricky times, lying up day after day, waiting to get through, and my colleagues, who had no experience of riding camels, developed agonisingly sore backsides and preferred to walk. Finally, we managed to get through the Egyptian defences at Sirwah. We went through three or four minefields, but the Yemenis had sussed these out very well indeed and the camels walked in each other's steps in one long, thin line. As we left Sirwah behind, we finally reached the mountains and an area free of republican and Egyptian domination; but we still had to be very careful of the large numbers of Egyptian helicopters and reconnaissance aircraft that were around.

On our arrival in the Khowlan, word was sent forward to Prince Abdullah bin Hassan, commander of the Fifth Royal Army, and as we approached the village of Gara, up a wadi, we met him and his tribesmen with great pomp and ceremony. These were all mountain men, quite a tough crowd, and were part of an army that fielded some 60,000 rifles of various types and all shapes and sizes. Abdullah bin Hassan was interested in us, not just because of the arms we were bringing in, but because of the

promise from our organisation that we would look at the position, support him when we felt it necessary, and even call in air supply of items he required to continue his fight.

As we settled in with Abdullah bin Hassan, it was decided that we should start reconnaissance as soon as we possibly could. To this end, I sent Dorman and Chigey off with one party, while Richardson and myself went off with another. Our aim was to find out the disposition of the Egyptian forces. This first reconnaissance was a short one – a five to 10-mile trek – to acclimatise ourselves with the high altitude. It soon became apparent to us that the Egyptians only held the low ground around Sana and that they were very, very reluctant to come out of their enclaves and go into the outlying towns and villages.

On our return, we saw the first Egyptian air raid on Gara – three Soviet-built Ilyushin 28s of the Egyptian Air Force dropping bombs and firing off 20mm rockets. Following the Ilyushins came Yak fighters, armed with rockets and machine guns, and these piston-engined aircraft were extremely manoeuvrable and able to get into the wadis. Later we were to see the Egyptians dropping gas bombs and napalm.

Having made the reconnaissance, we decided that the time had come to take action. Our plan was to put in a few mines, tickle up the opposition so that they would attack us, and then lead them into a pre-arranged killing ground. Little did we know what a big operation this was going to be.

We'd already started training the Yemenis with the weapons we'd brought in, especially the Bren-gun which is one of the simplest weapons to train the guerrilla on. We organised the men into little sections of between five and seven men each – gun sections or killing groups. Because of the language problem (the Yemeni hill dialects are extremely difficult even with a good knowledge of Arabic), we didn't go into tactics at all. We just showed them how to get down behind the gun, how to make the best use of cover, how long to fire your burst and how not to overheat your weapon. Purely the basics of a real first-time soldier. They were pretty good and knew

Right: A youthful Yemeni shows off a souvenir bomb splinter after an Egyptian air raid. When the Egyptians did sally forth from the protection of their enclaves they were constantly in peril of well-laid land mines. Under Cooper's direction, mines were set, and incidents such as the destruction of this truck goaded the Egyptians into launching operations along the lines of the ill-fated advance into the Wadi Thoul. A system of incentive was introduced for the mine layers: having been shown how to prime and conceal the weapon, the men were given two gold sovereigns. When the mine exploded, a further two were awarded.

how to keep their heads down and survive.

With this training, we set up an ambush in the Wadi Thoul to the east of Sana. The wadi came in and then split to form a 'Y' shape, and in the middle of the 'Y', up a steep slope, there was a small area of level ground about 50yds across. The two ends of the 'Y' both petered out into very steep escarpments and were unassailable. We positioned the royalist gun sections in foxholes in three well-camouflaged spots protected by rocks overlooking the small, flat piece of ground which we designated the killing area. Each position had a 'funk hole' to the rear for when the real 'shit' came in.

As the Egyptians reached the markers, our men opened up with devastating effect

At about 0900 hours the Egyptians moved into the wadi in great strength with a parachute battalion up front and a force of T-34 tanks and light artillery bringing up the rear. They were still unaware of our presence further up the wadi and were nosing around. Half way up the wadi, the tanks and artillery pulled up and the infantry advanced in extended order, packed shoulder to shoulder. They were carrying a lot of heavy clobber and were dragging heavy Russian machine guns along on wheels.

The royalist gun sections' orders were to hold fire until the Egyptians were well onto the killing ground below our positions, and stone cairn markers had been erected as a guide for the gunners. As the Egyptians reached the markers, our men opened up with devastating effect, knocking down the closely

Ambush at Wadi Thoul
August 1963

In June 1963 a mixed detachment of British SAS and French personnel flew out to Aden, transferred to a DC-3 airliner, and flew on to Beihan near the border with North Yemen. At Beihan, the detachment began a three-week long trek to join Yemeni royalist forces in the mountains near Sana.

By August, the detachment had put a training programme into effect, and the reinforced royalists were ready to take action against the Egyptian forces operating in the area. In Wadi Thoul, gun emplacements and a killing ground were prepared and the wait for the enemy began.

Egyptian attack

0900 A large Egyptian force, consisting of infantry with tank and artillery support moves into Wadi Thoul. As the force moves up towards the prepared royalist positions, the royalists hold their fire. The Egyptian artillery and armour halt and the rest of the force pushes up to the head of the valley.

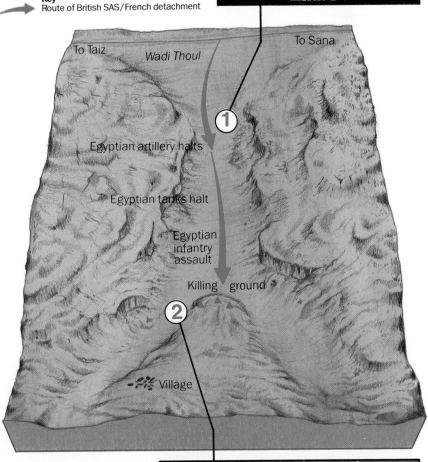

Key
→ Route of British SAS/French detachment

To Taiz — *Wadi Thoul* — To Sana

① Egyptian artillery halts
Egyptian tanks halt
Egyptian infantry assault
Killing ground
②
Village

Key
▲ Royalist Bren-gun positions
→ Egyptian forces

Firefight

As the Egyptian infantry reach the killing ground at the head of the wadi, the royalist forces open fire. The momentum of the assault is broken, and the Egyptian forces sustain heavy casualties. By nightfall the Egyptians have withdrawn.

EGYPTIANS IN NORTH YEMEN

Within a few hours of Colonel Sallal's proclamation of a republic in 1962, an advance guard of 3000 Egyptian troops landed at Sana airfield to support the new republican regime. By April of the following year, Egyptian strength had increased to 30,000 men. The Egyptians had the advantage of total air superiority and bombed and machine gunned at will. Their tanks controlled the main roads, but in the mountains it was a different story. Armoured patrols of the Egyptians, and their republican allies, were regularly ambushed by the royalists and the Egyptians preferred to remain within the confines of their well-defended enclaves. By 1965 Egyptian strength had reached 60,000 troops but Nasser's war was becoming increasingly unpopular in Egypt as casualties mounted. An offensive against Harad in the extreme northwest of the country, for example, had proved a costly failure in which half the force of armoured cars and 10 tanks was lost.

Egyptian forces remained in North Yemen until October 1967 when, in the wake of Egypt's disastrous defeat in the Six-Day War against Israel, Nasser decided to pull his troops out. The immediate consequence of Egypt's withdrawal was the fall of the republican leader Sallal.

packed infantry like ninepins. Panic broke out in the ranks behind and then their tanks opened fire, but their shells were exploding, not on our positions, but among their own men. The light artillery also joined in and most of the casualties they took during the 10-minute firefight were from their own guns.

For the rest of the day the Egyptians kept fire on the top of our hill but we were all well covered in our funk holes. The bodies that had fallen on the killing ground – we counted some 85 afterwards – were left where they had fallen and by nightfall the whole Egyptian force had left the wadi, returning to Sana with a very bloody nose indeed. Those bodies were to lie on that surface for over two years before an agreement was reached to allow the Red Cross to come and collect the skeletons.

The weapons and equipment lost by the Egyptians in the Wadi Thoul – radios, heavy and light machine guns, smallarms etc. – were all recovered by the royalists and taken into custody by the Fifth Army quartermasters, who placed them in one of the caves for future use.

Our next taste of action against the Egyptians was to be very different, but equally successful. We were given information that there was an Egyptian enclave of about two companies situated on top of a hill which was beautifully overlooked by still higher ground. The encampment was supplied by helicopter and was surrounded with barbed-wire and mines. Tents were well protected behind sangars and it was clear that the Egyptians had no intention of using it as a base for patrolling out of.

We went forward and did a reconnaissance with

glasses and soon realised that this was a 'master-piece' for a mortar attack. It was a beautiful soft target. Richardson, Dorman and I loaded up three camels with mortar bombs and the mortar, and took four Yemeni chaps along to be our bodyguard in case we ran into any trouble with the local tribesmen. We left our base in the very early morning so that we could get into position and open fire at first light. On the way in, we had a little bit of opposition from the locals when they saw us going through; they thought we would stir things up and then their villages would get bombed again. But the man that Abdullah bin Hassan had assigned to us convinced them that we had to give this camp a going over.

So we got down into position. We put somebody on the top with a direction finder – a stick held up in the air so that the mortar man could get the line. The map we had didn't give us much idea of the range, but Dorman was a real expert and would use the man on the hill to adjust his fire as necessary.

Left: An Egyptian infantryman wrestles with a recoilless rifle during an engagement with the royalists. The Egyptian forces in Yemen were well-armed and the royalists took every opportunity to capture enemy weaponry. Top right and above: Members of the Fifth Army get the feel of a captured Egyptian RPG rocket launcher and a light machine gun. Top left: While many weapons were new, some military methods were old. A Yemeni prepares mortar, using the time-honoured recipe of camel dung and mud for the building of a sangar in a mountain position.

We got the mortar set up and waited. At first light, as the Egyptians were just getting out of bed all sleepy-eyed and God knows what, we started firing. I think it was our second bomb that we got right inside the actual perimeter. Dorman banged away about 30 rounds and when these were finished we packed up the mortar, put it on the camel, and then the camels were away down the wadi heading for home.

Observed from the top, the panic was fantastic. They thought, at first, that they were going to be attacked by a force of infantry because they started to open fire all the way round. It was a long time before their artillery started to follow up the wadi behind. They were in a real state of turmoil and we were three or four miles away. They even shelled the wrong valley and kept the shelling up for the rest of the day. We had no idea how many casualties they had taken in the attack but, watching through the glasses, it was quite something – the confusion as the bombs landed among them.

By now time was beginning to run out on us. The SAS boys who had come in with me had only been given a month's leave and we had already been here over two months. We had to get out as soon as possible. Abdullah bin Hassan wanted us to stay, but I told him that I had to get out and make my report now that I realised that the Egyptians were running the whole show.

On the way out we had mixed fortunes until we got very close to Marib, where we ran out of water. This is a thing I never want to experience again: the feeling of having your mouth completely dried up when you haven't got a drop to drink. Well, we ended up in a wadi and a blinding sandstorm started blowing. Then one of the Yemeni stalwarts in our caravan volunteered to go into a nearby Egyptian position to get water. We remained in the wadi, under some bushes, thinking, 'God, what's going to happen now?' Without water, we'd had it. We went on waiting and then, suddenly, we heard a commotion coming down through the sandstorm, which was still blowing like hell. I fired a pistol into the air to give some idea of where we were and the man came in with two great big goat skins of water. It was brackish

Below: The boys come home. John Cooper (centre) leads the party back towards the border with Aden. But their problems were not yet over: soon after this picture was taken a violent sandstorm blew up and they ran out of water.

and mouldy and green and slimy, but my God did we enjoy it.

When the storm blew over we looked down towards the Aden border and there, only two miles away, was the Aden Federation army post! We were home.

THE AUTHOR Lieutenant-Colonel John Cooper was one of the original members of 'L' Detachment of the SAS and served throughout World War II, in Malaya and in the Jebel Akhdar campaign with the regiment. In 1963 he went into Yemen and commanded the eight-man team sent to reconnoitre and liaise with the royalist forces. On his return from the expedition, he was immediately sent back to Yemen to set up a radio communications centre. He remained in the country until 1966.

Top: The mixed SAS and French party takes a breather. Above: Chigey and Dorman, saddle-sore and foot-sore, trudge barefoot over the desert sands towards Aden.

107

After leading an eight-man intelligence-gathering team into the heart of war-torn North Yemen, Colonel John Cooper returned to the UK to report his findings. He did not stay long. Within weeks he was back among the Royalist forces with a new and important mission. Colonel Cooper tells the story of his second expedition to the Yemeni civil war

In the mountains of the Yemen. The author, Colonel John Cooper (left), poses for a photo with the co-ax radio aerial that formed the link with the outside world. Good communications were crucial to Cooper's mission, and without them the clandestine air drops of weapons and supplies in support of the Royalist war effort would have been impossible.

OUR MAN IN THE YEMEN

EGYPT, SAUDI ARABIA AND THE YEMEN

During the 1950s, with the rise to power of Egyptian President Gamal Abdel Nasser, relations between Egypt and Saudi Arabia were often strained. In 1958, for example, Nasser accused King Saud of plotting to assassinate him and frequent vitriolic verbal attacks were made by the Egyptians against the Saudi royal family and their whole system of conservative government.

When the Egyptian army arrived in the Yemen after the republican coup in September 1962, the hostility between Egypt and Saudi Arabia became even more acute. Egypt openly accused the Saudis of providing concrete support for the Royalist cause, which they were, while the Saudis responded with accusations that the Egyptians were bombing towns inside Saudi Arabia. Attempts by the United Nations to persuade the Egyptians to withdraw their forces from the Yemen, and the Saudis to withdraw their support for the Royalists, came to nothing. After an unsuccessful effort by the two countries in late 1964 to organise a provisional government in the Yemen, a ceasefire agreement was signed in August 1965 by Nasser and King Faisal. The halt in the war, however, was only temporary and fighting broke out again soon after.

Tensions between Egypt and Saudi Arabia continued thereafter and when Nasser was defeated by the Israelis in the 6-Day War of 1967, King Faisal did not conceal his pleasure – a pleasure derived not from an Israeli victory, but from the defeat of a Saudi opponent. In the aftermath of the Arab-Israeli war, Saudi Arabia agreed to help compensate the Egyptians for their financial losses resulting from the closure of the Suez Canal, but only at the price of a total Egyptian withdrawal from the Yemen. By early October 1967, Egyptian transports were taking their army home.

IN JUNE 1963 I commanded a small team of British SAS and French Deuxième Bureau men on an expedition into North Yemen. We were on a clandestine mission to gather intelligence on the prevailing military situation, and to provide support for the Yemeni Royalist forces engaged in a war against the republican regime of Colonel Abdullah al-Sallal. Sallal was in receipt of massive Egyptian military support, without which, I soon realised, the newly formed Yemen Arab Republic would be hard pressed to survive. I had seen the Royalist Zeidi tribesmen in action against the Egyptians. They were courageous fighters, but their weapons were antiquated and they lacked basic military training.

When I got back to the UK, I gave my assessment of the situation. I had been able to put together a very rough estimate of the number of Egyptian troops stationed in the Yemen, but, as yet, we had no hard information on their orbat (order of battle). Details of the formations deployed, their various strengths and how many tanks and artillery pieces they possessed were still unknown.

This particular intelligence was of special interest to the Saudis, who were extremely concerned about the military foothold that Egyptian President Gamal Abdel Nasser had established in the south of the Arabian peninsula. They were worried that Nasser might use the Yemen as a forward base from which to mount an offensive northwards over the border into Saudi Arabia and take possession of the rich oil fields, situated in the northeast of the country. Saudi concern found concrete expression in the form of financial support for the Royalist forces, whom King Faisal hoped would keep Nasser occupied in the Yemen and curb any expansionist ideas he might have towards Saudi Arabia. But the weapons and equipment that the Royalist tribesmen desperately needed to continue their fight against the Egyptians still had to be got into the Yemen. That was where I came in.

It was imperative that the content of my radio messages through to Aden was completely secure

On my second expedition, I was tasked with drawing up a detailed orbat of the Egyptian forces in the Yemen and, on the more practical level, with the taking of a series of air drops that had been planned to get arms and supplies through to the Royalists. Also, British intelligence was very keen to get hold of as much up-to-date Soviet-built radio equipment as they could, so I was asked to send out some examples, captured from the Egyptians. After re-equipping myself, I flew back to Aden alone. For the coming months it was to be a one-man show.

On arrival in Aden I was briefed by Squadron Leader Tony Boyle, who was then ADC to the High Commissioner, and learned that on my trip north to link up with the Royalists I was to be the money carrier. The Royalists were paid in gold, and the man carrying it was a prime target – not only for the Egyptians, but also for the tribesmen.

As a decoy, we put a number of boxes, rumoured to be containing the money but in reality packed with ammunition, at the front end of the camel caravan. I brought the real sovereigns with me. Fortunately, our bluff was not called and after a relatively uneventful journey I arrived in the mountains east of Sana, where I joined Abdullah bin Hassan, commander of the Fifth Royalist Army.

When I told the Royalist commander about the forthcoming airdrops he was over the moon. I was careful, however, not to tell him where they would be coming from – it was enough that he should know that material assistance was on its way 'from the Europeans'. It was to be some months, however, before the airdrops, codenamed Operation Mango, would begin and for the present I concentrated on the intelligence side of my mission.

I had brought with me an amateur radio set made by KW electronics of Dartford, a number of dry batteries and a charging engine. With Operation Mango coming up, it was absolutely imperative that the content of my radio messages through to Aden was completely secure. To this end, I used a simple but effective code, based on two different French dictionaries. The messages went out with each word encoded as a series of figures. The first digit in a series – either 01 or 02 – referred the translator on the other end to one of the dictionaries, while subsequent numbers pointed him to a page, then a column, and finally the line with the word I wanted to send. Thus, for example, 0143218 would indicate the dictionary designated '01', page 43, column 2, line 18. It was an old and laborious ruse (especially since I had to translate my messages into French before encoding them) but if you did not know which books were being used as the key to the code, and they could have been anything, anyone intercepting the transmission had little chance of understanding it. I was also transmitting on the edge of the amateur wave

The rugged, mountainous terrain of central Yemen (main picture) was ideally suited to the Royalist's style of guerrilla warfare. While the Egyptians fielded a modern, well-equipped army, and possessed total air superiority, among the crags and wadis of the mountains east of Sana they were at a distinct disadvantage. The Royalist Zeidi tribesmen (far left below) mined the roads, ambushed Egyptian convoys and harassed their enclaves with mortar attacks. Left: After months of operating alone with the Royalists, John Cooper (right of picture) was joined by a radio expert from 21 SAS, Cyril Weavers (centre). The Arab boy on the left, Ahmed, assisted Cooper with his medical work and became quite proficient. When Weavers and David Bailey joined Cooper in the Yemen they brought with them another radio and the group of Englishmen was able to split up. Below inset: Tribesmen work on the construction of a radio shack in the lee of a rugged outcrop. Above: Treating a wounded tribesman. This particular operation is being carried out by a French medic who preferred to remain with Cooper's group than with his own compatriots working in the north.

Below: While the Royalists were being supplied with weapons through the Operation Mango air drops, they were also able to utilise captured Soviet-built Egyptian equipment such as this wheel-mounted medium machine gun. Below right: Cyril Weavers poses for a picture with a captured Egyptian mortar and three Royalist tribesmen.

OUTSIDE INTERVENTION

The outbreak of civil war in the Yemen, following the declaration of the Yemen Arab Republic by Colonel Abdullah al-Sallal in September 1962, attracted many outsiders to the Royalist cause. Some came on intelligence-gathering missions, some brought in arms, money and medical supplies and some came as 'mercenaries'.

The first to arrive was Lieutenant-Colonel Neil 'Billy' McLean, the Member of Parliament for Inverness. McLean had made the journey on his own initiative and crossed the border into Yemen in October 1962. His self-appointed mission was to confirm the truth of reports that there was resistance to the newly formed republic. His telegram back to London, which indicated that at least half of the country was under Royalist control, resulted in the British government refusing to recognise the Sallal regime. McLean maintained a deep interest in the Yemen throughout the course of the war and made many personal visits to observe, assess and report on the situation.

In June 1963, Colonel John Cooper led a small party of SAS men (officially 'on leave') into the mountains east of Sana to review the progress of the war and to provide assistance and weapons training to the Royalist forces. Cooper was to spend nearly all his time in the country until 1966, radioing out intelligence, drawing up the Egyptian order of battle and taking air drops of supplies and equipment to the Royalists.

Also involved in the Yemen were a number of mercenaries. Although some were British, most were French or Belgian and included men who had fought for Moise Tshombe in Katanga in 1961 and 1962. The mercenaries, however, were there mainly to support the Royalists as tactical advisers, weapons instructors and radio operators and took little part in the actual fighting.

Medical assistance to the Royalist forces was another area in which outsiders were concerned. The International Red Cross operated mainly in the Republican areas, and the one mission it did send to the Royalists was situated near the northern border with Saudi Arabia at Uqd, a long way from the front. Desperately short of medical supplies and equipment, the Royalists were helped by Lady Birdwood, who set up a private relief organisation to channel essential medical aid into the areas where it was most needed.

band and at random intervals – we avoided fixed schedules – to further confuse any would-be eavesdroppers.

Keeping in regular radio contact with Aden and gathering information on the Egyptian forces was, however, only part of my work. I was also the local medic. The Royalists had no medical back-up whatsoever and there was a terrible shortage of drugs and dressings for treating men with battle wounds. Lady Birdwood was running a relief fund to try and get medical supplies through to the Royalist forces via Aden, but it was far from easy. On one occasion, a shipment of supplies was flown out by the RAF but then impounded in Aden until clearance for the supplies could be obtained from the local authorities. Lady Birdwood then came out herself to see what could be done, but the RAF stuck to their guns. She immediately contacted Tony Boyle and together they got into the stores where the shipment was impounded and sent out the essential items like morphia and field dressings.

With Lady Birdwood's supplies and the medical pack I had brought in, I set up a field hospital at Gara. I was also the surgeon. In the mornings I used to go round to villages within a 10 to 15-mile radius of my radio shack to treat the injured tribesmen. I was extremely fit and I used to run all the way, carrying the medical pack with me. Most of the wounds I had to deal with were napalm burns and injuries caused by

Above: Legendary French mercenary, Bob Denard, trains a Royalist soldier in the use of mortars. Right: David Bailey sets up a captured Egyptian recoilless rifle. Below right: Colonel Cooper's radio shack, set up in the ruins of a Yemeni building.

mortar shrapnel. I also set broken legs and performed all sorts of operations. When the work to be done was beyond my limited knowledge and the few books I had with me, I operated in conjunction with the 'radio doctor' down in Aden who talked me through the job. I am afraid I made some pretty glaring errors, especially in the mending of legs. As time went by, however, I became more proficient and I trained up a young boy called Ahmed to assist me, who became very good at giving injections. Vitamin injections were very important because the food was terrible. Tinned golden syrup and unleavened bread was about all I had to live on, though about once a fortnight we would get a piece of goat meat. Before Operation Mango got underway, and proper nourishment was flown in, my weight went down to under eight-and-a-half stone.

A particularly unpleasant aspect of the war in the Yemen was the gas-bombing carried out by the

Egyptians against our positions in the mountains. The gas canisters were dropped from Ilyushin 28s and on hitting the ground would disgorge a pall of thick white smoke. This vapour had a terrible effect on the eyes and many of the men were blinded, some permanently. On one particular morning we were holed up in some caves in a very deep wadi near Gara. The caves provided very good protection against bombing attacks, but not against napalm or gas. Leaving my refuge for my morning constitutional and to relieve the call of nature, I walked about a mile and a half down the wadi. Suddenly, out of the sky came two Egyptian Ilyushins, flying low at about 500ft as they swung into the valley. The aircraft dropped their gas bombs, and as the canisters hit the floor of the wadi the deadly white vapour swirled up the steep, rocky sides and into the caves. Before long, some 200 blinded tribesmen came out of the caves, yelling and carrying on. It was deplorable. All I had to hand was some Optrex eye wash, but that was absolutely useless. From then on we used the caves as little as possible.

All the time, the Royalists kept up a campaign of

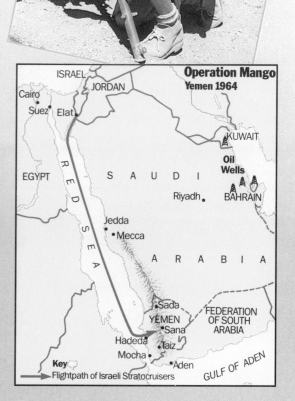

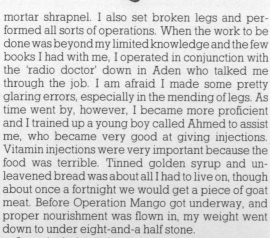

harassment against the Egyptian forces, mining roads and launching guerrilla-style ambushes and attacks on their enclaves. Despite their total air superiority and their modern weapon systems, the Egyptians were extremely wary of us and there were times when we exploited their extreme caution with very amusing results. One day, just before dawn, we laid a dummy mine, constructed out of an old tin can with an object resembling a detonator attached to the top. We then positioned ourselves on the mountain-side overlooking the mined road and waited for the Egyptians to arrive. Lo and behold, after two hours a vehicle appeared, moving gingerly along the road. Seeing the 'mine' ahead, the troops jumped out and inspected the contraption and then turned round and drove off the way they had come.

About an hour later, out came a whole convoy of vehicles with a tracked armoured personnel carrier (APC). Engineers were sent forward to observe the object again and, having debated at length on what to do, they dug round the sides and put a cable round it with the other end attached to the APC. Then, they all squatted down and started shooting at the mine. Of course, nothing happened, and by this time we could hardly control our mirth. Finally, they winched it out onto the road. I have never seen such hysterics. Some of the younger officers could see the funny side of it, but I don't think the older ones did because there was a hell of a lot of shouting going on down below. We never repeated this ruse but it was a great deal of fun and it certainly kept the Egyptians on their toes.

The Israeli authorities were extremely concerned that the whole operation should run like clockwork

After nearly 11 months of working on my own with the Royalists I finally got word that I was to be reinforced with two more men and that Operation Mango could now go ahead. The two new men were Cyril Weavers and David Bailey. Weavers was a radio and communications man from 21 SAS and Bailey came from the Sussex Regiment. I had not heard of Bailey before but apparently he had pestered Billy McLean endlessly to be allowed to go out and support the Royalist cause and, after a vetting by the 'club' back in the UK, it was finally agreed that he could come out and join me.

We now had two radios and started operating separately. I put Bailey in one area and Weavers came with me. We also began our preparations for Mango. The reason behind the strict blanket of

security surrounding the air drop operations was that they were, in fact, being flown by the Israeli Air Force. If this information was to get out... well, one can imagine the political repercussions!

Anyway, we started to set up a test for the Mango communications and although at first we could not always hear the Israelis on the other end, the radio link became better and better with practice. The Israeli authorities were extremely concerned that the whole operation should run like clockwork and asked for a complete breakdown of my experience of taking air drops before they would consider proceeding. Fortunately, I was an old hand at the business, having taken numerous supply drops in France in 1944 when I was with the SAS, and again in Malaya. I had also done a number of courses on the various procedures and techniques of lighting, communications and so on, and eventually the Israelis were satisfied that I could handle the job.

When they reached the port of Hadeda, they swung the aircraft inland towards the mountains

To make the drops the Israelis had converted a Stratocruiser with a roll-off exit at the rear for pushing out the canisters with their 'chutes. At our end the equipment was less than sophisticated – the only lighting gear we could raise to mark the drop zone was a couple of car headlamps, running off two old batteries, and a series of petrol and diesel fires. The drop zone itself was only 400yds long so the Israelis were going to have to be on the ball and pretty accurate.

During the week running up to the first drop we were in contact with them on a four-hourly basis to make sure that our communications equipment was working at all times, right up to the moment that the plane took off.

On the night of the first drop the Stratocruiser took off from Elat and flew down the Red Sea with Egypt on its right and Saudi Arabia on the left. They had to come in almost at sea level to avoid detection by Egyptian radar and then, when they reached the port of Hadeda, they swung the aircraft inland towards the mountains and climbed to a height of 10,000ft. Throughout the flight they maintained strict radio silence until they reached the 10,000ft mark, when a message came through, 'We are approaching. Will be with you in 10 minutes.'

Shortly after that, I received the signal to light the fires. Up went the car headlamps and David Bailey lit

Below left: With Cooper in the Yemen were two members of the French Deuxième Bureau, one of whom is shown talking to a group of tribesmen. Tragically, the French were victims of an Egyptian gas-bombing and were blinded. With no sophisticated medical aid available, they had to be shipped out to Aden, riding blind with a Yemeni camel caravan. Above: Much of the equipment dropped to the Royalists during Operation Mango was of German origin dating back to World War II. Shown here is a 7.92mm MG machine gun, fitted with a drum magazine. Below: An Egyptian T34 tank lies abandoned after a Royalist ambush. The roads in the Yemen were not made up, making it very easy for the Royalists to conceal mines, while the wadis and mountain passes provided perfect cover for ambush parties. Right: A lone tribesman looks out over a deceptively peaceful landscape.

the beacons. Then we heard, 'Got your visual. Dummy run.' The Stratocruiser came in low over the flare path at about 250ft and turned away. The Israelis had muffled the engines and it was very quiet. Then the huge aircraft came in for the actual drop, and as it passed 60 parachutes spewed out of the back. It really was excellent dropping, real professional stuff. As he started pulling out, the pilot said, 'Last parachute for you. Report.' 'Bullseye', I replied. Then he said, 'Best of luck. Cheerio.' That was the last communication we had with the aircraft as it disappeared and dropped down from the mountains for the return flight up the Red Sea.

Well, everybody went wild. They had bullock carts, everything out, collecting the containers and taking them under cover. The next morning the Egyptians had an aircraft up over the mountains but they were not looking in the right place. They had

obviously heard or seen something during the night and were alerted to the fact that someone had flown over. But who had been there, and where they had gone remained a complete mystery.

Abdullah bin Hassan was delighted. He now had the mortars and bombs he needed, and a plentiful supply of smallarms, including German Schmeissers, Spandaus and rifles. The source of these weapons was brilliantly concealed. Every serial number on the arms had been scored out, the parachutes were Italian in origin and even the wood-shavings used in the packaging had been imported from Cyprus. No-one, not even an expert, could have worked out the source of the shipment. The last container to be dropped carried our personal mail, up-to-date English newspapers and a bottle of whisky. A superb gesture! I had not touched a drop of alcohol for a year, and the whisky tasted absolutely vile. But David, Cyril and I sat round in our little hideout and devoured the bottle and then fell asleep.

This was the first of nine Mango air drops we were to receive. As time passed, we became more proficient and the Israelis dropped the gear in fewer,

and much larger, containers so that we did not have so much work to do rounding up the equipment on the drop zone.

At this stage in the game, with our increasing military strength and know-how, Abdullah bin Hassan decided to go on the offensive and surround the capital, Sana, cutting it off from the main port of Hadeda. I sent Bailey off to cover the left flank, and Weavers the right, while I remained at the Royalist HQ with Abdullah bin Hassan. The operation was a great success. We cut off the roads, stopping all traffic, and were able to hold our own in the rugged passes where smallarms fire could be brought to bear with devastating results on the roads below. The Egyptians, who were cooped up in their enclaves and spread all over the country, could do little to combat this tactic on the ground. They did, however, increase the level of air activity against us, using bombs, napalm and poison gas. But their bombing was terribly inaccurate and often they would be dropping ordnance several miles away from our actual positions.

At this stage, tragically, we suffered a big setback. One day, the Egyptians dropped a gas bomb on our radio station and the two French Deuxième Bureau men, who had come in with me on my first visit to Yemen, were blinded in the attack and had to be sent back to Aden on camels. It was also time for me to take a break. The timing, however, could not have been worse.

I was immediately tracked down to where I was staying in Moreton and surrounded by journalists

As I arrived back in the UK, a series of letters was splashed all over a Cairo newspaper, purporting to be evidence of British 'interference' in the Yemeni civil war. The letters, variously addressed 'Dear John', 'Dear Major Cooper' and 'Dear Abdul (Black)' – my codename in the Yemen – were then investigated by the *Sunday Times* newspaper's 'Insight' team and appeared in that paper in July 1964. I was immediately tracked down to where I was staying in Moreton, Essex, and surrounded by journalists. I was hounded relentlessly but they never got to grips with me. I was picked up in a mini by Fiona Frazer, then secretary to our organisation, while my brother-in-law took my car and headed off in the opposite direction with all the reporters in hot pursuit. Changing cars, I went straight to Heathrow airport, boarded a plane and, once again, headed east for Aden and the mountains of the Yemen.

Despite the revelations in the press, I had achieved my goal. I had drawn up the full Egyptian orbat, right down to the names of the commanding colonels, the divisions, brigades and battalions deployed. I was also able to report in detail on the aircraft the Egyptians were operating, and the squadrons committed. Apart from the intelligence, London was also very glad to receive a modern Soviet field radio which I had shipped out on one of the camel caravans.

THE AUTHOR Lieutenant-Colonel John Cooper was one of the original members of 'L' Detachment of the SAS and served throughout World War II, in Malaya and in the Jebel Akhdar campaign with the regiment. He spent three years in the Yemen during the civil war, gathering intelligence and acting as a military adviser providing technical expertise to the Royalists.

SAS

In April 1965 a nine-man patrol from 22 SAS fought a bloody battle for survival against superior numbers of rebel tribesmen in the heart of the Radfan mountains

This page: Members of an SAS team load their rucksacks on the back of a truck prior to making a sweep of the Radfan in search of rebel tribesmen.

EDWARDS' PATROL

UNDERCOVER IN ADEN TOWN

While their comrades battled it out in the Radfan, several SAS undercover teams operated in the teeming alleyways and streets of Aden against Yemeni-trained hit men who were striking against British Special Branch operatives and their contacts in the Arab community. With the schedule of British withdrawal from Aden settled, there was little chance of 'turning' captured terrorists against their erstwhile comrades and the SAS had to go it alone with little help from the local population.

After a tough course in urban undercover work, selected SAS men, often Fijians who could more easily pass for Arabs, were sent out into the town on a regular basis to tackle the terrorists on their own ground. The men who took to the streets were equipped with the heavy, 13-round Browning pistol, a weapon relatively easy to conceal under traditional Arab clothing.

The SAS unit, usually no more than 20-strong, worked from Ballycastle House, a barracks for married military men close to Aden town's Khormaksar airport. From this seemingly innocent location, SAS teams, usually of two or three men, would move into the capital's Crater district, the centre of the enemy's activities. Often, one of the men would wear British military dress in an attempt to lure the terrorists into making a move.

Although the SAS groups made regular forays into the Arab quarter, it was rare for them to capture a terrorist. However, on a number of occasions they were successful in preventing attacks on 'soft' targets, in particular groups of civilians and schoolchildren.

The value of the SAS undercover operations in Aden is difficult to evaluate, but it is certain that their very presence forced the enemy onto their guard. In addition, the hard intelligence gathered by the teams enabled the security forces to score some notable successes against the terrorists.

DURING THE EARLY, evening of 29 April 1965, as the sweltering heat of the desert day was giving way to the bone-chilling cold of the night, a small convoy of armoured cars rattled through the gates of the British base of Thumier, some 60 miles inland from Aden town, and headed northwards along the dusty Dhala road, pushing ever deeper into the Radfan mountains. On board the swaying vehicles the nine men of 3 Troop, A Squadron, 22 SAS – all veterans of the counter-insurgency wars in Malaya and Borneo, with the exception of the troop commander, Captain

Above: Thumier, the centre of British activity in the Radfan.
Right: A patrol moves out.

Robin Edwards, and his signaller, Trooper J.M. Warburton – checked their weapons and equipment: 60lb packs, 80 rounds of ammunition apiece for their SLRs, extra bandoliers of smallarms ammo and over 1000 rounds for the detachment's Bren gun. Ahead lay a short journey to the troop objective – an undistinguished but strategically vital piece of high ground known as 'Cap Badge'.

Edwards and his team were the spearhead of a large-scale operation that was to involve Royal Marines, paras, units of the Royal Horse Artillery and the Royal Artillery, an armoured car squadron with Saladins, and units of Aden's Federal Regular Army (FRA). The intention of the regular forces was to occupy in strength Cap Badge and a second position, 'Rice Bowl', and from these halt the flow of weapons from neighbouring Yemen to the rebel Quteibi tribesmen. Before the main moves could be made, the SAS team was to establish a secure drop zone for the paras at Cap Badge. Once in position, Edwards' men would establish a tight perimeter and prepare flares and lamps to guide in the paras. Their descent was scheduled for the night of the 30th; the SAS had 24 hours to get into position.

Some distance out of Thumier the SAS convoy turned off the Dhala road and moved into the Wadi Radwa. As the cars slowed to negotiate the difficult, rock-strewn terrain, they suddenly came under heavy and continuous fire from concealed sangars dotted about the surrounding heights. Clearly, the tribesmen were alerted to the SAS team's presence. To avoid damage to the vehicles, Edwards ordered his men to dismount and climb towards Cap Badge

under cover of darkness. Despite heavy loads and a hard climb up precipitous slopes to the 3900ft summit of the Djebel Ashqab, progress was good. Only Warburton gave cause for concern. Crippled by agonising stomach cramps, he began to lag dangerously behind. Aware of Warburton's fate should he be captured, Edwards halted to allow the young signaller to catch up, and then redistributed his load, including the 45lb radio, among the rest of the men. An hour later, Warburton had dropped behind.

By now it was 0200 hours, 30 April, and dawn was less than three hours away. To be caught in the open by the accurate rifles of the enemy snipers would spell the end of the mission; Edwards resolved to hole up in a safe position and then resume the march after dusk. Although they were three miles from Cap Badge and behind schedule, there was still some cause for optimism: the worst of the agonising climb was over, the team was in sight of the djebel's summit, and only a downhill trek stood between them and the objective. Scouring the surrounding slopes through the gloom, Edwards spotted two unused stone sangars that seemed to fit the bill. Behind hard cover, he and his men would be able to get some rest, safe from prying eyes. At 0230, Edwards radioed the squadron commander back at Thumier, emphasising that there seemed no cause for alarm. However, when dawn broke, the team's situation was found to be less than ideal. The sangars were little more than 800yds from the rebel village of Shab Tem, from where tribesmen regularly moved out to occupy their hill-top vantage points, and both were dominated by a ridge less than 100yds away.

The team's luck ran out at about 1100 hours when they were forced to deal with a goatherd who almost stumbled on their position. A single, well-aimed round took care of the immediate danger but the commotion attracted dozens of puzzled tribesmen from Shab Tem. The rebels appeared to believe that the noise had been caused by an accidental dis-

After reaching their area of operations by motor transport (above), lightly equipped troops armed with SLRs and GPMGs make the hazardous climb to a hill-top post (above left).

charge from one of their own rifles, and they advanced towards the sangars without taking cover. Several paid the price for their lack of caution as the SAS sought to even up the odds, but the rest dived for cover, searching out the source of the firing. Spying out the high ground close to the sangars, a number of tribesmen crept into position.

Edwards was equal to the threat. Through Warburton's radio, he was in direct, if shaky, communication with the squadron's second-in-command, Major Mike Wingate Gray, who had a direct telephone link with the RAF liaison officer at Thumier, Squadron Leader Roy Bowie. Two hours after the patrol had been discovered, four Hawker Hunters pounced on the tribesmen holding the ridge, spraying their ranks with cutting bursts of cannon fire. The ridge was quickly cleared but, surrounded by the rebels, the SAS men could not escape the accurate fire of the enemy. The slightest movement above the sangars attracted a vicious burst of shots. Only the Hunter strikes, guided to their targets by a recognition panel spread out over the ground between the two sangars, and much-needed artillery fire, kept the tribesmen from overrunning the SAS team's position.

As the afternoon dragged on, however, the RAF

Edwards' Patrol
Aden, April–May 1965

Ordered to hold a landing strip members of 22 SAS climbed into the Radfan, only to be faced by overwhelming enemy forces. Suffering heavy losses, they had to make a fighting withdrawal back to the British base at Thumier.

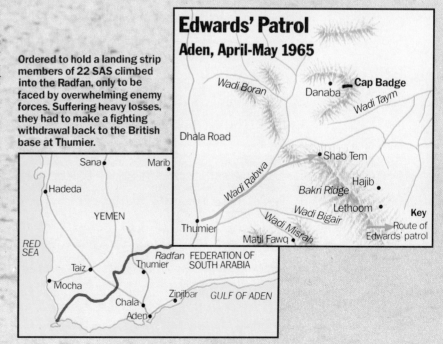

119

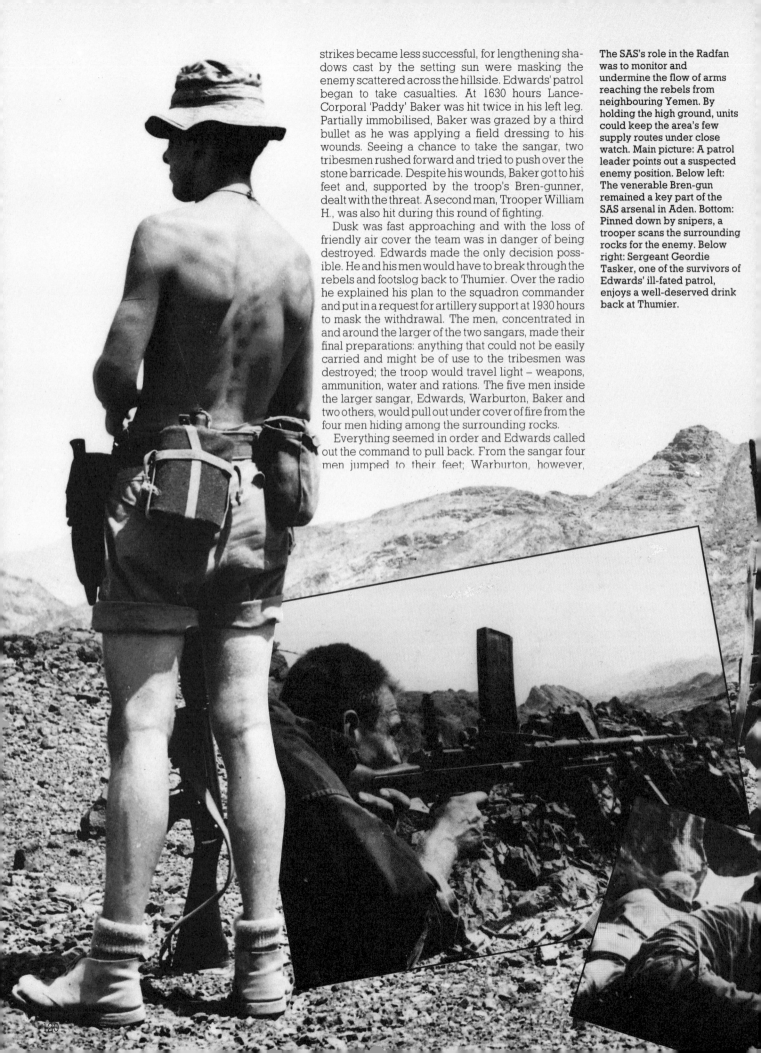

strikes became less successful, for lengthening shadows cast by the setting sun were masking the enemy scattered across the hillside. Edwards' patrol began to take casualties. At 1630 hours Lance-Corporal 'Paddy' Baker was hit twice in his left leg. Partially immobilised, Baker was grazed by a third bullet as he was applying a field dressing to his wounds. Seeing a chance to take the sangar, two tribesmen rushed forward and tried to push over the stone barricade. Despite his wounds, Baker got to his feet and, supported by the troop's Bren-gunner, dealt with the threat. A second man, Trooper William H., was also hit during this round of fighting.

Dusk was fast approaching and with the loss of friendly air cover the team was in danger of being destroyed. Edwards made the only decision possible. He and his men would have to break through the rebels and footslog back to Thumier. Over the radio he explained his plan to the squadron commander and put in a request for artillery support at 1930 hours to mask the withdrawal. The men, concentrated in and around the larger of the two sangars, made their final preparations: anything that could not be easily carried and might be of use to the tribesmen was destroyed; the troop would travel light – weapons, ammunition, water and rations. The five men inside the larger sangar, Edwards, Warburton, Baker and two others, would pull out under cover of fire from the four men hiding among the surrounding rocks.

Everything seemed in order and Edwards called out the command to pull back. From the sangar four men jumped to their feet; Warburton, however,

The SAS's role in the Radfan was to monitor and undermine the flow of arms reaching the rebels from neighbouring Yemen. By holding the high ground, units could keep the area's few supply routes under close watch. Main picture: A patrol leader points out a suspected enemy position. Below left: The venerable Bren-gun remained a key part of the SAS arsenal in Aden. Bottom: Pinned down by snipers, a trooper scans the surrounding rocks for the enemy. Below right: Sergeant Geordie Tasker, one of the survivors of Edwards' ill-fated patrol, enjoys a well-deserved drink back at Thumier.

remained motionless. He and his radio had been hit several times during the most recent exchange of shots. There was nothing to be done and the other four ran for the covering group. Edwards, in the centre of the party, was the target of a vicious fusillade. Hit by several rounds in the space of a few seconds, he fell to the ground, where the rebels pumped shots into his lifeless body.

Although barely able to walk due to his leg wounds, Baker and the two other survivors from the sangar took up position some 15yds to the rear of the original covering party, whose turn it was now to fall back. Luckily the tribesmen

were still blazing away at the deserted sangars and the party crept into the night without coming under fire. By keeping to the high ground that criss-crossed the hillsides, the team expected to avoid pursuit and any further clashes with the enemy. Moments later, and still on schedule, the battered party was heartened to hear the whistle of shells as the

FIGHTING FOR RADFAN

In the years before the final independence of Aden, scheduled for November 1967, the SAS formed part of a regular force drawn from the British armed forces that attempted to keep a number of warring factions, many backed by Egypt and the Soviet Union through the Yemen, from undermining the legitimate local authorities.

The specialist skills of the SAS were used in two main areas: Aden town itself, and in the Radfan mountains close to the Yemeni border. When a state of emergency was declared in late 1963, the SAS consisted of two squadrons, A and D. The unit's involvement in the conflict started in early 1965. At that time, D Squadron was on a tour of duty in Borneo and, as luck would have it, A Squadron had arranged to begin a tour of Aden during May. The commander of the squadron suggested that his men form part of the force earmarked for a Radfan operation. His request was granted and the regiment began its long association with Aden and the Radfan. For security reasons, the first SAS teams arrived in great secrecy and even their families believed that they were on training exercises on Salisbury Plain. After their acclimatisation courses the men settled into a routine of undercover, anti-guerrilla work that was to last until the British finally left Aden in November 1967. Operating with the regular forces, the SAS worked with helicopters.

Like most counter-insurgency wars, the campaigns in Aden and the Radfan were hard and long, with the SAS winning few clear-cut victories against the enemy, yet the regiment made a significant contribution to the military operations. In a constant round of often dangerous patrols, the men helped to contain the worst excesses of the rebels. It was a thankless task, and when the SAS finally pulled out shortly before independence, few men regretted leaving the embattled protectorate.

Royal Artillery pounded the area around the sangars with high explosive. Although accurate, the fire did little damage to the enemy, for the tribesmen had retired with the bodies of Edwards and Warburton. Later the two men were decapitated and their heads put on display in the Yemen.

Unaware of the gruesome fate awaiting the bodies of their two comrades, the survivors continued the long trudge towards Thumier. After more than 24 hours in action and a day spent under the intense heat of the sun with dwindling supplies of water, the men were close to exhaustion. Short of stamina, their bodies aching with fatigue, they stumbled over scree slopes, ever alert for the presence of the

Below: SAS men draw water from a well under the walls of a native village. Below left, inset: Gathering intelligence from the locals was a major part of the SAS's brief in Aden. Bottom: A British mortar responds to a night attack.

enemy. Led by their two sergeants, the team made slow progress. The two wounded men, Baker and Trooper William H., brought up the rear, hobbling and staggering as best they could. A halt was called. The medic dropped back to attend to Baker, whose blood-soaked field dressings had worked loose to expose his leg wounds.

The march was resumed, with the men sticking to the high ground above the Wadi Radwa. Suddenly, the lead sergeant signalled a halt. In the dim distance there seemed to be an encampment. Not wishing to investigate further, the sergeant ordered the group to climb higher, taking a path away from the direct route to safety. Having worked round the camp, the men discovered that what they had been avoiding had been nothing more than several large rocks. Danger, however, was close at hand. Baker, again in the rear, heard the sound of someone trailing the group and dropped further back to investigate with Trooper H. Taking position behind a bush, they peered through the night, looking back down the track. Four men, unmistakably Arabs, loomed out of

the night. Coolly, Baker and his companion held their fire until their quarries were level with their cover.

Calling on every ounce of their strength, the two ambushers jumped to their feet and opened up on their unsuspecting targets. The four men were bowled over, hardly aware of what had hit them. Baker kept pouring fire into the bodies until he was sure the job was done. Up front, the rest of the team waited for the two men to return, and as a parting shot one of the sergeants loosed off a few bursts from a Bren gun to discourage any other Arabs who might have ideas about continuing the pursuit.

Moving off once again, the SAS men resumed their nightmare journey with Baker and Trooper H. taking up position as the rearguard. After an hour or so, they picked up the sounds of two men – probably enemy scouts. Settling into an ambush position, Baker and Trooper H. bided their time until they were sure of their targets. Again a sustained round of firing ended the threat. It was about 0230 hours on 1 May; the weary party had been on the move for over nine hours and were close to the point where they could climb down to the Wadi Radwa. From there it was but a short haul to Thumier and safety. Slithering and sliding down the hillside, the team finally came to rest in the wadi, where they were able to slake their raging thirsts with muddy water from a stream. Having come so far and with help in sight, the sergeants reluctantly but correctly decided to hole up until daylight to avoid any brushes with the FRA soldiers who were known to be in the area. Having trekked through miles of hostile territory, no-one relished being shot by his own side.

The wounded men were placed in the Saladin for the journey back to base

As the sun rose that morning the slumbering men were roused to begin the march into Thumier along the line of the wadi. Thirty minutes later the seven heard the unmistakable growl of an armoured-car engine. Climbing out of the dry water course, they flagged down the vehicle. The two wounded men were gently placed in the Saladin for the short journey back to base but the remaining five walked the final mile. The operation was over and although it had to be counted as a failure, the SAS team had come through an ordeal by fire with great skill and courage in the face of overwhelming odds. Baker, the man who did so much to prevent the tribesmen from destroying the survivors during the retreat from Shab Tem, won a much-deserved Military Medal.

The exploits of Edwards' patrol were only the beginning of SAS involvement in the Radfan during the run up to the independence of Aden. Much of the time, small teams would be inserted into hill-top hides to monitor the movement of the rebels and their supply columns down the camel tracks from neighbouring Yemen. It was dirty, often unrewarding work and out-and-out successes were few. Yet despite the difficulties of tracking down a wily enemy who was operating in small groups in some of the toughest country of the Middle East, the men of the SAS did score several victories in the protracted counter-insurgency campaign that preceded Aden's independence.

THE AUTHOR William Franklin has contributed military articles to a number of specialist publications and has a particular interest in the world's elite combat forces.

Officer, 22 SAS, Aden 1960s

Dressed in loose-fitting jungle green trousers and khaki shirt, this soldier is armed with a 7.62mm L1A1 SLR. Other equipment comprises a pair of '44 pattern waterbottle covers (used as pouches), a non-regulation belt, a jungle hat and a pair of rugged desert or chukka boots.

AUSTRALIAN SAS

The Australian Special Air Service Regiment (SAS) originated as the 1st SAS Company in July 1957, and was raised and formed at Campbell Barracks, Swanbourne, Western Australia. The company was, at the outset, an Infantry Corps element and in 1960 became part of the Royal Australian Regiment. At that time, it had some 120 men on strength. On 4 September 1964, the unit was elevated to full regimental status and consisted of Headquarters and Base Squadron (Training Cadre), the 1st and 2nd Sabre Squadrons – these were the fighting element – and the 151st Signals Squadron.

The regiment was put through tough training programmes in New Guinea, Thailand and on the island of Okinawa and then, in February 1965, the two squadrons were deployed to Borneo. The 1st Squadron went to Brunei while the 2nd Squadron was based in the Kuching area on the coast of Sarawak.

The first Australian SAS troops to enter Vietnam did so as part of a 30-man Australian Army Training Team in mid-1962. These few men were the forerunners of an Australian SAS involvement which was to bring great distinction to the relatively new formation in the Australian armed forces. By 1966 a third Sabre Squadron had been formed, and in July of that year the 3rd Squadron arrived in Vietnam. Each Sabre Squadron and signals troop undertook two tours of duty in Vietnam until the Australian withdrawal from the war in October 1971.

In the jungles of Vietnam, the Sabre Squadrons of the Australian SAS proved highly effective in the hard-fought war against the Viet Cong

WHEN THE MEN of the 1st Battalion, The Royal Australian Regiment (RAR), sailed for the war in South Vietnam in May 1965, they were told that mess dress would be needed. A year later, as the newly formed 3rd Sabre Squadron of the Australian Special Air Service Regiment (SAS) prepared to join their compatriots at Nui Dat in Phuoc Tuy province, they were

told the same – but when they arrived, they found that they were living under ponchos, battered and drenched by daily tropical downpours. It was a fitting introduction to the five years of active service in Vietnam that were to come.

But the regiment was no stranger to the rigours of jungle warfare. In February 1965, the 1st Squadron was sent to Borneo as part of the Commonwealth forces involved in the 'Confrontation' between Malaysia and Indonesia, and there they were to gain invaluable experience in tactics and fighting methods that would stand them in good stead for

their later tours of duty in Vietnam. Five months before the close of ops in Borneo, the 3rd Squadron was deployed to Phuoc Tuy, where they operated until February 1967. From then on, each of the three squadrons served on a yearly rotational basis, operating out of a special area of Australian Task Force Headquarters Nui Dat, known to the men as 'SAS Hill'. This inner sanctum was exclusive to SAS personnel and stringently enforced, tight security kept any snoopers out.

When the SAS first arrived, it saw its function as an intelligence-gathering and surveillance unit, to provide headquarters of the Australian Task Force with information for the deployment of larger, regular RAR forces in the Australian area of responsibility. But their mission soon broadened to encompass not only undercover recon and observation patrols, but also fighting recons and ambush work. Normally, five

men – lead scout, patrol leader, second-in-command, signaller and medic – were used for recon work, but if an ambush was to be laid, the five-man patrol would be beefed up; the largest single patrol was carried out by 30 men.

The SAS soon became masters of the art of fighting reconnaissance and were to achieve the highest kill ratio of any unit of its kind operating in Vietnam since the war fought in Indochina by the French. During their first tour of duty, the 3rd Sabre Squadron tried out a wide range of new techniques, which were to be developed further by the squadrons that followed them. In that one year, the 3rd mounted 134 patrols and made 27 contacts with the enemy: 46 enemy were killed, four possible kills were noted, 13 were wounded and one enemy soldier was taken prisoner. The only SAS man killed by enemy fire during the five years of commitment to Vietnam died after this tour – Trooper R. J. Copeman was hit by hostile smallarms fire during a contact and died of his wounds three months later in Australia.

On the ground, the SAS operated in tough terrain in the midst of enemy-infested territory. Phuoc Tuy province is partly coastal, with several ranges of mountains. Old, overgrown rubber plantations, jungle, and expanses of secondary growth with large

areas of spikey bamboo, made the going difficult but provided excellent cover for clandestine SAS surveillance operations and surprise ambushes.

One day in 1969, an SAS patrol, on a typical recon

The men of the Australian SAS are trained to fight in a wide range of environments and are familiarised with varying techniques of insertion by air, sea and land. Above: On the Assault Swimmer Course, SAS men make a 'wet' jump. Below: The SAS Canoe Course. Right: Into action – a trooper emerges from the bush with an SLR during an ambush training exercise.

SABRE SQUADRONS

mission, made contact with the enemy when five Viet Cong (VC) were spotted heading towards a guerrilla camp. When the enemy soldiers had approached to within 15m of the patrol, one of the VC spotted their position but was killed immediately with a shot to the chest. The patrol scout then engaged another soldier, who was similarly despatched. The remaining three VC opened up but were quickly silenced with SAS smallarms fire.

An hour later, as the SAS moved on, they found themselves in the middle of a well-used track complex, and some 10 VC were observed moving northwards, only 10m away. Suddenly, another 19 appeared on the scene, moving northeast at a distance of 25m, only to be followed by a further six. As one of the VC approached the hidden SAS men, he was taken out by the patrol signalman and the rest of the patrol then engaged the two groups, pinning them down with a barrage of smallarms fire.

Disappearing into the dense foliage, the SAS continued to reconnoitre the area and, an hour or so later, passed close to the perimeter of a reinforced VC company position. Almost immediately, nine VC were seen approaching, and when they had got to within 20m the SAS opened up. The leading soldier was stopped dead in his tracks but the others began to return strong, effective smallarms fire. The SAS raked the area with rifle fire and 40mm high-explosive grenades from their M79s, which kept the enemy's heads down. After these brief, but incisive, close-quarters firefights, the patrol was winched out by helicopter. Sergeant J. M. Robinson, the patrol leader, was later awarded the Distinguished Conduct Medal.

In these dangerous circumstances silence, stealth and infinite patience were crucial

But not all recons were quite so eventful and there were days when a patrol would move no more than about 500m. As a rule, patrols operated mainly in the daytime, preferring not to work blindly. Moving out after breakfast and a recce of their immediate surroundings, they would move stealthily until mid-morning. From then until the middle of the afternoon, they observed what they called 'pak time' – a period when there was increased VC movement and activity. During pak time, the patrol would deploy on either side of a track known to be used by the enemy, where they would observe VC movements and gather as much intelligence as they could. Communication between the troops was strictly by hand signal, and in these dangerous circumstances silence, stealth and infinite patience were crucial.

So skilful were the SAS at personal concealment that on one occasion, so the story goes, a trooper lying in a hide found himself being urinated on by a passing Viet Cong soldier who was blissfully unaware of his presence. The SAS soldier accepted the warm rain without complaint! On another mission, an NCO moved in so close to a VC camp that he suddenly found himself right in the middle of their jungle firing range – an alley carved out of the thick jungle – and was forced to remain holed up in the

When the SAS squadrons first arrived in Vietnam, their mission was essentially one of deep-penetration reconnaissance rather than direct combat. But they soon found themselves in the thick of battle. On patrol, two main smallarms were used – the SLR (far left and left) and the M16 (left centre).

Phuoc Tuy

To Saigon
Song Thi Vai
SOUTH VIETNAM
RUNG SAT SPECIAL ZONE
Song Chau Pha
• Ngai Giao
PHUOC TUY
• Nui Dat
Phuoc Le   Ba Ria
Dat Do
Vung Tau   SOUTH CHINA SEA

South Vietnam
LAOS
• Da Nang
THAILAND
Quang Ngai
CAMBODIA
SOUTH VIETNAM
Phnom Penh •
Nha Trang
Saigon • Nui Dat
SOUTH CHINA SEA

COMBAT KIT

In Vietnam the SAS used a wide range of smallarms and support weapons in their operations in Phuoc Tuy province. Individual weapons included the M16 assault rifle, the CAR15 Colt Commando – the short-barrelled version of the M16 with a telescopic stock – and the SLR rifle. Generally, the 7.62mm SLR was preferred for its range and hitting power over the 5.56mm M16. Testament to this can be found in the Sergeants' Mess at Swanbourne, where an SLR with six inches lopped off its barrel hangs in a place of honour. This relic of the Vietnam War is 'affectionately' known as 'The Bitch'! For heavier firepower, the M79 40mm grenade launcher was used, and the SAS armoury also included Brens and GPMGs. In addition, the SAS used a variety of combat shotguns, pistols, mines and grenades. The choice of weapons, as is usual with the SAS, was left to the individual trooper. In the field, the SAS usually wore US Special Forces uniform, tiger stripes or olive-drab greens. Although bergens were carried at times, on operations the SAS carried most essential equipment on their belts. To summon up helicopters when a patrol needed to get out of an area quickly, the URC-10 bleeper/signal transmitter was used. Another favourite item of kit was the sniper veil/neck-band bandana. The SAS would also carry lengths of nylon fishing line, for signalling to each other. The length of line was attached to a finger of each patrol member and signals could be passed down the line in absolute silence by a gentle tug on the connecting nylon. Mirrors were also used for signalling.

undergrowth for three days until the coast was clear and he could make a safe getaway.

The SAS operated mainly in the so-called 'free-fire zones' of South Vietnam, where it was assumed that anyone moving around was the enemy. To carry out their deep-penetration recons, the SAS had to get in quickly and were usually inserted by choppers of the 9th Squadron, Royal Australian Air Force, accompanied by helicopter gunships should the dropping point turn out to be 'hot'. The 9th Squadron, based at 'Kanga pad' at Nui Dat, flew specially modified choppers, mounting twin M60 machine guns and fitted with a winch for insertion and extraction of men on the end of a rope. The SAS could also parachute into a general area where they would rendezvous with armoured personnel carriers to insert them into their area of operations.

The choppers were also a vital means of getting a patrol out, should the men on the ground find themselves up against a force too large to handle. But such extractions under fire were often as dangerous as the firefights on the ground. Late in 1969, after a very heavy contact, a patrol was extracted by rope and, during the lift-out, Trooper D. J. Fisher fell 30m into the jungle below. A company of the 9th Battalion, RAR, and another SAS patrol were despatched to search for him, but Fisher was never seen again. He was posted 'missing in action, presumed dead'.

Later in the same year, a New Zealand patrol was being pulled out after a similar heavy brush with the

VC when, suddenly, the extraction chopper came under heavy fire. The stricken bird dragged the patrol nearly 100m before crashing to the ground. The SAS gave the stunned aircrew first aid and then led them out on foot.

During the course of their tours in Vietnam, the Sabre Squadrons were often called upon to perform specialist tasks, or to carry out one-off missions in addition to their routine recon work. Such missions included the demolition of a water-tower, a suspected enemy observation post that air attack had failed to destroy, and the so-called 'tractor job'. On

One of the keys to successful SAS-type operations is the ability to deploy at speed, and the SAS employ a wide range of transport to get them in and out of the battle area. To negotiate rough terrain, motorcycles are used (above left) while for the longer-range insertions typical of the Vietnam War, choppers from the 'Kanga pad' took the SAS patrols in (above right). One of the main tasks in Vietnam was to observe movements of Viet Cong forces while remaining undetected (top) but if the SAS ran into a force too strong to handle on their own, troops from the Royal Australian Regiment (right) were called up to take on the enemy. Far right: Clad in wet suits and camouflage, SAS men practise insertion by canoe.

this operation, mounted during the later stages of the 1968 Tet Offensive, a patrol was tasked with the destruction of an enemy tractor and trailer, known to be operating in the vicinity of a friendly firebase. Two SAS corporals designed, built and laid the explosive charges which destroyed the tractor, and the whole mission resulted in the death of 20 enemy soldiers and the capture of a large quantity of enemy weapons, including a recoilless rifle.

On another occasion, a 12-man patrol located a VC workshop, later identified as the Ba Long Province Armoury Workshop. The patrol attacked the camp, which was defended by troops, fitters and armourers, while a stand-by patrol was winched into the

camp, carrying explosives. Large ammunition caches were destroyed, along with a number of camp structures.

After the demolition, the two patrols returned to the camp to inspect their handiwork, only to unearth further weapon and ammunition dumps. It soon materialised that the camp was, in fact, a major complex. The stand-by patrol was winched out with the captured weapons, while the men left behind were reinforced by Australian and South Vietnamese infantrymen. The discovery of the Ba Long workshops led to a major operation against VC in the area by infantry units of the Australian Task Force.

But not all SAS ops went so smoothly. On one operation, known as Overboard, the SAS set up an ambush against a number of sampans being used by the enemy in the coastal rivers southeast of the Task Force headquarters. A net was strung across the Rai river to stop the boats but, as a sampan struck the net, it gave way, and before the ambush party could open fire, the crew of the sampan went over the side and into the water. The sampan was taken into custody and loaded with enemy equipment. The SAS then set out across the river to link up with the ambush detail on the far bank, but capsized on the way, sending both the captured and the SAS men's kit to the bottom.

A 'killing house' is maintained for training troopers in the arts of close-quarters combat

Despite such 'upsets', the Australian SAS emerged from the war as one of the most successful special-operations units. Their repertoire of long-range, ambush, harassment and recon patrols had considerable influence on the setting up of the US Army Long-Range Reconnaissance Patrols (LRRPs) and SAS personnel also taught at the MACV Recondo (reconnaissance commando) school established at Nha Trang in September 1966. At times, the SAS operated in conjunction with US Special Forces – the Green Berets – and the US Navy SEALs on special clandestine missions.

The Australian SAS views its operations in Borneo and South Vietnam together. In these two campaigns, more than 1400 patrols were completed, with the movement of some 5600 enemy troops reported. In 298 contacts, SAS patrols killed more than 500 of the enemy, for the loss of only one man who died of wounds sustained in action. Fourteen Australians were wounded in combat, one was posted missing, and eight men died from causes unrelated to the fighting.

Today, the Australian SAS strives to maintain the unrivalled standards of its record in Borneo and South Vietnam, while keeping a close eye on the ever-changing requirements of modern warfare. One squadron is now devoted to specialist anti-terrorist work, and at Swanborne, the SAS HQ in a suburb of the city of Perth, a 'killing house' is maintained for training troopers in the arts of close-quarters combat and dealing with hostage situations. The selection process for entry into the SAS is very stringent: only one out of every six officers seeking to join the regiment is taken on, and only one out of every four applicants for non-commissioned ranks is accepted.

The Australian SAS have become specialists in a wide range of sophisticated operational techniques, and their training covers everything from high-altitude parachuting to amphibious assault tactics and underwater work. The training is tough and realistic, and it is a telling fact that many more SAS men have died during training than on actual combat missions.

THE AUTHOR Pat Burgess is an Australian writer and broadcaster, and has compiled several programmes from his researches into Australian military history.

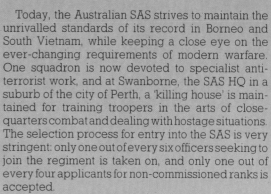

Below: On the SAS selection course, prospective recruits to the regiment have to make a 20km route march, loaded up with 30kg of kit plus an SLR rifle. The Australian SAS selection course is particularly tough, and only the best men are taken on after the gruelling series of tests. The fact that far more men have died during SAS training than in actual combat is a testament, not only to the stringency of the preparatory courses, but to the fighting abilities of the individual men when faced with an enemy.

SAS
JUNGLE FIGHTERS

In the shadowy, secretive war during the 'Confrontation' between Indonesia and Malaya in 1965, the superb professional skills of the SAS came into their own in the jungle

'I REGARD 70 troopers of the SAS as being as valuable to me as 700 infantry in the role of hearts and minds, border surveillance, early warning, stay behind, and eyes and ears with a sting!' So wrote Major-General Walter Walker in January 1964.

In the early hours of 28 April 1965 a four-man team of soldiers from the 22nd Special Air Service Regiment (22 SAS) waited patiently, SLRs at the ready, by the side of a river located some 9000 yards inside Indonesian territory. The team, led by Captain Robin Letts, had been ordered to reconnoitre the area around Berjonkong and Achan, where the Indonesians were known to have forward bases. During his 'recce', Letts discovered a waterway used by the enemy to ferry men and supplies to the border, and decided to set up an ambush. Positioning his men inside the loop of the river, with one man to his right, one to his left, and the other covering the left flank, Letts awaited the arrival of Indonesian boats.

He did not have to wait long. At 0815, two-and-a-

Previous page: Clutching an American Armalite rifle and weighed down with a heavy rucksack, an SAS trooper moves cautiously across a bamboo bridge in Borneo. Below: Stripped to the waist in the humid tropical conditions of Borneo, an SAS detachment launches a narrow riverboat loaded with weapons and kit at the outset of a patrol. In the dense and often impenetrable rain forest, craft such as these were invaluable as transport and in the countless waterways the SAS often employed the services of local tribesmen as guides and steersmen.

half hours after the team had taken up their position, a boat appeared, followed by a second and then a third. Each boat contained three soldiers, two paddling and the other standing astern with weapon cradled, acting as sentry. As the first boat reached the man to Letts' right, the second Letts himself, and the third the man to Letts' left, the SAS team opened fire. It was all over within four minutes. Four Indonesian bodies lay floating atop the water, blood oozing into the reddening stream. Two more lay dead in their boats, while two others lay prostrate on the river bank; the ninth enemy soldier had fled in panic into the adjacent swamp. The ambush had succeeded. Letts' team collected their bergens and 'scooted' back towards the safety of Malaysian territory, happy in the knowledge that they had made the enemy feel insecure even on his own home ground.

That the SAS had been given such a mission was no real surprise, since by that time 22 SAS had spent over two years on the jungle frontier which divided Indonesian Borneo (Kalimantan) from Malaysian Borneo. Indeed, almost as soon as the SAS arrived in Borneo, in January 1963, it had been deployed along the border to act as a defensive intelligence network. At the time, the Commander British Forces, Borneo,

THE SAS IN BORNEO

Between December 1963 and August 1966 the mountainous island of Borneo, sparsely populated and covered by dense jungle, became a theatre of armed warfare. The former British colony of Malaya, west of Borneo, was pressing for the formation of a major new political entity in the area. To be known as the Federation of Malaysia, it was to comprise British North Borneo (now Sabah), Sarawak, Brunei, Malaya and Singapore. Though Britain endorsed the future that Malaya proposed for her territories, President Ahmed Sukarno of neighbouring Indonesia bitterly opposed the plan as a threat to his ambition to expand the Indonesian frontiers.

In December 1962 a rebellion led by anti-Malaysian elements erupted in the Sultanate of Brunei, though British forces arrived and suppressed the revolt before Sukarno could profit from it. Four months later, however, Sukarno began to infiltrate insurgents from Kalimantan (the Indonesian southern part of Borneo) into the British colonies. When Sabah and Sarawak (though not Brunei or Singapore) became officially incorporated into Malaysia in September 1963, the infiltrations were stepped up. In response, the British organised a border guard of Malaysian, British and Commonwealth troops to contain the insurgents. A prominent constituent of this force was the SAS.

So effective was the Allied force that the Indonesian incursions seldom penetrated much beyond the actual line of the border. As time passed the cost of 'Confrontation' came to be considered too high by the Indonesian people and they lost faith in their president's vision of an aggrandised Indonesia. Sukarno was overthrown in March 1966 and five months later Indonesia abandoned Confrontation and made peace with Malaysia.

Major-General Walter Walker, faced the twin threat of an internal uprising from the Clandestine Communist Organisation (CCO), a subversive movement based mainly on Chinese settlers in Sarawak, and of external invasion from Kalimantan. Apart from a small number of local forces, Walker had only five battalions of men available to meet these threats, an insufficient force to maintain internal security over the 80,000 square miles of territory on his side of the border, and at the same time to guard against possible attack from the other side. In the event, Walker decided to hold back the bulk of his men as a reaction force, ready to respond to troubles from within or incursions from without. At the same time he decided to deploy the available SAS squadron (about 70 men) along the border to warn of any Indonesian incursions.

The SAS had been allotted a most difficult task. One squadron, totalling not even 100 men, was being asked to keep watch along a jungle frontier almost 1000 miles long, a frontier so wild and rugged that in some places it had not even been mapped. But then the SAS had extraordinary qualities. More so than any other regiment, the SAS possessed the ability to operate in inhospitable terrain for long periods of time, living off the land without regular re-supply; moreover, having taken part in the counter-insurgency campaign of the Malayan Emergency (1948-1960), many SAS troopers spoke or understood Malay, the *lingua franca* of the frontier tribes. These attributes proved to be invaluable, because in practice the only effective means of controlling the border was to enlist the support of the border tribes, the native people who lived in settlements located on hillsides or in river valleys.

133

Fortunately for the SAS, many of these tribes were well disposed towards the British. Nevertheless, the tribesmens' loyalty could not be taken for granted, particularly as the favourite sport of some of them was headhunting. In an effort to win them over, SAS personnel operating in small teams of three to four men went into the settlements and stayed there for weeks or even months, helping with the planting, harvesting and weeding of crops, giving medical assistance and at all times respecting the customs and traditions of the natives. In return, the natives provided the SAS teams with news of any useful findings, such as spoors or bootmarks left in the jungle by the Indonesians.

Such information was relayed back to squadron headquarters on high-frequency radios and was supplemented by other information – about border-crossing points, jungle tracks, potential sites for ambushes and helicopter landing, and so on – gathered by the SAS teams on the patrols they carried out in their respective areas. So successful were these activities that by the time the Indonesians began their cross-border incursions, in April 1963, the SAS had already won over many of the tribes and had provided the security forces with 'eyes and ears' along the frontier.

The SAS continued their frontier duties, winning 'hearts and minds'

In the months that followed, the SAS continued their frontier duties, winning 'hearts and minds', collecting intelligence and detecting and tracking enemy incursions, as well as helping to train a force of native irregulars called the Border Scouts. Inevitably, though, as the Indonesians stepped up their guerrilla incursions, the regiment's role was modified. By early 1964 SAS personnel were not only detecting incursions but were also helping infantrymen to intercept the infiltrators; the infantry, deployed from forward bases or dropped into the jungle by helicopter, were guided into ambush positions by SAS

Main picture: A fortified SAS hill outpost with a large helicopter pad for bringing in supplies and launching heliborne operations. Below left: An SAS trooper on foot patrol moves stealthily through thick vegetation. Below right: A patrol cooks up rations on a solid fuel stove deep in the jungle. The SAS had to carry everything they needed and could not rely on resupply during operations.

Below left: Troopers halt to take stock of their position and examine the map. Below right: A four-man patrol leaves the sparse shelter of a native hut and sets out into the jungle on a reconnaissance mission.

teams. Later that year SAS teams led ambush parties or 'killer groups' over the border into Kalimantan, to hit the enemy before he could penetrate Malaysian territory.

These offensive forays, ultra-secret operations codenamed 'Claret', called for the utmost skill and care. Any trace of British presence on Indonesian soil could have caused severe embarrassment to the British government. After all, Britain was not at war with Indonesia and wanted to avoid any accusation that she was escalating the conflict (it was for this reason, and also because of the risk of killing friendly tribesmen, that air strikes into Kalimantan were ruled out). Claret missions were, therefore, subject to definite limitations. They were to be undertaken only by experienced jungle troops and were to be guided by the SAS and the Border Scouts, who were to reconnoitre the target areas beforehand. They were also limited in terms of depth of penetration – initially to 3000 yards.

By the end of 1964, Claret operations had proved to

be politically acceptable and militarily feasible. Consequently, when Walker learnt of a divisional strength build-up of high quality Indonesian troops opposite the First Division (the western part of Sarawak) in December 1964, he sanctioned Claret missions to a depth of 10,000 yards. The Indonesians seemed to be planning a major offensive against the First Division, and Walker believed that by threatening their forward bases and lines of communication he would force them to concentrate on defensive rather than offensive plans. In effect, Walker saw Claret operations as a means of denying the Indonesians the military initiative.

At first, during December 1964 and the early months of 1965, Claret teams were ordered to concentrate primarily on reconnaissance, a natural prerequisite to strikes in that the Kalimantan side of the border with the First Division had not previously been investigated to any great extent. Accordingly, SAS teams went over the border to identify Indonesian bases, infiltration routes (actual and potential)

Left: The SAS test their weapons in preparation for an operation against Indonesian infiltrators. One of the troopers has fixed an improvised grip to the handguard of his Armalite to provide a steadier hold for automatic fire.

and lines of communication, by land and water.

Perhaps typical of such operations was a four-man patrol that set out early in January 1965 to recce the area south of Gunong Brunei, where the Koemba river ran close to the border. This patrol, led by Trooper Bennett, had to negotiate steep hills, thick jungle, rocky streams and a 300-yard wide swamp before reaching the river. All the same their endeavours were worthwhile. They brought back valuable information about the area and also managed to earmark ambush positions – particularly promising in the latter respect was a high rock from which movements along the river, and along an established track linking Seluas and Siding, could be watched. Bennett's team made no attempt to engage the enemy, though some 'recce' teams – like Letts' – found targets they felt were too tempting to leave unscathed.

If Letts' team had carried out a 'recce' that ended up as an engagement, it was not long before such engagements became standard practice. By early May 1965, Major-General George Lea, who had succeeded Major-General Walker two months previously, had decided that Claret operations should begin in earnest. One of the objectives chosen was a major supply route, the Koemba river near Poeri. A four-man team of SAS troopers led by Don Large was ordered to investigate river traffic near Poeri and to engage a suitable target.

Large's team had taken on a well-nigh impossible mission. Six previous attempts had been made to reach this sector of the Koemba river – and each had been foiled by heavy going across swamps. The general feeling in headquarters was that this new attempt would also fail, but Large himself remained optimistic, even though soon after setting out from a landing position, on 10 May 1965, the patrol ran into difficulties. On their second day in the jungle the team heard enemy soldiers ahead; they had to take a detour through thick undergrowth, and to do so without making a noise or leaving tracks, an endeavour that tested their jungle skills to the limit.

Worse was to follow. After crossing undetected over a main jungle track on the third day, and another main track (possibly used by the Indonesians for cutting off Claret teams) on the fourth day, the team made for a loop in the river, where Large believed they would find the tail of a spur leading to the river bank. To their chagrin all they found was more swamp – and each probe they made seemed to lead them into deeper swamp. After spending the night on a mud island, the team pressed on westwards, hoping to find higher ground. As they inched their way forward they heard the sound of boat engines – heavy diesels – but saw no sign at all of the spur. Failure began to seem inevitable, but Large refused to admit defeat. Taking breakfast on dry land, the team talked over their predicament and decided to persevere – to go back into the swamp and to head downstream with a view to finding a causeway to the river.

Having at last found his objective, Large wasted no time in setting up an observation post

Progress was painfully slow, though they were at least encouraged by the sound of diesel engines, which indicated that they must be close to the river. And then, to their surprise and amazement, they found high land rising to 30ft above the swamp. It was the spur! They emerged from the swamp and began to negotiate the spur, soon entering a narrow belt of jungle. After crossing the jungle, they came to a rubber plantation. Skirting round this they saw before them the Koemba river, fast-flowing and some 40 yards wide.

Having at last found his objective, Large wasted no time and proceeded to establish an observation post. He discounted the area to his right because there was little cover near the bank, and also rejected the area to his left, which, although well covered, was the first place the enemy would expect them to go. He settled for the area to his front, a

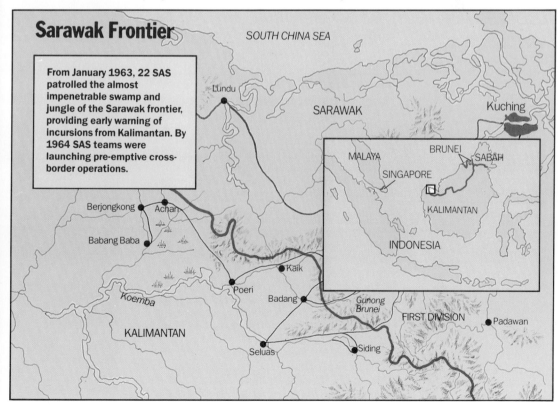

Sarawak Frontier

From January 1963, 22 SAS patrolled the almost impenetrable swamp and jungle of the Sarawak frontier, providing early warning of incursions from Kalimantan. By 1964 SAS teams were launching pre-emptive cross-border operations.

SOUTH CHINA SEA

Lundu

SARAWAK

Kuching

MALAYA
BRUNEI
SABAH
SINGAPORE

KALIMANTAN

INDONESIA

Berjongkong   Achan

Babang Baba

Kaik

Poeri   Badang

Koemba   Gunong Brunei   FIRST DIVISION   Padawan

KALIMANTAN

Seluas   Siding

HEARTS AND MINDS

During the early stages of the Borneo campaign the Indonesian communist guerrillas held all the trump cards: they had intimate knowledge of the jungle and its dangers, knew how to live off the land, and used the local tribesmen as informants and providers of food. The small SAS patrols could not off-set these advantages by military action alone, and adopted a 'softly-softly' approach to the problem.

The lynch-pin of their strategy was the 'hearts and minds' programme; a system of mutually beneficial exchanges between the local people and SAS teams. With this technique the SAS aimed to break up the guerrillas' supply network and deny them the use of native villages. The way to success was gaining the confidence and trust of local tribesmen and the key figure was the patrol's medic who had to be prepared to deal with everything from gunshot wounds to births.

Although the precise nature of a particular operation might vary, patrols followed a similar pattern of methods. They would enter the village unannounced and then seek out the headman. While some of the men engaged him in conversation, the medic would set up his surgery. Later, small presents would be exchanged and any urgent needs signalled back to base. The tribesmen would also be paid for any work they undertook for the SAS team. After a meal and more talk, the patrol would withdraw. Within the week, however, the SAS would reappear to take the next steps on the road to friendship.

SAS aid was not, however, purely altruistic; it produced military benefits. Villages were a valuable source of food, security and intelligence. If the locals could provide these facilities, the SAS would be free to concentrate on their primary task; the destruction of the guerrilla forces operating in the jungle.

10ft-high river bank with a ditch on the near side. This position had its disadvantages, the greatest of which was that the team would have to pull back across open ground on their way out. But it afforded a good view of the river, a ditch in which to rest, and reasonable cover (in the form of scrub and a tree) for both bank and ditch. It was also the sort of place the enemy would least expect an ambush site, or so Large hoped.

He decided that he would wait until a boat negotiated the river bend, and then rake it with fire

During the afternoon Large observed movements on the river and planned his ambush. He came to the conclusion that the best means of fulfilling his strategic objective – to make the enemy feel that their major supply lines were threatened – would be to destroy a boat carrying war cargo. As regards tactics, he decided that his best bet would be to wait until a boat had negotiated the river bend and then rake it with fire from astern; this would offer a good chance of causing serious damage and would limit the crew's opportunity to return fire. His plan of action was for his team members – Walsh, Millikin and Scholey – to move forward to firing positions, three yards apart; he himself would move in behind them to direct the firing, to watch out for other boats and to keep an eye on the rear.

Having established their positions and plan of action for the ambush, Large and his team settled down to an unpalatable meal of uncooked meat-blocks – they were unable to use their solid-fuel

stoves or light a fire for fear of giving themselves away – and then managed to catch some sleep. They were to spend the next day fulfilling the first part of their orders – to establish the pattern of river traffic. It

Far left: Maintaining good relations with local people in Borneo was one of the ground rules for SAS operations. Here a trooper exercises his medical expertise on a villager, cleaning a gash prior to stitching. Far left, below: An SAS team moves onto high ground to prepare an ambush. Left: An SAS radio operator at a forward operations base.

Corporal, 22nd SAS Regiment, Borneo 1965-66

This SAS soldier wears typical tropical kit for the fighting in Borneo: olive-green trousers, shirt of un-identified origin and battered jungle hat worn over a cloth-scarf sweat band. On his back he wears a bamboo carrier, capable of lifting a wide variety of loads. A 58-pattern web belt is worn around the waist, upon which is fixed – from left to right – an AR-15 ammunition pouch, 44-pattern compass pouch, AR-15 ammunition pouch and a 44-pattern water bottle carrier. Armament comprises the US-manufactured AR-15 Armalite assault rifle, fitted here with twin magazines. A highly effective weapon for close-quarters jungle fighting the AR-16 proved popular with specialist troops such as the SAS and the Gurkhas. Unlike the regular forces, specialists such as the SAS can pick and choose those weapons and items of equipment they deem most suitable; and, consequently, they have been issued with an exotic range of weapons.

soon became apparent that headquarters was fully justified in its assumptions about the importance of the river. Among the vessels the team saw go past were a military supply launch and a 45ft-long luxury motor yacht. The latter was a tempting target, but it appeared to be the flagship of some VIP. Large was mindful of the political consequences that might result from the destruction of such a vessel and so let it alone. He also let pass a 40ft launch that carried soldiers, confident that a more suitable target would appear the next day – something it would be well worth while waiting for.

Within half a minute they unleashed 60 rounds against their target, killing the two sentries

The next morning, having radioed for permission 'to engage opportunity target', Large and his col-leagues waited eagerly. He allowed free passage to a two-man canoe and to a 30ft launch in the hope that a bigger prize might present itself. Five hours later none had done so, and as the sun became obscured behind thick cloud and rain began to pour down, Large's team-mates began to curse their leader's decision to let so many boats past on the previous day. But just then, with visibility fading, another launch appeared. It was a big one too, about 40ft long and 8ft wide; there were two sentries astern, it appeared to be carrying cargo, and soldiers were resting beneath its large canopy. As the launch passed by, 45 yards distant, Large beckoned his men to their firing positions. Within half a minute they unleashed 60 rounds against their target, killing the two sentries and holing the boat. The stricken vessel listed in the water. As smoke belched from it, soldiers emerged from beneath the tarpaulin and jumped overboard in haste. Seconds later the whole vessel was engulfed by flames.

Mission accomplished, the SAS men collected their effects together and took off along the spur as quickly as possible. However, there was a shock in store for them as Large found his path blocked, at head level, by a deadly snake – a king cobra – but fortunately the snake decided not to attack, and the team made rapid progress. By evening they had crossed the cut-off path. On the following day, having signalled for a helicopter on the SARBE (search and rescue beacon), they were winched out of the jungle and flown back to base. Large's sortie had accomplished a great deal. The team may only have destroyed one launch, but the psychological effect was devastating. The Indone-sians now felt that their main supply routes were insecure and were compelled to re-deploy troops to guard them.

Other cross-border raids took place during the succeeding months, forcing the enemy further onto the defensive. In these subsequent raids, the role of the SAS was to act as guides, rather than sole participants, but that hardly mattered. The SAS men had done their bit. They had pioneered a tactic that was to force the Indonesians to abandon their for-ward bases and, in truth, to deny them any real chance of success.

THE AUTHOR Francis Toase is Senior Lecturer in the Department of War Studies and International Affairs at the Royal Military Academy Sandhurst and has contributed to *British Military Operations 1945-1984, Armed Forces and Modern Counter-Insurgency* and the forthcoming *Modern Guerrilla Warfare*.

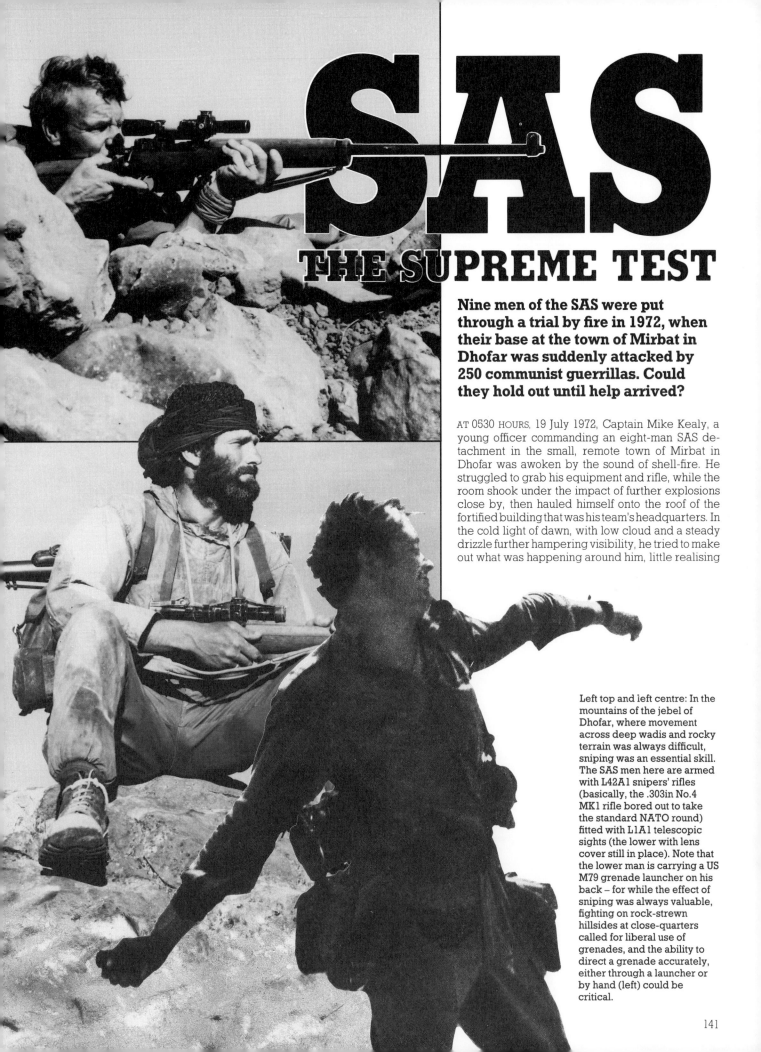

SAS
THE SUPREME TEST

Nine men of the SAS were put through a trial by fire in 1972, when their base at the town of Mirbat in Dhofar was suddenly attacked by 250 communist guerrillas. Could they hold out until help arrived?

AT 0530 HOURS, 19 July 1972, Captain Mike Kealy, a young officer commanding an eight-man SAS detachment in the small, remote town of Mirbat in Dhofar was awoken by the sound of shell-fire. He struggled to grab his equipment and rifle, while the room shook under the impact of further explosions close by, then hauled himself onto the roof of the fortified building that was his team's headquarters. In the cold light of dawn, with low cloud and a steady drizzle further hampering visibility, he tried to make out what was happening around him, little realising

Left top and left centre: In the mountains of the jebel of Dhofar, where movement across deep wadis and rocky terrain was always difficult, sniping was an essential skill. The SAS men here are armed with L42A1 snipers' rifles (basically, the .303in No.4 MK1 rifle bored out to take the standard NATO round) fitted with L1A1 telescopic sights (the lower with lens cover still in place). Note that the lower man is carrying a US M79 grenade launcher on his back – for while the effect of sniping was always valuable, fighting on rock-strewn hillsides at close-quarters called for liberal use of grenades, and the ability to direct a grenade accurately, either through a launcher or by hand (left) could be critical.

22ND SPECIAL AIR SERVICE REGIMENT, OMAN 1972

The badge of the SAS was formally approved in January 1942. It was chosen by Major David Stirling, originally of the Scots Guards, who had set up the oddly named 'L' detachment of a non-existent Special Air Service Brigade in 1941, using men from a commando force that had been disbanded. He chose the sword of Damocles and wings to symbolise what he determined would be the role of his unit: raids by small groups of men, often dropped by parachute, behind enemy lines. The 1st Special Air Service Regiment was formally recognised in January 1943, and in April of that year the 2nd Special Air Service Regiment was established. These regiments fought in Sicily, Italy and Northwest Europe until 1945. After the war, the SAS regiments were disbanded, but in 1947, 21 SAS, part of the Territorial Army and successor to the Artists' Rifles, came into being. In 1950, a unit named Malayan Scouts (SAS) was set up to take the war against communist guerrillas in Malaya into the jungle; men from 21 SAS were attached to B Squadron of the scouts, and in 1952 the scouts formally became 22 SAS. Since then, they have served Britain all over the world – and no campaign was more important than that of the early 1970s in Dhofar.

that he was about to take part in an action that would demonstrate beyond all doubt the fighting ability of the SAS; for without the courage, weapons skill and tactical acumen of all the SAS men involved, Mirbat would surely have fallen to the vastly more numerous enemy.

As always in their operations, the SAS in Dhofar were keeping a low profile, but using their experience and expertise to support a government allied to Britain. The Sultanate of Oman, of which Dhofar was the isolated southern province, had a long history of association with the British – indeed, in 1959 SAS troopers had spearheaded a decisive assault on the mountain fastness of rebels within Oman itself. The sultan's domains were of great strategic importance in that their northern tip dominates the mouth of the oil-rich Gulf. In 1969, in fact, some SAS men had been deployed when it was suspected that a few Iraqi-trained guerrillas might be operating there.

The people living in the mountainous hinterland of Dhofar, were quite distinct both in their language and culture, from the other subjects of the sultanate. Said bin Taimur, sultan since 1932, was a very conservative ruler. Every aspect of modern life – from radios to spectacles, from medicines to bicycles – was banned. Some Dhofaris, however, had found work abroad, and inevitably realised that the enforced backwardness of their homeland was largely due to the reactionary sultan. Swayed by the ideals of Arab nationalism, a group of exiles formed the Dhofar Liberation Front in 1962. In 1965 they started a small-scale guerrilla war in Dhofar.

A well-armed foe was steadily undermining an ally of Britain

The Sultan's Armed Forces (SAF), comprising the Muscat and Northern Frontier Regiments, were able to contain the insurgency at this stage, deploying about 1000 men in Dhofar, with British officers and Baluchis from Pakistan in the ranks.

In 1967, however, South Yemen, a Marxist state, began to aid the Dhofari insurgents, who were, in any case, similar to the Yemenis in language and culture. The Dhofari insurgents now had a safe base, and began to receive a flow of weapons from the communist bloc; they were also given better training. The mountainous hinterland (known as the jebel), in which deep wadis, limestone caves and the lack of effective roads gave guerrillas natural advantages, was soon out of the control of the SAF.

Sultan Said's response to the revitalised insurgency was to redouble stern repressive measures. Prisoners were publicly executed and their bodies hung up for days, while villages suspected of sympathising with the rebels were attacked, and their wells concreted over. The latter in particular was a vindictive measure in a land where water is at a premium. Soon the population of the jebel had been alienated, and the SAF could only defend the coastal plain.

Things went from bad to worse. The town of

For the SAS in Dhofar during the early 1970s, weight of equipment was not the key to victory. Transport might be by jeep (right top) but patrolling in the mountains involved wearying marches on foot (bottom right). There was some artillery support (centre right above, a 25pdr gun-howitzer manned by the SAS) but the most important task was to win the trust of the *firqat*, tribally based forces often composed of former rebels (centre right below, a *firqat* patrol).

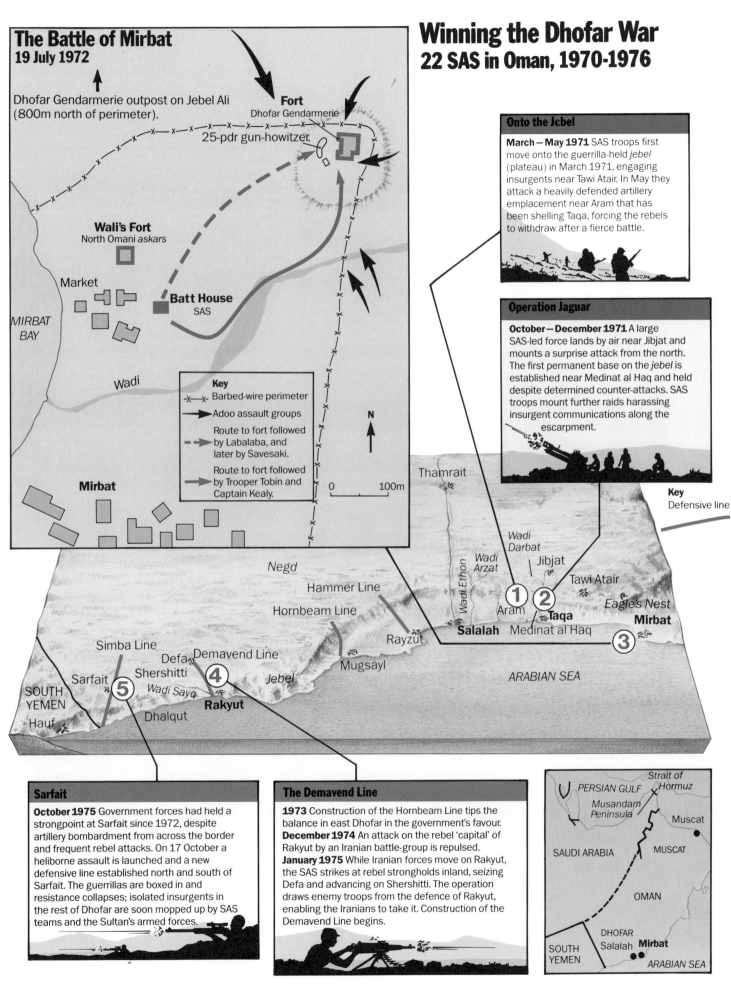

The Battle of Mirbat
19 July 1972

Dhofar Gendarmerie outpost on Jebel Ali (800m north of perimeter).

Fort
Dhofar Gendarmerie

25-pdr gun-howitzer.

Wali's Fort
North Omani *askars*

Market

MIRBAT BAY

Batt House
SAS

Wadi

Mirbat

Key
- ✕—✕— Barbed-wire perimeter
- ➤ Adoo assault groups
- Route to fort followed by Labalaba, and later by Savesaki.
- Route to fort followed by Trooper Tobin and Captain Kealy.

N

0   100m

Winning the Dhofar War
22 SAS in Oman, 1970-1976

Onto the Jebel

March — May 1971 SAS troops first move onto the guerrilla-held *jebel* (plateau) in March 1971, engaging insurgents near Tawi Atair. In May they attack a heavily defended artillery emplacement near Aram that has been shelling Taqa, forcing the rebels to withdraw after a fierce battle.

Operation Jaguar

October — December 1971 A large SAS-led force lands by air near Jibjat and mounts a surprise attack from the north. The first permanent base on the *jebel* is established near Medinat al Haq and held despite determined counter-attacks. SAS troops mount further raids harassing insurgent communications along the escarpment.

Key
Defensive line

Thamrait

Wadi Darbat
Wadi Arzat
Wadi Ethon

Jibjat
Tawi Atair

Negd

Hammer Line
Hornbeam Line

Aram   ① ②
Taqa   *Eagle's Nest*
Salalah   Medinat al Haq   **Mirbat**
③

Rayzut

Mugsayl

ARABIAN SEA

Simba Line
Demavend Line
Defa
Shershitti   ④
Jebel
Wadi Sayq
Sarfait   ⑤
Rakyut
SOUTH YEMEN
Dhalqut
Hauf

Sarfait

October 1975 Government forces had held a strongpoint at Sarfait since 1972, despite artillery bombardment from across the border and frequent rebel attacks. On 17 October a heliborne assault is launched and a new defensive line established north and south of Sarfait. The guerrillas are boxed in and resistance collapses; isolated insurgents in the rest of Dhofar are soon mopped up by SAS teams and the Sultan's armed forces.

The Demavend Line

1973 Construction of the Hornbeam Line tips the balance in east Dhofar in the government's favour.
December 1974 An attack on the rebel 'capital' of Rakyut by an Iranian battle-group is repulsed.
January 1975 While Iranian forces move on Rakyut, the SAS strikes at rebel strongholds inland, seizing Defa and advancing on Shershitti. The operation draws enemy troops from the defence of Rakyut, enabling the Iranians to take it. Construction of the Demavend Line begins.

Strait of Hormuz
PERSIAN GULF
Musandam Peninsula
Muscat
SAUDI ARABIA
MUSCAT
OMAN
DHOFAR
SOUTH YEMEN   Salalah   **Mirbat**
ARABIAN SEA

THE *ADOO*

The *adoo*, the guerrillas who fought against the sultan's forces, were a brave and resourceful foe whose possession of automatic weapons, especially the Russian Kalashnikov assault rifle, gave them formidable firepower. The original Dhofar Liberation Front was a broad grouping with radical Arab nationalist ideals. When, however, South Yemen became the main supplier of arms and protection, a Marxist ideology was adopted and the Liberation Front was subsumed into the People's Front for the Liberation of the Occupied Arabian Gulf (PFLOAG).

Most Dhofaris were not interested in Marxism as such. They were concerned about material progress (in particular the lack of it under Sultan Said), while remaining fiercely tribal, especially in the mountains, and firmly Moslem. This gave Sultan Qaboos' modernisation programme and the tribally-organised *firqat* a great attraction for many of the *adoo* offended by the extremes of PFLOAG ideology.

Nevertheless, at the peak of the insurgency there were probably 2000 full-time guerrillas ready for action, backed up by a 3000-strong militia. Their support weapons were mainly portable Soviet equipment, such as RPG-7 rocket launchers and 12.7mm heavy machine guns, but they possessed heavier equipment in the form of some 122mm Katyusha rocket launchers. They also made use of Western material where they could get it, as the deployment of a Carl Gustav rocket launcher at Mirbat demonstrated. The *adoo* were determined fighters with a tradition of resistance to central authority. And as they showed at Mirbat, they could look death in the face without flinching.

Rakyut, administrative centre of western Dhofar, fell to the *adoo* (as the guerrillas were known) on 23 August 1969. The capital of Dhofar, Salalah, was little more than a fortified enclave, containing the town, the sultan's palace and an RAF base. A well-armed foe was steadily undermining an ally of Britain; but it seemed little could be done.

In the spring of 1970, some senior SAS officers considered the problem of insurgency in Dhofar. The SAS had made great use of good relations with local populations during the campaigns in Malaya and Borneo, and the senior officers concluded that a concerted attempt to win the 'hearts and minds' of the Dhofaris by establishing medical and veterinary centres, coupled with a concentration on collecting the good intelligence that is the key to counter-insurgency, were the essential first steps in reversing the tide.

It was evident that under the rule of Sultan Said, such a programme was impossible, but in July 1970 a palace coup (during which the old sultan shot himself in the foot) removed Said's control from the affairs of state. His son Qaboos, Sandhurst trained and with experience in the British Army, enthusiastically set about implementing a new policy. He expanded his armed forces to include more fast patrol boats, more helicopters and 12 Strikemaster jets; the SAF grew from 2500 to 12,000 men, led by some 600 British officers and a few specialist NCOs, some on loan from the British Army and some under contract to the sultan. A whole series of measures was put into operation to improve the lot of the Dhofaris and, crucially, an amnesty was offered to any of the *adoo* who changed sides.

Forty members of the SAS penetrated the mountainous hinterland, and stayed for 12 days' fighting

The first SAS team arrived in Dhofar within hours of the coup. One of their tasks was to act as a bodyguard for the new ruler, but they also took a leading role in the implementation of the new strategy. The SAS detachments were officially named 'British Army Training Teams' (BATTs) so that it could be denied that any British combat troops were present. The first two training teams were based at Taqa and a small town some 70km east of Salalah: Mirbat.

About 200 *adoo* surrendered between September 1970 and March 1971 alone – mainly due to disagreements between Marxists and more traditionalist Moslems. Qaboos was persuaded that these individuals could be used in a counter-insurgency role; and the SAS teams were to play a major role in this process.

The guerrillas who had surrendered were deployed in *firqat,* units of indeterminate size. Their loyalty was often in doubt, and the motives of many were questionable. Nevertheless, they formed an essential link with the local population, a link critical in the new strategy. In March 1971, the *firqat* showed that they could fight when a force of 60, together with 40 members of the SAS, penetrated the mountainous hinterland, and stayed for 12 days of almost constant fighting.

The broad sweep of government strategy was to show they could maintain control of eastern Dhofar while gradually establishing a presence in the mountains. Once the east was secure, and the guerrillas were no longer safe in their mountain strongholds, then a general move west could begin. To initiate this policy, two SAS squadrons led an offensive (Operation Jaguar) in October 1971, by *firqat* and SAF units, setting up a base inland, near Jibjat.

The attack on Mirbat was well planned. It was to take place during the monsoon, when air support was difficult if not impossible

The decision of the guerrillas to attack Mirbat was their response to the fact that government forces were gaining the initiative. What better way to demonstrate the foolishness of changing sides and the continuing power of the *adoo* than by taking over a town in the east of Dhofar, and holding it for a few hours before substantial SAF troops could be moved in; a town moreover in which a British Army team had trained the local *firqat*?

The attack on Mirbat was well planned. It was to take place during the monsoon period, when low cloud made air support difficult if not impossible (the town of Rakyut had fallen during the monsoon period when no air support had been available). A force of 250 guerrillas (far more than had ever been used in one operation before) had been assembled, and their support weapons included not only mortars and

Left above: The roof of the Batthouse, the base of the SAS team stationed in Mirbat. It was from here that the SAS poured fire onto the rebel *adoo* advancing towards the perimeter wire. Left below: The Batthouse seen from the pit in which Lance-Corporal Harris manned the mortar. Below: The Gendarmerie Fort, seen from the sea, with the gun-pit where the 25pdr was sited to the right. This photograph was taken by Captain Kealy himself. Bottom: An SAS trooper in Dhofar mans a 0.5in Browning machine gun, an old but dependable weapon. Harris' mortar, a GPMG, and a Browning were the support weapons that the SAS in Mirbat deployed against the attacking rebels.

heavy machine guns, but also 75mm recoilless rifles, and one Carl Gustav 84mm rocket launcher. In order to weaken the *firqat* at Mirbat, a small group of *adoo* had allowed themselves to be observed near the foot of the mountain escarpment, and so a large proportion of the 60-strong *firqat* had been sent out to investigate. Finally, the attackers had reckoned on the advantage of surprise as they stealthily surrounded the town and the fortified perimeter to its north during the night of 18/19 July. They were undisturbed as they made for their start lines, and, as dawn began to break, the first elements began to move forward.

Had total surprise been achieved, the attackers might well have won an easy victory. As it was, however, there was an outpost on a hill known as Jebel Ali, about 800m north of the barbed-wire perimeter. This was manned by a patrol of the Dhofar Gendarmerie, and, fortunately for the defenders at Mirbat, this patrol noticed the *adoo* creeping up and opened fire. Four of the gendarmes were killed and four managed to escape, but their alertness meant that firing had begun rather earlier than the insurgent leaders had hoped. The support weapons opened up, wakening the SAS detachment. Kealy himself rushed to the roof of the 'Batthouse' as the BATT headquarters was called.

Kealy had only recently joined the SAS as a troop commander. At 23 years old he was rather less experienced than the eight men from B Squadron he had under his command. These eight men, having completed their three-month tour of duty, were due to be relieved and so far at Mirbat they had passed a relatively uneventful time, training the local *firqat* and enduring just three short bombardments; but

now, as their commander joined them on the roof, all thoughts of a peaceful return to Britain vanished in the desperate need to fight off the guerrilla attack. The gendarmerie patrol had given them a brief warning; now they had to make their expertise tell.

From the roof the SAS laid down a murderous pattern of fire upon the advancing guerrillas

When Kealy reached the roof, the whole area around seemed full of noise, smoke, and pandemonium. Corporal Bob Bradshaw, whose calmness and shrewdness under fire were to be some of the most important assets of the defence, pointed out the direction from which enemy mortar shells were coming, and the lines along which the *adoo* themselves were advancing. The captain tried to take stock of the situation. He knew that 100m to the northwest, near the sea, was the Wali Fort, held by about 30 *askars* (armed tribesmen) from northern Oman. They were returning guerrilla fire, but were armed with rather dated .303in rifles, hardly a match at close quarters for the Soviet-made Kalashnikov assault rifles that the *adoo* were carrying. About 700m to the northeast lay a larger fort held by about 25 more of the Dhofar Gendarmerie. They too were returning enemy fire. In a gun-pit beside the fort was a World War II vintage 25-pounder, manned by an Omani gunner. One of the SAS team, Trooper Labalaba, a Fijian, had already gone across to assist him. It was clear that the *firqat* in the town itself, weakened by the earlier dispatch of the patrol, would be of little immediate use as it struggled to organise itself; but it might be effective later.

Trooper, 22 SAS, Oman 1971-75

Olive green fatigues are worn by this SAS trooper and include a jungle hat with brim folded under around the sides to form a peak at the front. His personalised belt holds water-ammunition-survival-escape/evasion kit, and over his back a Bergen rucksack is carried. Instead of the standard British Army SLR the trooper is armed with a US 5.56mm M16 rifle, a small-calibre automatic weapon with a maximum effective range of 400m. The M16 is considerably lighter than the SLR (3.86kg to 5kg, loaded with 20-round magazines) and its full automatic capability makes it a useful weapon for close-quarters fighting.

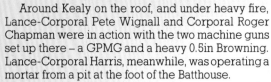

Around Kealy on the roof, and under heavy fire, Lance-Corporal Pete Wignall and Corporal Roger Chapman were in action with the two machine guns set up there – a GPMG and a heavy 0.5in Browning. Lance-Corporal Harris, meanwhile, was operating a mortar from a pit at the foot of the Batthouse.

All in all, these seemed puny defences against the weight of firepower that the guerrillas were deploying. But it was obvious that the key to the action would be the Dhofar Gendarmerie Fort, and in particular the 25-pounder pit. If that position fell, then further resistance would be futile. But if it could be held, then there was hope that help, in particular in the form of air support, might eventually arrive.

Over the gunfire Kealy heard from the other Fijian trooper, Savesaki, who was manning the short-range radio, that Labalaba at the fort had been shot in the chin. The captain agreed to Savesaki's request to take medical aid to him. This involved a run of 700m over open ground but Savesaki, a top-class rugby player, set off confidently, weaving through the hail of bullets that seemed to bar his way. To the relief of those on the Batthouse roof, he fell panting and unharmed into the gun-pit.

The relief of the SAS men was short-lived, for their attention was suddenly taken from this act of considerable heroism by groups of well-armed rebels seen advancing towards the perimeter wire that defended the encampment on three sides. The *adoo* opened up with automatic weapons and their support weapons concentrated on the Gendarmerie Fort with devastating effect. Now the technical expertise of the SAS came into play. From the Batthouse, Wignall and Chapman laid down a murderous pattern of fire on the advancing guerrillas, firing furiously and accurately as they screamed for more ammunition, while their gun barrels steamed in the early morning drizzle. The *adoo* managed to reach the wire in considerable numbers, but to cross barbed wire is difficult, and the guerrillas had nothing more than their bodies or a blanket to throw across. They were now extremely vulnerable. Bradshaw was able to pick them off with his SLR as they became entangled in the wire; in particular he cut down one officer who was bravely urging on his men while astride the wire himself. But still some got through, and made for the fort.

What Kealy needed now was reinforcements and support. During the confusion he had almost forgotten the long-range radio. He called headquarters in Salalah for a helicopter to casevac Labalaba and for jets to attack the advancing rebels, but with the clouds still so low he realised there was little chance of the Strikemasters managing an attack for some time.

In spite of the great bravery shown by the *adoo*, and in spite of the damage done to the Gendarmerie Fort by the bombardment, it was clear after about 0700 hours that the first crisis had passed. The initial assault had been held by a combination of physical courage (Savesaki's dash to the gun-pit) and solid experience, notably Bradshaw's efficient direction of the mortar and machine-gun fire that had chopped away at the guerrilla advance and given the SAS troopers a short breathing space.

The SAS were still in grave danger, however. The main anxiety now was that the gun-pit was not responding to repeated radio calls. Kealy told Bradshaw to take command at the Batthouse, while he and Trooper Tobin investigated the situation in the gun-pit. As Kealy was about to set out, Bradshaw, smiling, pointed out that he still had his 'flip-flops' on – in the excitement he had forgotten to change out of them. The rather embarrassed young captain went back to his room for his boots.

Kealy and Tobin, taking a less direct route than Savesaki, stealthily began their approach along a shallow wadi at the back of the Batthouse. However, as so often in war, strange almost humorous events ran parallel to extreme peril. Kealy and Tobin, intent on their task, had to pass a laundry house. As they did so, an old man came out and insisted on shaking hands. The two SAS men stayed for a moment to exchange civilities before continuing. But now they had to race for the gun-pit under fire, covering each other as they went. Tobin reached the pit safely while Kealy took refuge in a nearby ammunition bay. Tobin immediately applied a drip to the badly wounded Omani gunner as Labalaba painfully crawled towards Kealy to explain that Savesaki, although badly wounded in the back, was covering the left-hand side of the fort.

Suddenly, there was an almighty explosion. Through the smoke, Savesaki called to Kealy that more rebels had penetrated the wire and were heading towards them. The attack was on again with a vengeance, and the second crisis of the Battle of Mirbat had arrived.

Kealy spotted a grenade rolling over the lip of the gun-pit. He braced himself for his last moment

Labalaba, in spite of his wounds, continued to man the 25-pounder. He fired one shell at the *adoo* and reached down for another which he put in the breach; but he was never able to use this round, for he was killed instantly by a bullet. Kealy's position was now under intense fire. The captain shot down one eager rebel who had appeared round the corner of the fort, at point blank range, and was delighted to see that Tobin had taken over the 25-pounder and was firing away. Delight was short-lived, however, as Tobin in turn was shot – mortally wounded as it later turned out.

Kealy radioed back to the Batthouse for Bradshaw to bring down mortar and machine-gun fire on the enemy who were now closing on the fort in considerable numbers. Calm as ever, the corporal directed the machine-gun support, and assured Kealy that jets were on their way. Mortar support was more difficult – the range was just too short for effective firing. Whatever reassurance Kealy felt from this message was cut short when he spotted a grenade rolling slowly over the lip of the gun-pit. He braced himself for what he anticipated would be his last moment. But, to his disbelief, like an ill-packed firework, the grenade failed to explode. Moments later Strikemaster jets of the SOAF, with cannon firing, screamed in at low level to attack the rebels.

Under this air attack, the *adoo* began to pull back, and once again SAS expertise made itself felt, as Kealy from the fort and Bradshaw from the Batthouse directed the air strikes onto the most important areas, to inflict maximum damage on the enemy. Another set of air strikes at about 0915, concentrating on the *adoo* heavy support weapons on the Jebel Ali, furthered hampered the attackers and by now, too, those members of the *firqat* who had remained in the town were in action against the guerrillas who had moved to the southeast of the town.

The situation was still serious; only the air strikes, which had been carried out at very low altitude and at great risk to the pilots, had prevented the second major assault from carrying the day. But now, however, support in the form of fresh troops arrived. As luck would have it, 23 members of G Squadron, 22 SAS had landed in the Oman only 24 hours before and were about to move to the hills for acclimatisation training when they were alerted to the situation at Mirbat. They flew by helicopter from Salalah to the seashore southeast of Mirbat and joined the intense battle. The rebels were amazed at the ferocity of the new attack (the reinforcements were few in number, but carried nine GPMGs between them), and began to pull back. Mirbat was relieved.

The SAS lost two men at Mirbat – Trooper Labalaba and Trooper Tobin who later died of wounds – and suffered two seriously wounded. Over 30 guerrilla dead were found on the battlefield, but many more died later of their wounds. The action had been a triumph of courage and expertise against enormous odds, and in a very real sense marked a turning point in the war. Had Mirbat fallen, then the government's credibility would have collapsed; its successful defence proved the worth of Sultan Qaboos' policies, and led to vicious arguments within the guerrilla movement.

After Mirbat, SAS teams in Dhofar continued their work of training *firqat* and taking the fight against the guerrillas into the mountains. Dealing with the *firqat* was never easy and there were many criticisms of the system. But the gradual erosion of support for the guerrillas among the population would certainly have taken longer without the SAS-led *firqat*, and it was the success of the 'hearts and minds' programme spearheaded by the SAS that underpinned the drive west as government forces gradually took the initiative.

SAS numbers in Dhofar were always small – often under 50 men and rarely over 100 – and, in comparison with the 15,000 or so troops (including contingents from Jordan and Iran) that took part in the offensives of 1974 and 1975, SAS involvement may therefore seem puny. But the role of the Special Air Service Regiment was to act as a backbone, a stiffening for much larger forces; and in this they were invaluable. Whenever the going got tough they could be relied upon to provide all support necessary – as in January 1975, for example, in the attack on the guerrilla supply dump at Shershitti, when SAF troops caught in an ambush were relieved by SAS teams, after three days' hard fighting.

The war in Dhofar came to a practical end after the SAF won an unexpectedly easy victory at Sarfait in October 1975 and the taking of the Dorra Ridge in December of that year; by March 1976, the People's Democratic Republic of Yemen had come to an agreement with the Sultanate of Oman, and the Dhofari rebels were deprived of the safe haven and automatic re-supply that had been essential to their earlier success. There were still some isolated incidents, but the last SAS personnel left late in 1976. Since the arrival of units of the regiment in 1970, they had lost just 12 men killed, including the two who had died at Mirbat – the battle in which a 23-year-old captain and eight men had held off 250 heavily-armed guerrillas.

THE AUTHOR Max Arthur has written for TV, stage and films as well as military history. He is at present working on a series of first-hand accounts of the Falklands War.

THE HEROES OF MIRBAT

The nine members of the SAS at Mirbat upheld the traditions of the regiment in exemplary style, and set new standards for others to follow. Captain Kealy (above), awarded the DSO for his part in the battle, had never been in action before. His bravery was matched by his ability to 'read' what was happening around him – in particular he was always aware of the problems that might arise if the Dhofar Gendarmerie or the local *firqat* panicked, or felt betrayed. Tragically, Kealy died on exercise in the Brecon Beacons in 1979. Corporal Bradshaw, awarded the MM, was calmness and efficiency personified, directing support and interdiction fire from the Batthouse. Trooper Tobin, who courageously assisted Kealy in the defence of the gun-pit, was awarded a posthumous DCM, while Trooper Labalaba, also killed in defence of the gun-pit, received a posthumous Mention in Despatches. Of the other members of the team, Trooper Savesaki made the dash under fire to keep the 25-pounder in action and covered the left-hand side of the Gendarmerie Fort, although badly wounded; Lance-Corporal Harris continued to provide mortar support in spite of ranges being so short that he had to support the mortar barrel with his legs; Lance-Corporal Wignall and Corporal Reynolds provided support from the roof of the Batthouse throughout the battle; while Corporal Chapman, in addition to manning one of the machine guns during the first *adoo* assault, also played a key role in the arrival of support by guiding in the first Strikemaster.

In 1979 a column of Rhodesian SAS men infiltrated into Zambia to strike at the nerve centre of ZIPRA – Joshua Nkomo's personal command post in the heart of Lusaka

SAS
STORMING THE BASTILLE

THEY CALLED Operation Bastille Rhodesia's own Entebbe; so dramatic and unbelievable was the mission, that when the SAS commander, Major Dave Dodson, briefed his men, one trooper stood up, uttered a soldier's well-known expletive, and asked the officer if he was totally mad. As the bold plan unfolded, the SAS realised that their commander was not joking and that they were indeed going into the heart of the Zambian capital, Lusaka, to the home of Joshua Nkomo, leader of the Zambia-based Rhodesian nationalist group ZIPRA (Zimbabwe People's Revolutionary Army). If all went well, they would assassinate Nkomo and reduce his personal command post to rubble.

The situation in Rhodesia by the Easter of 1979 was critical. The war had escalated considerably since the signing of a political agreement by Ian Smith (the Rhodesian prime minister) and three internal black leaders, and although black majority rule was about to become a reality, both Joshua Nkomo's ZIPRA and Robert Mugabe's rival ZANLA (Zimbabwe African National Liberation Army) had refused to take part in the elections and had threatened to disrupt them by force.

Then, fresh intelligence warned of a far more serious threat. Joshua Nkomo, who had always held the majority of his men back in Zambia, had put his army on a conventional footing and was now poised to mount an invasion. Eight of ZIPRA's regular battalions were said to have regrouped northeast of Lusaka and another was reported to be near the Rhodesian border. To counter this apparent threat, the government forces were immediately deployed along the border to monitor crossing points and defend the countryside. Within Rhodesia itself, some 60,000 men were called up to protect voters as they went to the polling booths. Despite these precautions, the Rhodesians considered it imperative

Below: The Rhodesian SAS at war. Below left: Heavily laden with weapons and kit, a group of SAS men pose for the camera after the completion of an operation in the bush.

RHODESIA'S ELITE

In the early 1950s Major Mike Calvert arrived in Rhodesia to recruit men for his Malayan Scouts; some 100 Rhodesians, 90 civilians and 10 regulars, were selected for the Far East Volunteer Unit. The volunteers were to be known as C Squadron Malayan Scouts (SAS) and would wear Rhodesian shoulder flashes.

Two men, Peter Walls and his second-in-command, Lieutenant Ron Campbell-Morrison, were ordered to knock the squadron into shape, and once in Malaya a British-trained major would take command of the men. In the event, no-one could be found to take charge of the squadron so Peter Walls himself led the force in Malaya.

The Rhodesian commitment in Malaya lasted two years and the squadron returned home, with most men returning to civilian life. However, several men including Walls stayed in the army, using their recent experience to train units in counter-insurgency methods.

The early 1960s saw the Rhodesian armed forces undergoing expansion and a small team of men from the original squadron was ordered to select and train recruits after taking part in a refresher course with the British SAS. Returning home, it was decided to form six Sabre (combat) Troops with a total strength of 184 men. After Rhodesia's unilateral declaration of independence from Britain in late 1965, the Rhodesian SAS began to carry out operations against black nationalist groups.

For most of the war, the SAS carried out hit-and-run raids into neighbouring Mozambique, Zambia and Botswana. Never more than 200 strong, units attacked the enemy with an audacity that produced results out of all proportion to their size. In 1978, the unit was retitled 1 Special Air Service Regiment (Rhodesia). However, majority black rule and the political success of Robert Mugabe, led to the disbandment of the regiment in late 1980; many members moved to South Africa, some taking up arms in the South African Defence Force.

that the threat of invasion be removed by decisive, pre-emptive action: the very heart of the ZIPRA organisation would have to be attacked.

Yet the odds against carrying out a successful attack in the centre of the Zambian capital were formidable. Nkomo lived in a well-to-do suburb just two kilometres from the Zambian Army barracks; there were armed guards at the Zambian president's official residence, a stone's throw from Nkomo's sprawling bungalow, and guards at the target itself. The SAS team might also have to deal with the Zambian police and air force. The unknown factor facing the SAS was the Zambian reaction to an attack in the capital. This imponderable meant that the strike force would have to be flexible, have a lot of firepower and be completely mobile.

There was only one solution to the question of mobility: they would have to drive to Lusaka in their own transport, and do so at night. It was decided to use Sabre Land Rovers, the SAS's redundant pre-bush war specialist vehicles. By giving them a dark-green colour scheme with yellow paint splodges, it was hoped that they would resemble Zambian security force vehicles. A commercial ferry, the *Sea Lion*, would take the Sabres across Lake Kariba to the Zambian shore and from there the strike force would follow a rough track and a dirt road until they reached the main Lusaka road for the drive into the Zambian capital. The biggest hurdle facing the SAS would come long before they reached Lusaka, however. They would have to cross a river bridge at Kafue that was reportedly guarded by a strong detachment of the Zambian Army, supported by several heavy weapons. If the SAS men had to fight their way across this bridge the extent of their casualties would decide whether they aborted the

mission or not. After the initial briefing, the assault teams were put through exhaustive rehearsals for the operation, with everything being worked out down to the finest detail. The Sabres were made serviceable for the 200km trek to Lusaka, and then driven to the ferry. There were seven vehicles in the convoy which was to carry 42 men. As well as the hit on Nkomo, two other targets, a Liberation Centre housing several southern African nationalist groups, and an arms store, would also be attacked.

Eventually, the strike force was ready. All they needed now was the word. An externally-based undercover agent was to alert them when Joshua Nkomo was home and 'all go' was eventually flashed to the SAS waiting on the ferry on 12 April. There was still a bit of daylight left and the commander, Major Dave Dodson, decided to risk landing in Zambia as soon as possible. The ferry nosed into a deserted

150

landing spot and a protection party went ahead to secure the beach-head. It was just after 1800 hours; the attack was scheduled for 0200 hours on the 13th. The strike force drove off and set course for Lusaka. Their vehicle lights were on and the bright moon helped the drivers to negotiate the dirt track. Most of the men were apprehensive, but acknowledged that they were so well-armed that they would be able to deal with almost every problem – except, perhaps, the Zambian detachment at the Kafue bridge.

For the first 10km they made good time, but then the track deteriorated and, at times, faded away completely. It was necessary to use a lot of four-wheel drive and fuel, but the commander had anticipated most of the problems and each vehicle carried three times the fuel it needed. By this stage the men's initial excitement had faded and there was very little talk. Everyone settled down to a long, hard slog on

the poor track. The drivers bounced their vehicles through the mud and, where the track was washed away, they felt more like sailors than soldiers, as the passengers put their weight on one side, then the other, to stop the listing vehicles sinking into the morass. Then, one vehicle broke down completely, and Major Dave Dodson had no option but to order the six passengers to stay behind. It meant that their task, an attack on the arms store, would have to be abandoned. Leaving six very unhappy men behind, the remaining vehicles moved off into the gloom of the night. They were now running very late, but the commander decided he was ready to continue and risk being caught in Lusaka at first light.

As they approached Kafue bridge, the machine guns were placed on their mountings and the men took the safety catches off their rifles.

Then came the biggest surprise of the entire operation. There was nothing and no-one to hinder their progress: no Zambian troops, no heavy weapons, and no barriers. The SAS sped across the bridge hardly daring to believe their good luck. They headed for Lusaka. There was far more traffic than they had been expecting and the men deliberately kept their faces averted to avoid their features being recognised in the glare of the on-coming lights. When a vehicle pulled up behind them, Captain Martin Pearse stood up and waved the driver on. The man obeyed and pulled out, hit the accelerator and disappeared without suspecting a thing. Soon, an orange glow ahead warned that they were approaching Lusaka. Traffic rolled on its way and, off in the distance, the SAS could make out the blink of traffic lights. As the 36 Rhodesians drove into Lusaka under the full glare of the city lights, their watches showed 0240 hours. Lieutenant Rich Stannard, who was to lead the attack on the Liberation Centre, was at the back of the convoy and turned off with two vehicles to his target, leaving the others to continue to Nkomo's home.

Driving through Lusaka was an eerie experience, as Major Dave Dodson remembers:

Top: Joshua Nkomo, leader of the Zambian-based ZIPRA and target of Operation Bastille. Centre: Nkomo's residence and command post in Lusaka after the SAS raid. Bunker bombs and machine-gun fire reduced the building to ruins but a tip-off from a well-placed ZIPRA spy warned the African leader of the impending attack and his life was saved. Far left: For the clandestine raid into Zambia, the SAS painted their Sabre Land Rovers to resemble Zambian security force vehicles. Centre left: SAS troopers check their kit aboard the ferry *Sea Lion* during the trip across Lake Kariba. Left: The Rhodesian SAS column moves northwards through the bush.

'There we were, fairly well gunned-up – two machine guns and an RPG-7 per vehicle – each gun having 1500 rounds in it; troops in the back, helmets on and blackened-up. The traffic lights were working and, to keep the convoy together and delay any suspicions of the locals drifting around, we stopped at the lights. A bloke pulled up next to us; we half waved at him and he half waved at us.'

The lights changed to green, the drivers slowly let out their clutches, and the blackened-up Rhodesians were on their way again. Soon, the SAS were closing in on Joshua Nkomo's home which was screened from view by a wire security fence covered with hessian. The convoy stopped briefly, while Dave Dodson gave his last command. Then the vehicles

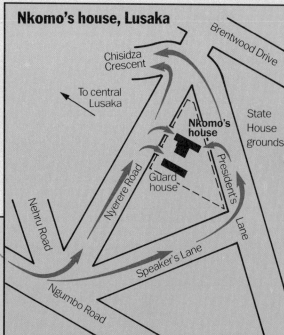

Nkomo's house, Lusaka

Below right: Lieutenant Rich Stannard, leader of an attack on one of the secondary targets in Lusaka – the Liberation Centre. After knocking out the operations room Stannard's men rigged the centre with explosives and the building was totally destroyed. Bottom: The SAS column makes a brief stop during the journey through the bush.

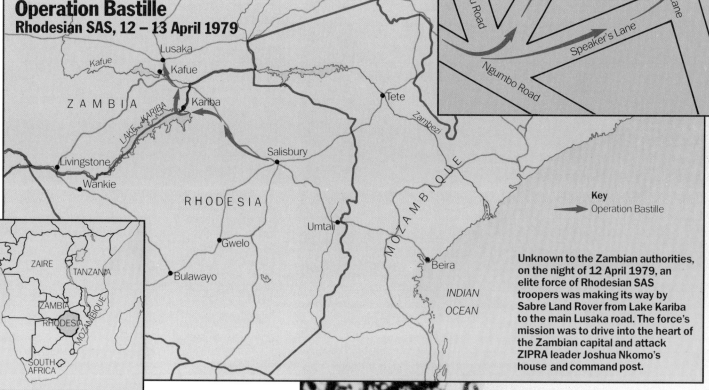

Operation Bastille
Rhodesian SAS, 12 – 13 April 1979

Key
→ Operation Bastille

Unknown to the Zambian authorities, on the night of 12 April 1979, an elite force of Rhodesian SAS troopers was making its way by Sabre Land Rover from Lake Kariba to the main Lusaka road. The force's mission was to drive into the heart of the Zambian capital and attack ZIPRA leader Joshua Nkomo's house and command post.

roared off at speed, two in one direction and the third in another. It was 0255 hours. The plan was for Martin Pearse to breach the security wall, then lead a team into the house to assassinate Nkomo. Dave Dodson and a sergeant-major were to breach the two main gates, then bunker bomb and rocket their side of the bungalow, leaving Pearse to get on with the house-fighting. Six men would be in a reserve vehicle on Dodson's side to watch for outside interference.

Martin Pearse's vehicle came screeching up, but, even before it stopped, a guard behind the security fence began firing. Pearse's rear gunner opened up in response, letting rip at a cluster of security huts and emptying his first belt in record time. Pearse leapt from his Sabre and raced to the fence to attach an explosive charge to blast an entrance. However, there was a problem with the attachment, and so he whipped out his wire-cutters to force an entrance big enough to take a man with webbing. The twinkle of lights could be seen from Nkomo's house, and once the enemy fire was neutralised near his entrance, Pearse led two other men into the garden.

On the opposite side of the target, the two front gates had been breached and the SAS were

machine-gunning the house, the vehicles and anyone they saw moving. There was some return fire, but the SAS quickly suppressed all opposition from the 30 or so guards. Fifteen bodies lay sprawled around the grounds and the remainder of the guards wisely kept a low profile. Then, everyone on the commander's side of the house began rocketing and bunker bombing the bungalow. Dave Dodson lobbed a bunker bomb into the main building and the lounge burst into flames. Masonry and timber were sent crashing to the floor, and the lights were blown out. Fire quickly took hold, and smoke, dust and flames rose over the residence. The noise from the exploding bunker bombs, machine guns, rockets and smallarms was fantastic. It was a spectacular sight; the machine guns had one tracer in three rounds, so the SAS could see the red sheets of tracers hitting the target.

At the nearby Zambian president's palace, the presidential guard began firing, their red and green

tracer criss-crossing and ricocheting across the night sky. But it was merely a token show; nothing and no-one came near the raiders. Elsewhere in the capital, Zambians ran into the streets in their night-clothes, alarmed at all the commotion.

Martin Pearse was by now racing to Nkomo's bedroom, but his original plan to throw in a bunker bomb was frustrated as the window was barred. He doubled around to the back door, blew the lock off and hurried inside with his team. Faced with a two-sided passageway and four doors, they set about clearing the choking smoke and dust-filled house with chilling precision. They had 15 minutes to do the job. Aided by a torch strapped to the underside of his AK rifle, Pearse fired into every likely hiding place in Nkomo's bedroom. But there was no sign of their man. The bathroom and storeroom were cleared but, again, there was no sign of life.

Pearse and the corporal then returned to the room and killed the two enemy soldiers

As the SAS burst into the last remaining room, a guard opened up on them from under a bed and another man shot at them from inside a cupboard. Pearse and his corporal grenaded the room, and the third team member fired a very long burst from his cut-down RPD machine gun. Pearse and the corporal then returned to the room and killed the two enemy soldiers. Pearse called the overall commander on his radio to report that he had finished. The Bastille had fallen, but the SAS reluctantly came to the conclusion that Nkomo had not even been in the house. Although the Zambian-based undercover agent had seen him go into the house, he had not seen Nkomo leave.

Martin Pearse had done an excellent job, and had Nkomo been there that night, there is no doubt what the outcome would have been. Later, Joshua Nkomo's claim that he had escaped by climbing through a toilet window was met with hilarity by the Rhodesians. The truth, however, was not so funny. Nkomo survived, not through bad luck on the SAS's part, but because he had been tipped off by a well-placed spy. It was the closest the Rhodesians were to come to assassinating Nkomo, for the operation was the last attempt on his life. The entire operation had been pulled off in 25 minutes and all the detailed planning had made it unnecessary to give orders during the raid as everyone knew what to do at each stage.

The first Zambian reactions to the attack had been picked up by the SAS radioman as the assault team hurried from the ruins to their waiting vehicles, meeting up around the corner to reorganise. In quick time, they were on their way again, passing several military vehicles heading towards Nkomo's suburb. However, the Sabres were on the other side of the carriageway, and the Zambians showed no interest in the convoy as it observed the speed limit and made its way out of town to rendezvous with Lieutenant Rich Stannard and his team who were attacking the Liberation Centre. By now, the city lights were doused and air-raid sirens whined across the capital as the Zambians thought that the Rhodesians were about to carry out an air strike.

Rich Stannard and his demolition teams had already hit the enemy operations room, and were rigging up their charges and lighting their safety fuzes. The ops room was still blazing furiously as they roared off at high speed, well away from the forthcoming fireworks. At the rendezvous point, the men

TACKLING THE MEN AT THE TOP

The assassination of a high-ranking enemy official or military commander has often been seen as a legitimate act during wartime. In World War II, both the Allied and Axis commanders authorised raids against their opposite numbers. Two attacks in particular highlight this approach to the conduct of war: the British commando raid on Rommel's North African HQ in November 1941, and the German swoop on Tito's mountain base in May 1944. Both failed, but most commentators agree that the potential advantages to be gained far outweighed the risks involved. However, few armies would ever seriously contemplate such acts unless the removal of the enemy's 'head' would have immediate and profound consequences on the course of the conflict. Like the attacks on Rommel and Tito, the raid on Nkomo's HQ, if successful, would have dealt a massive blow to the enemy's morale and severely compromised their ability to co-ordinate their activities in the field.

All three men were regarded as charismatic leaders who inspired an almost religious fervour in the men under their command.

The essence of all three missions was the use of highly trained forces that had been given every piece of available intelligence during the planning of the operation. However, no matter how much preparation took place, the likelihood of failure remained high, and luck played an essential part in determining the outcome. Although the element of surprise was present in all three cases, the raiders were unable to succeed in their tasks. Both Rommel and Nkomo were absent and Tito was able to flee before the assault groups reached his hideaway. Nevertheless, the use of small commando-type teams to take out the enemy's leadership is still regarded as a viable military option as was shown by the solo British helicopter attack on the Argentinian headquarters in Port Stanley during the Falklands campaign of 1982

RAID ON BEIRA

Operating mainly in the border areas during Rhodesia's long bush war, the Special Air Service (SAS) was called upon for clandestine missions. As the conflict escalated, the SAS was used in Zambia, Botswana and Mozambique, from where nationalist guerrilla groups were operating.

Their single largest economic target was Beira, a well-defended city on the coast of Mozambique. The destruction of Beira's giant oil-storage depot would deal a crippling blow to the country's already faltering economy.

Aerial reconnaissance by Captain Bob McKenna, the strike-force commander, showed a well-illuminated target, and the attack was planned for 23 March 1979. After silently making their way through the back streets of the city, McKenna divided his force into three groups. Captain Colin Willis, after laying a suitcase bomb on a large oil pipeline, took charge of the first group and set up a position on the far side of the depot. The second group,

under Lieutenant Peter Cole, peeled off to lay explosives against an electricity pylon, before rejoining McKenna's main attack force next to the fuel tanks.

At 0015 hours, having waited anxiously for Willis to get into position, McKenna initiated the attack using an RPG-7 rocket launcher. Moments later, Willis's raiding party followed suit. Under a relentless cross-fire of rockets and armour-piercing bullets, the fuel tanks erupted, pouring smoke and flames into the night sky. The depot's anti-aircraft gunners and guards, convinced that they were under air attack, fired into the night sky. Their mistake allowed the raiders to make good their escape.

Confident that the attack had succeeded, Captain McKenna gave the order to pull out. Suffering only two casualties, the raiders disappeared silently into the night, the suitcase bomb exploding behind them. Within a few hours, the charges on the electricity pylon would detonate, cutting off the city's power supply. Mission accomplished.

who had attacked Joshua Nkomo's home heard the sudden rumble of heavy vehicles. Was the Zambian Army reacting? Would Rich Stannard's escape route be blocked? But they saw no sign of the Zambians and within minutes Stannard and party had joined them. Seconds later, a massive orange mushroom billowed into the sky, followed by an enormous thunderclap as the Liberation Centre went up.

Frightened civilians came streaming out of their homes heading for the safety of the bush, their suitcases and chattels stacked high on their heads. It was also time for the SAS to take their leave. It was 0400 hours, and light enough for them to be seen. However, on the long journey south there was no-one to stop them. They crossed the Kafue bridge without incident, picked up the six men left behind with the broken-down vehicle, drove to the ferry and then set sail for home. It was 18 hours since the ferry had

Top left: The officers who led the three assault groups at Beira. From left to right are Captain Colin Willis, Lieutenant Pete Cole and the commander of the op, Captain Bob McKenna. Top right: Willis (left) goes over the details of the suitcase bomb that was used to blow the pipeline; with him are Cole and Les Clark. Above right: Captain Martin Pearse, the officer who led the house fighting on Operation Bastille.

delivered the SAS to the Zambian shore and now the prospect of a couple of hours well-earned sleep lay ahead.

One of the most dramatic operations of the war was over. Later the Rhodesian elections went ahead without too much disruption and Nkomo did not begin developing his invasion strategy until seven months later. But it was his old foes, the SAS, who finally put paid to his plans in a series of further slick pre-emptive strikes into Zambia that repeated the successes of the earlier raids.

THE AUTHOR Barbara Cole is married to a former Rhodesian SAS officer and has written a book entitled *The Elite: the Story of the Rhodesian SAS*. It has been hailed as a classic in counter-insurgency writing and Cole is currently working on a pictorial edition.

SAS
SIEGE BREAKERS

Terrorists held 26 hostages at gunpoint in the Iranian embassy at Princes Gate in London in May 1980 – and then the SAS moved in

NUMBER 16 Princes Gate, home of the Iranian embassy, stands overlooking the peaceful green expanses of Kensington Gardens in the heart of London's fashionable SW7. Today the house, once the scene of the busy comings and goings of the diplomatic community, stands empty; its doors chained and secured with a heavy padlock. On the first floor the elegant facade is crumbling and charred – the only remaining visible evidence of the events of 5 May 1980. In the early evening of that Bank Holiday Monday, several crashing explosions and the sharp crackle of automatic fire resounded along the terrace of houses at the climax of a tense siege which had kept the British government, its security forces and the public on tenterhooks for six days.

It was immediately supposed that the gunmen inside were blowing up the embassy, and slaughter-

Right: The SAS go in. Armed with a 'Hockler', the Heckler and Koch MP5A3 sub-machine gun, an SAS man springs across the embassy balcony.

THE 22ND SPECIAL AIR SERVICE REGIMENT

The present-day SAS, the direct descendant of the World War II SAS, was formed in 1952, and began its career with a series of campaigns against guerrillas operating in the difficult terrain of countries such as Malaya, Borneo and Aden. In recent years, however, the SAS has become more associated with the war against terrorism.

In May 1972 they were involved in a 'wet-jump' in the mid-Atlantic to board and search the Queen Elizabeth II for a bomb. Following the massacre of Israeli athletes at the Munich Olympics in September 1972, the British authorities ordered the creation of specifically-trained anti-terrorist units.

Over the last 15 years the main strength of the SAS has been deployed to combat the IRA, both on the British mainland and in Northern Ireland, but it was not until January 1976 that the government announced publicly the use of a full squadron in the South Armagh border region. Terrorism, however, has an international face, and it has become common practice for the SAS to liaise with other European security forces. In May 1977 they helped Dutch marines and police to deal with a train-load of hostages hijacked by South Moluccan terrorists, and five months later a two-man team lent their expertise to the West German GSG9 anti-terrorist squad to free hostages held on a hijacked airliner.

By May 1980 the SAS could draw on the experience of many years of counter-terrorist operations.

ing the hostages they had taken. Moments later, however, several dark silhouettes plunged into view. Vaulting agilely over the balcony from the house next door, they blasted their way through the window of the embassy with explosives. A pall of smoke belched from the shattered window, and the mysterious figures, dressed from head to toe in black, slipped inside. For the astonished onlookers at the front of the building, this was their first, and most likely their last, view of the 22nd Special Air Service Regiment going into action.

Unidentified gunmen had burst in through the front doors of the embassy after spraying the outer glass door with bullets

The handling of sieges where hostages have been taken can never be a text-book operation. In every case hundreds of different factors have to be taken into account: who are the gunmen, what do they want, and will they really kill their hostages if their demands are not met? In many cases security forces have painstakingly negotiated a peaceful outcome, and a basic pattern of siege handling has been developed over the years. The provision of food, cigarettes, medical supplies and access to the media for the release of ideological statements are the results of hard bargaining. The position of the police is that they will never give anything away without getting something back in return – usually the release of a hostage. The question of a full-frontal assault by the police or army is never far from the minds of both security forces and the gunmen, but in recent years both parties have been haunted by the Munich massacre of 1972. Then, the German police

attacked the terrorists on an airfield runway and the hostages, 9 Israeli athletes, met a tragic end as their Palestinian captors despatched them with a handful of grenades.

British security forces, however, have a first-rate record in the business of dealing with terrorist groups: the Spaghetti House restaurant siege of 1975 was ended without casualties, and, later that year, IRA gunmen gave themselves up at a flat in Balcombe Street, London, without harming a middle-aged couple they had taken hostage. In the latter siege, a mention, on the BBC, of the SAS being in the vicinity, was believed to have brought the terrorists out. But the situation at Princes Gate proved far more complex and infinitely more dangerous.

At 1132 hours on the morning of Wednesday 30 April, a group of unidentified gunmen had burst in through the front doors of the embassy after spraying the outer glass door with bullets. The terrified occupants of the five-storey building were quickly rounded up – in addition to the 19 Iranians in the embassy there were seven non-Iranians, including two men from the BBC and Police Constable Trevor Lock from Scotland Yard's Diplomatic Protection Group.

With sirens blaring and lights flashing, police units were on the scene within minutes – Lock had succeeded in transmitting an emergency signal through to the Yard before being overpowered by the raiders. They were soon joined by the more specialist units at Scotland Yard's disposal: D11, known as the 'Blue Berets', an elite unit of police marksmen, took up positions around the building, followed by C13, the anti-terrorist squad, while the Special Patrol Group and members of C7, the Yard's Technical Support Branch, were also quickly on the scene. The latter were in charge of the surveillance equipment that monitored everything that went on

Left: 1250 hours on Friday 2 May, the third day of the siege. A brief glimpse of one of the gunmen as he appeared at the front door of the embassy to pick up a package of food. Negotiations at this point were going well and the gunmen are said to have complimented the police on the quality of the meals sent in. Left below: The SAS in training for anti-terrorist operations. One of the key aspects of their training is to prepare them to deal with any terrorist situation whether it be in the heart of London or in the wilds of South Armagh in Northern Ireland. Right: Since the gunmen spoke little English, hostages relayed their demands to the police. Here PC Trevor Lock and the Lebanese journalist Mustapha Karkouti speak on the gunmen's behalf. Below: The weapons of the SAS – the Heckler and Koch MP5A3 sub-machine gun and the 9mm Browning HP automatic pistol. (Weapons not shown to scale.)

BATTLEDRESS AND WEAPONS

The 22nd SAS Regiment, unlike most units of the regular British Army, allows its men a degree of personal choice in both the weapons and clothing used on active service.

At the embassy the need was for light, comfortable clothing that would not interfere with movement. The men wore tight-fitting black combat clothing with high patrol boots and 'Northern Ireland' gloves, and a black-covered flak vest covered the torso. Headwear consisted of a standard-issue army respirator and a grey anti-flash hood – both helped to reduce the effects of smoke and heat generated by the explosions and subsequent fire during the assault on the embassy.

A black belt held an open-top holster for the 9mm Browning automatic pistol and a series of pouches that contained magnesium-based 'stun' grenades and 30-round magazines for the Heckler and Koch sub-machine gun.

The 9mm Heckler and Koch MP5A3 was perhaps the most effective part of the SAS arsenal deployed at Princes Gate. Of West German origin, it was pressed into service after two SAS men had witnessed its effectiveness in close-quarter combat during the GSG9 assault on an airliner at Mogadishu. The 'Hockler', as the MP5A3 is known to the SAS, is light (2kg), short (32.5cm) and can fire at a rate of up to 650rpm or, if need be, single shots to take out individual targets.

157

inside the embassy. By mid-afternoon plainclothes SAS men were also present – their arrival, however, was considerably more discreet.

With the embassy effectively sealed off and surrounded, the police received the gunmen's demands over the telephone at 1435. The gunmen identified themselves as the Group of the Martyr. In opposition to the harsh Islamic Iranian regime of the Ayatollah Khomeini, they were fighting for the liberation of Khuzestan, an oil-rich district inhabited by Arabs in the southwest of Iran, that had a history of revolt against Iranian domination. Their demands included the release of 91 Arab prisoners held in Iran, their immediate transfer from gaol to London, and a request for Arab ambassadors to mediate with the British authorities. Noon the next day was the deadline – if it was not met they threatened to blow up the embassy and execute the hostages.

In Zulu Control, the main police headquarters set up further down the terrace, the Yard mulled over the immediate problems of the situation. In both the Spaghetti House and Balcombe Street sieges background knowledge of the men involved had proved invaluable in wearing them down. The police, however, knew little of the Group of the Martyr, and, as far as they could see, only one of the gunmen could speak English. The police were also unaware as to how many hostages had been taken, and, although they later discovered there were 26, held by six terrorists, it was difficult to fix their location in the rambling building. The authorities began their tense negotiations almost immediately, and, because of the obvious difficulties, adopted the tried and tested 'softly-softly' approach.

Meanwhile the SAS were making their own preparations to deal with the situation. At a barracks in Regent's Park a scale model of the besieged embassy had been constructed, to familiarise the men with every detail of the layout of the building they would have to assault if police negotiations broke down.

Operation Nimrod, as it became known, was nothing new to the SAS. Since the early 1970s, SAS training procedures had placed great emphasis on counter-revolutionary warfare and the fight against international terrorism. The Munich massacre had proved the need for specially-trained squads of men ready to deal with any eventuality at a moment's notice. This meant coping with the hijacking of aircraft, trains or ships at any time of day, anywhere in the world. It also meant dealing with the armed takeover of buildings where hostages were involved.

SAS training involves stretching a man's endurance to the limits

At Bradbury Lines, the SAS headquarters at Hereford, a close-quarter battle (CQB) house had been constructed for the purpose of training troopers in the use of small arms in enclosed spaces. Members of the SAS are trained to burst into rooms, recognise their terrorist adversaries, and shoot them down before they have time to react. In the CQB house, SAS men sit in a room with a number of 'terrorist' straw dummies while their colleagues storm in and riddle the dummies with live ammunition from their silenced Sterling sub-machine guns and Browning automatics. It is not an exercise where mistakes can be made. Lightning reflexes, and the ability to shoot accurately and lethally while running, crouching or rolling across the floor, are the keys to such combat skills.

Their marksmanship is only part of the story, however. First of all, the SAS have to get into the area where the hostages are being held. While SAS training involves stretching a man's resources and endurance to the limits, it also teaches him all the basic assault techniques, including abseiling – part of the mountain-training programme – and the use of explosives to blast a way into sealed buildings. Equipment, specially developed for these particularly hazardous operations, is also crucial to their success. 'Frame charges' were used to break through the strengthened glass of the embassy's windows. These are large rectangles of plastic explosive that are placed flush against the glass, so that the whole window is blown in when the charges are detonated. Then 'stun' grenades would be used.

→ 34 ▮ → 34A ▮ → 35 ▮ → 35A ▮

Above left to right: 1923 hours on Monday 5 May. The SAS frontal-assault team moves into position with 'frame charges' and blows out the embassy windows. As the smoke clears the black-clad figures disappear into the building on their way to the second-floor telex room and an appointment with the terrorists.

The stun grenade had been specially developed by the SAS for just such an operation as Nimrod. When detonated, it produces a blinding flash, a deafening bang and a cloud of smoke. It is in the moment after the explosion, when gunmen are temporarily blinded and disorientated by the smoke and the noise, that the SAS man must act. These grenades had been supplied by the SAS to the German GSG9 anti-terrorist unit, were used successfully in an assault on a hijacked Lufthansa aircraft on the runway at Mogadishu in Somalia in 1977, and were perfectly suited to the Princes Gate operation.

To assist in the assault, preparations were also being made at the embassy itself. In order to determine the exact position of the gunmen, Scotland Yard's C7 installed a number of microphones and surveillance devices in the chimneys and walls of adjoining buildings. To cover the noise of this installation work, a barrage of road drills was set up in nearby Enismore Gardens – the Gas Board was supposedly carrying out emergency repairs after the report of a gas leak in the street. Unknown to the gunmen inside, a section of wall between the embassy and the house next door was also being removed. As quietly as possible the bricks were removed one by one, leaving only a thin sheet of plaster for an assault team to kick their way through.

Outside in the street things were not going so well. Patient negotiations on the part of the police had secured the release of several hostages, food and cigarettes had been passed in to the gunmen, and two deadlines had passed without incident. By the evening of 1 May, the second day of the siege, the gunmen had discarded their demand for the release of the 91 prisoners in Iran, hoping that, through the mediation of the requested Arab ambassadors, they could negotiate a safe passage out of the country. The British government, however, was taking a firm stand on the questions of mediation and safe conduct, and, to the fury of the gunmen, radio news had made no mention whatsoever of their demand for Arab mediators. Frustrated and jumpy, the gunmen threatened to kill hostages unless their demands were broadcast in full. For several tense minutes they sat listening to Capital Radio's nine o'clock news bulletin. The demand for the mediators was stated and the crisis was temporarily averted, but the mediators failed to materialise.

By the morning of the sixth day, Monday 5 May, the situation was deteriorating rapidly. With the government refusing to make any concessions, the police had little bargaining power left, and had lost the precious confidence of the terrorists. Inside the building, the strain of the past days was beginning to tell. The gunmen had grown pessimistic of their chances of escape, and a raging political argument, which had broken out between them and several of the Iranian hostages the night before, brought the situation to the brink of catastrophe. At 1140 hours, Constable Lock appeared at the window to say that his captors would start shooting the hostages unless news of the Arab mediators was immediately forthcoming. Desperately playing for time, the police persuaded the gunmen to wait until the mid-day BBC news. The BBC bulletin, however, made little impression on the gunmen and at 1331 three shots were heard from inside the embassy.

Faces masked with respirators, the SAS men stormed the building

For the gunmen, surrender was now the only realistic way out, but at 1850, after having restated their demands, three more shots were heard and the dead body of the embassy press officer was pushed out of the front door onto the pavement. The police responded at once. Seemingly giving into their demands, the negotiators made contact with the leader of the gunmen, offered him safe conduct and an aircraft to take the group out of the country. But as the terrorist leader discussed the details of the bus to the airport he was also giving away his position to the waiting SAS assault force.

At 1923, the black-clad assault team crashed into the embassy. Their faces masked with respirators, the SAS men stormed the building from three sides. The initial assault came from the back. Abseiling down ropes from the roof, the first pair reached the

Assault on the Iranian embassy

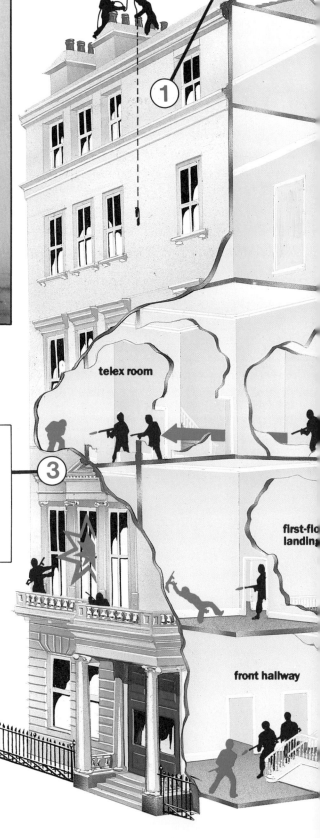

Microphones and surveillance devices are lowered down the chimney to monitor the movements of the terrorists and hostages inside the embassy.

① ②

telex room

Members of the frontal-assault group blast their way through the first-floor windows with 'frame charges' and lob in a 'stun' grenade. Reaching the telex room, the SAS burst in and shoot two terrorists dead.

③

first-floor landing

front hallway

terrace at the back of the embassy, but were unable to detonate their frame charges because of a colleague entangled in a rope above them. A second pair dropped to the first floor back balcony and both teams were forced to hack their way in through bullet-proof glass. A stun grenade was thrown in and the SAS made for the telex room on the second floor where they knew, from the C7 surveillance, that a number of the hostages were being held.

On the first-floor landing the terrorist leader was with Trevor Lock, and as an SAS man appeared at the window he raised his gun to fire. Lock sprang into action, hurling himself at the gunman and grappling with him until the SAS man was able to put him away. Meanwhile at the front of the building, in full view of the TV cameras, the SAS blasted through the first floor window and lobbed in a stun grenade. Flames poured from the window, and out of the thick smoke came the first of the hostages, the BBC man Sim Harris, into the welcoming hands of an SAS trooper. A third team stormed through the thin sheets of plaster where the bricks had been removed.

Racing through the burning building, the SAS converged on the telex room. Hearing the mayhem of the assault, the gunman guarding the hostages turned his gun onto them – killing one and wounding two others. When the SAS burst in, he and two colleagues had mingled with the hostages scattered around the floor of the room. The room was full of smoke, and in the confusion the SAS demanded to know which ones were the terrorists. As they were pointed out the SAS shot two of them dead.

The actual sequence of events in the telex room at Number 16 Princes Gate has never been fully estab-

Left: Covered by an SAS 'Hockler', Sim Harris, first of the hostages to appear, makes a dramatic escape from the burning building. Right: Clearing up after the operation. On Wednesday 7 May firemen went in to remove the bodies of the gunmen found inside the embassy. Wrapped in a body bag, a corpse is lowered from the second-floor front window of the embassy.

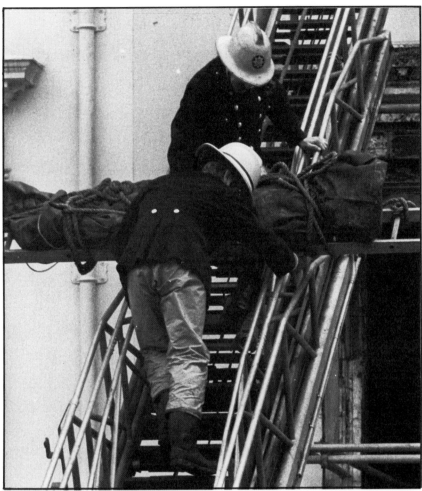

An SAS assault force abseils down from the roof in pairs. On the way down a flailing boot breaks a back window and the element of surprise is almost lost. One of the team becomes entangled in a descent rope and the SAS are unable to use 'frame charges'. They hack their way in through the strengthened-glass windows on the first and ground floors and toss in a 'stun' grenade. Entering the building, they shoot a gunman in the front hallway and race towards the telex room.

lished. Several of the hostages interviewed afterwards said that the gunmen tried to surrender, but, in the heat of the battle, amid the smoke and confusion and wailing of the hostages, the SAS took what action was deemed necessary.

In the wake of the assault the bodies of five of the six gunmen were carried out of the embassy; two were taken from the telex room, one from an office at the back, one from the embassy hallway near the front door and the fifth from the first floor. All had died from firearm wounds to the head and chest. As for the SAS, they suffered no casualties and left the area in two Avis vans.

The Iranian embassy siege gripped the nation's imagination for six long days, and, thanks to television, everyone in the country had a grandstand view of the unfolding drama. It was on this dangerous and dramatic stage that the SAS made their public debut. Negotiation by the police kept the hostages alive, but it was the SAS, in a brief 17-minute exchange, who brought them freedom. The operation at Princes Gate was carried out with almost surgical precision, and, although the gunmen killed one of the hostages in the final shoot-out, SAS training in anti-terrorist techniques was shown to be second to none.

THE AUTHOR Jonathan Reed is a historian with a special interest in revolutionary warfare and modern counter-insurgency techniques. He has contributed articles to a number of military publications on subjects including the Palestine Liberation Organisation and counter-insurgency operations in Central America and Vietnam.

THE SAS TODAY

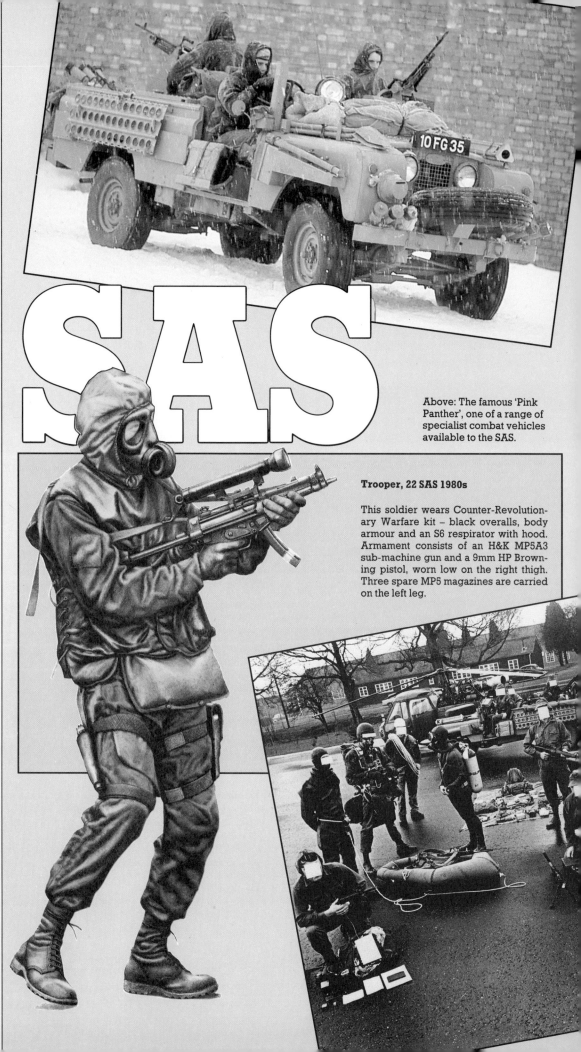

The Special Air Service (SAS) consists of three regiments: the regulars, 22 SAS, and two Territorial Army (TA) regiments designated 21 and 23. Each of the three regiments comprises four squadrons. The SAS squadrons are subdivided into troops, which in turn are further broken down into four-man patrol teams. In the regular regiment, however, the size and organisation of the troops varies according to the specialist roles they are assigned. 22 SAS is also provided with a fifth squadron, composed of reservists, from which specialist personnel can be drawn for particular missions. In addition, a regular SAS signals squadron supports the requirements of 22 SAS, while a TA signals squadron provides for the two territorial regiments.

The SAS of today is a small, tightly knit organisation with the emphasis on quality not quantity. To achieve the level of fitness and the skills required for their dangerous and often sensitive missions, the selection and training process is necessarily ruthless and tough in the extreme. Physical, intellectual and technical skills are developed to the full, along with a good measure of initiative and the ability to improvise in a crisis. Highly realistic exercises are also staged to familiarise the SAS troops with every conceivable terrorist situation. However, while the popular press tends to focus on the 'heroics' of siegebreaking, it must not be forgotten that their strategic role – raiding, intelligence gathering and sabotage – is often as equally demanding and is every bit as important, even if it does not appear quite so glamorous to the public eye.

Above: The famous 'Pink Panther', one of a range of specialist combat vehicles available to the SAS.

Trooper, 22 SAS 1980s

This soldier wears Counter-Revolutionary Warfare kit – black overalls, body armour and an S6 respirator with hood. Armament consists of an H&K MP5A3 sub-machine gun and a 9mm HP Browning pistol, worn low on the right thigh. Three spare MP5 magazines are carried on the left leg.

Generally acknowledged as the world's foremost experts in the business of fighting terrorism, the SAS of today has a wide variety of specialist roles – from clandestine surveillance to hostage rescue

IN THE INITIAL period after World War II the primary task of the Special Air Service (SAS) was to counter insurgency in Britain's former colonial possessions such as Malaya, southern Arabia and Sarawak. Since then, however, its role has changed to cope with a more modern problem – the threat of international terrorism. The SAS has had to adapt its techniques to fight a new and ruthless enemy wherever he may strike. Counter-Revolutionary Warfare, as the battle against terrorism and insurgency is sometimes known, has become one of the most important aspects of SAS work and the regiment is now recognised as the foremost exponent of siege-breaking and hostage-rescue techniques.

The SAS is one of the smallest corps in the British Army, but by its professionalism and adherence to the original principles of its founder, David Stirling, it has produced astonishing results. Stirling insisted on the exploitation of surprise, deception and professional cunning; and so does the SAS of today. Daring has always been the watchword. This quality was demonstrated, for example, by the pioneer role played by the SAS in military free-fall parachuting, and more particularly by one remarkable feat during a training exercise. Sergeant Reeves climbed down the static line of a learner's parachute, which had

Below left: Equipment on display. Trained to operate in any environment, the SAS troops are equipped for underwater, airborne, amphibious, mountain, desert, jungle, arctic and urban warfare. Right: An SAS skier. The SAS do not use rifle slings – the weapon must be ready in the hand at all times – but this trooper has improvised one with a length of cord.

TROUBLE SHOOTERS

become entangled in the aircraft's tail, and cut the man free. He dropped clear with him, deployed the man's reserve parachute, and then with but a few seconds in hand, released his own parachute. Such cool courage and initiative were absolutely at one with the finest traditions of the SAS.

In the mid-1960s the then CO of 22 SAS, Colonel Wingate-Gray, pointed out that whatever sort of operations the British Army might be engaged in, whether counter-terrorist, limited war or general war, there would always be an important role for the SAS, simply because of their special skills. His contention has been borne out by events in Dhofar, in Northern Ireland, at the Iranian Embassy in Princes Gate, and in the South Atlantic, while the SAS is at all times ready, if necessary, to fulfil its NATO role.

The SAS sub-unit is made up of four men, and the regiment as a whole consists of a number of squadrons, each of which is divided into troops. Each troop has four of these small self-contained four-man groups. Every man can drive, swim and parachute. They all possess the basic skills of combat survival, close-quarters fighting, resistance under interrogation, and knowledge of weapons, including foreign models. As far as possible all are trained in radio, explosives, demolition techniques and medicine. In addition, many SAS men speak the languages of those regions where they may have to operate – for example, Arabic, German and Swahili.

Over and above these individual capabilities, the squadrons themselves, by virtue of special training or experience, are ready for deployment in extreme environmental conditions, such as desert, mountains or snow. Free-fall parachuting and a capability for amphibious warfare increase their versatility. But even this is not the limit of their training: police Special Branch work, bodyguard skills, industrial sabotage and VIP escort duties can be undertaken too. It was reported, for example, that the Counter Revolutionary Warfare Group (as it is known in the press) was involved in the tight security arrangements for the wedding of HRH Prince Andrew and Miss Sarah Ferguson in July 1986. Moreover, and this is most significant, the regiment is capable of simultaneously carrying out a number of operations, independent of each other, worldwide, with the further advantage of secure communications.

In short, 22 SAS has the ability to conduct special operations of many sorts – surveillance, intelligence gathering, counter-guerrilla work, clandestine offensive and raiding missions, sabotage – in all sorts of country and conditions. No wonder they have been so much in demand. And when in the 1970s the secret war of international terrorism got under way, the regiment was ready to meet this new challenge.

That they were ready had much to do with the foresight shown by the SAS commanders in the late 1960s. It was then that they turned their thoughts to the potential need to back up either MI5 (responsible for security within the UK) or MI6 (sometimes known as the Secret Service or Secret Intelligence Service, responsible for security matters external to the UK) with military help. They could not do so, however, unless they were provided with adequate

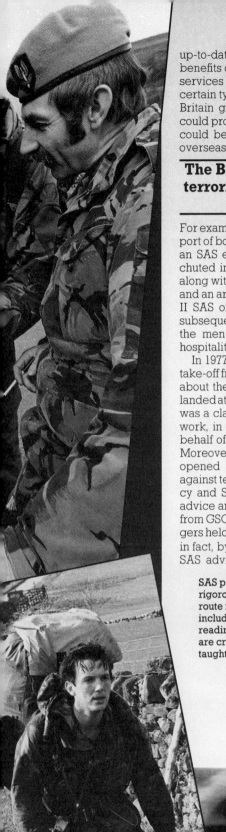

up-to-date information and intelligence, and the benefits of closer collaboration between the secret services and the military. Those responsible for certain types of security and intelligence matters in Britain gradually came to recognise that the SAS could provide armed back-up for MI5 and MI6, and could be called upon to help both in Britain and overseas as necessary.

The British government has an anti-terrorist ace, ready to be played at a moment's notice

For example, the regiment was undismayed by a report of bombs on board the liner *Queen Elizabeth 2*; an SAS explosives expert was immediately parachuted in a 'wet jump' operation into mid-Atlantic along with two men from the Special Boat Squadron and an army captain. As a distinguished World War II SAS officer, Colonel Brian Franks, put it: 'The subsequent search of the ship revealed no bomb, but the men enjoyed a luxury cruise and unlimited hospitality from the passengers.'

In 1977 a Lufthansa flight was hijacked soon after take-off from Majorca and after four days of shuttling about the Gulf and the Mediterranean, the aircraft landed at the Somali capital of Mogadishu. The hijack was a classic example of international terrorism at work, in that a group of Palestinians was acting on behalf of the West German Baader-Meinhof gang. Moreover, as Tony Geraghty has pointed out: 'it opened a new phase of European co-operation against terrorism through the use of British diplomacy and SAS specialists.' Two SAS men gave both advice and help to the German anti-terrorist squad from GSG9, sent to Mogadishu to rescue the passengers held captive by the Palestinian gunmen. It was, in fact, by using two stun-grenades supplied by the SAS advisers as a prelude to their storming the

SAS physical training and selection is extremely rigorous and new recruits have to make extensive route marches with full kit (left) while further training includes precarious rope work (left centre). Map-reading skills (above) and demolitions work (far left) are crucial to SAS work, as are the combat skills taught in the battlefield training exercises (below).

aircraft, that the GSG9 commandos gained just enough time, merely a few seconds while the four Palestinian terrorists were incapable of action, to kill three of them and wound and disarm the fourth. The risks were clear enough, for the stun-grenades could have ignited the aviation fuel and alcohol that the hijackers had scattered about the cabin, but, in the event, speed, daring and surprise won the day.

Such co-operation with other European anti-terrorist commando forces has now become part and parcel of the West's tough stance against the terrorist. The SAS has been involved with the training of Spain's crack Groupo Especiales Operaciones (GEO), and helped the Italians set up a similar unit, the Nucleo Operativo Centrale di Sicurezza (NOCS). Such training was to prove invaluable to both forces – the Spaniards successfully rescued more than 200 hostages during a bank siege in Barcelona in 1981, and NOCS in 1982 rescued the kidnapped American General James Dozier from the Red Brigades. There are also links with the US anti-terrorist unit, Special Forces Operational Detachment Delta, or Delta Force, and American secret service operatives. In 1985, for example, it was reported that US personnel, including members of President Reagan's personal bodyguard, were involved in exchange visits to Hereford, while SAS officers made similar trips to the United States. Strategy, new techniques and training programmes are discussed – and past experience in the war against terrorism.

The Iranian Embassy siege of May 1980 was resolved in the full glare of radio and television coverage, and was an absolute vindication of SAS doctrine, training, and readiness for action. But it is important to understand the very severe restrictions under which the SAS operates when called upon to help the police in terrorist incidents. The SAS does not have a free hand, but may only employ as much force against the terrorists as is necessary to rescue the hostages. This is a matter for fine judgement. In the case of the Princes Gate siege, the SAS prepared for a violent solution from the outset. The possession of an elite unit able to apply force skilfully in resolving hostage incidents has given the British government an anti-terrorist ace, ready to be played at a moment's notice.

This professionalism is the result of the most profound study of terrorism and continuous practice in thwarting it. Imagination and realism are watchwords in SAS training exercises. And as members of the SAS play the part of terrorists in training scenarios there is no shortage of difficulties for the 'home side' to cope with. (Indeed during one simulated aircraft hijacking, a Home Office official, negotiating with the 'terrorists', was distressed when a 'body' was hurled from the aircraft and he himself was splashed with tomato-juice blood.) If such incidents could be

Right: 18 May 1972. Sergeant Clifford Oliver of 22 SAS parachutes into the Atlantic, watched by passengers from the deck of the *QE2*. The bomb scare on the luxury liner proved to be a hoax, but the authorities were taking no chances. Bottom: The SAS's most spectacular, and most public, operation was the storming of the Iranian Embassy in London in May 1980.

resolved by patient and peaceful negotiation there would be no need for SAS involvement. Alas, it is not possible. Luckily the SAS, who can win conflicts by perseverance and persuasion, are also very good with guns.

There is, however, one operation where their efforts have not been crowned with palpable victory, and that is in Northern Ireland. Surveillance, intelligence-gathering, even the elimination of Provisional IRA gunmen have made little progress towards ending the troubles, which in fact have no military solution, but only a political one. Victory, in the accepted military sense of the word, is unattainable. The SAS will, however, continue to do its duty in Northern Ireland for as long as is necessary.

The elite nature of the SAS gives its members a great opportunity for experimentation with all sorts

of new technology which may prove to be useful to the men in the pursuit of their specialist roles. At their disposal are many different forms of transport – helicopters, powered hang-gliders, transport aircraft, amphibious assault and reconnaissance craft, Range Rover-type vehicles, special cars and so on. Their radio equipment, however, which demands very long-range and secure communications, is the envy of many other organisations. During a crucial moment in the SAS CO's negotiations with General Menéndez for the Argentinian surrender in the Falkland Islands in 1982, whereas the SAS were able to talk direct from Menéndez's office by satellite link to higher headquarters, Menéndez himself had to go to another building where his communications centre was. The SAS enjoys exclusive use of all equipment suited to its purpose, for no matter how high the quality of the individual SAS soldier, he needs to use the very best that technology can provide for the

Main picture: An SAS undercover surveillance party, escorted by troops from other British units, boards a helicopter after an operation in South Armagh, Northern Ireland. Bottom: Two British soldiers stand over the covered body of Captain Richard Westmacott, the first SAS man to die at the hands of the Provisional IRA. In early May 1980, Westmacott's team attacked a house in Belfast's Antrim Road, occupied by eight members of the IRA. The IRA men were armed with an American M60 machine gun (seen here poking from a first-floor window) and it was a burst of fire from this weapon that killed Westmacott. Despite the killing of their officer, the SAS team succeeded in taking all eight IRA men alive.

In recent years the majority of terrorist actions have been related to the Palestinian question in the Middle East, and are becoming steadily more frequent. Many of the bombings, kidnappings and hijackings, however, have occurred outside the Middle East on a world-wide basis – attacks with grenades and sub-machine guns on the El Al check-in desks at Rome and Vienna airports in December 1985; a Libyan bomb in a Berlin discotheque in April 1986; and the hijacking of a Pan American 747, and the subsequent bloodbath, in September 1986 at Karachi airport.

In Western Europe, anti-terrorist agencies are faced with a number of different terrorist organisations. Apart from nationalist groups such as the Basque ETA in Spain and the IRA in Northern Ireland, there are presently several extremist left-wing revolutionary organisations active on the terrorist scene. These include the Red Army Faction and the Revolutionary Cells in West Germany, Action Directe in France, the Combative Communist Cells and the Revolutionary Front for Proletarian Action in Belgium, the Popular Force of 25 April (FP25) in Portugal, the Red Brigades in Italy and GRAPO in Spain. In January 1985 Action Directe announced an alliance with the Red Army Faction to attack NATO targets in Europe, and links between the alliance and the Belgian Combatant Communist Cells have also been established. Widespread bombing attacks on NATO-linked targets and the murder of military personnel and prominent industrialists in Europe would indicate that international terrorism, far from being a thing of the past, still presents a very real and serious threat to Western security.

three basic elements of combat: shooting, moving and signalling.

Apart from the overt and covert combat operations undertaken by the SAS, the regiment has proved itself capable through ingenuity and intellect of carrying out 'hearts and minds' programmes among peoples as far removed as the inhabitants of southern Arabia and the jungles of Malaya and Sarawak. In one operation in the Middle East, a group of SAS parachuted, free-fall and at night, into a wadi only 800m long, surrounded by mountain ridges which were 1000m higher than the altitude at which parachutes were opened. Then, apart from seeking out guerrilla bands, they gave aid to the local tribesmen, building schools and medical centres, planning roads, making airstrips and producing maps of the whole area.

The SAS is also reported to be involved in general training programmes for foreign armed forces. In early 1986, sources in Botswana in southern Africa confirmed that 90 SAS men were to conduct joint training exercises with the 3500-strong Botswana Defence Force (BDF). The aim of this training is to provide the BDF with the capability of repelling any incursions into Botswana by the South Africans in search of members of the African National Congress. In June 1985 South African troops had killed 12 people during a cross-border raid on Gaborone, the capital of Botswana.

The SAS was formally deployed to Northern Ireland in 1976 where much of its work involves surveillance and the setting up of ambushes in 'bandit country' – South Armagh – against the IRA. As the troubles continue, the SAS is quite predictably tight-lipped about the nature of its work there, but several successful missions are known to have been carried out, including the capture in 1978 of one of the most wanted IRA men of the time, Francis Hughes. Below: Armed with an SLR, a trooper keeps a low profile, down from the skyline, as an Army Scout helicopter moves out of the area of operations.

With the new climate of inter-governmental co-operation in the business of fighting terrorism, the role and potential deployment of the SAS has reached new heights. During the terrorist campaign in Paris in the autumn of 1986, the SAS was placed on standby to aid the French authorities should its services be required, and intelligence information was supplied. But while the regiment moves closer to the limelight in the war against terrorism, the SAS man himself remains an enigma. Avoiding any form of publicity, he tends to be a nameless, faceless figure, hiding out anywhere in the world, from the Arabian desert to an anonymous London office. The various qualities of the unit, however – instant readiness, elusiveness, and sheer ruthless professionalism – will never cease to excite the public imagination. And while the regiment's reputation for excellence endures, it will always be needed – and always be ready.

THE AUTHOR Major-General John Strawson served with the 4th Hussars during World War II and was Chief-of-Staff, United Kingdom Land Forces before retiring. He has written several books, including *A History of the Special Air Service Regiment*.

SAS

In the Falklands campaign of 1982, the 22nd Special Air Service Regiment was deployed on dangerous behind-the-lines missions during which all their arduous training, their legendary fighting skills, and their reputation were put to the test

FALKLANDS BATTLEFIELD

THE SAS DEPLOYED no less than one and a half of its four squadrons during operations to re-take the Falklands in 1982. Their tasks included the traditional strategic ones of infiltration for surveillance and intelligence-gathering, together with tactical ones concerned with diversionary attacks and seizing key features in front of the main attacking force. Moreover, they did once again what David Stirling and his original 'L' Detachment had done some 40 years earlier – mounted raids to destroy enemy aircraft on their airfields.

Above: At war in the Falklands. When news first came through on the BBC that the islands had been invaded, Lieutenant-Colonel Mike Rose, CO of 22 SAS, put one squadron on stand-by, ready for the call to head south.

The first job which D Squadron undertook was part of Operation Paraquet, the recapture of South Georgia, and as the Task Force commander, Rear Admiral John 'Sandy' Woodward, required information about enemy dispositions at Leith and Grytviken in order to plan his attack, D Squadron was invited to find out about Leith. It was getting ashore that was to prove the most hazardous undertaking.

South Georgia rises steeply out of the South Atlantic, a long ridge of jagged peaks at the very edge of Antarctica. The weather conditions fluctuate with terrifying rapidity, from watery sunshine to the full ferocity of an Antarctic blizzard. There was time only to insert SAS observation patrols by helicopter – scaling the cliffs and glaciers would have taken time and could not be attempted.

The first insertions were near disasters. Accompanied by a radar-equipped Wessex helicopter, two Commando Wessex of C Flight, 845 Royal Naval Air Squadron, succeeded on 21 April in landing an 18-man SAS patrol on the Fortuna Glacier in the face of 60-knot winds. That night a storm with Force 10 gales and driving snow forced the patrol to abandon their operation.

The next day, the three helicopters returned. In their first attempt to fly the patrol out a sudden whiteout caused Lieutenant Mike Tidd to crash into the mountainside, having quickly 'flared' his aircraft to minimise the impact. The eight men on board – only one was slightly injured – were put into the other two helicopters, which then flew through the whiteout on their radar alone. One of these then hit a ridge and also crashed, with only one injury – to the same man hurt in the first crash! The remaining Wessex shuttled the patrol back onto HMS *Antrim* without further incident.

Supported by naval gunfire, the raiders shot up the aircraft with smallarms and rockets

Later the SAS managed to get ashore by Gemini landing craft. There was not a great deal of fighting to do, for the Argentinians had been persuaded by the effective use of naval gunfire support, directed by a Forward Observation Officer, that British intentions were serious. But there were some lively incidents, as Corporal Davey of 19 Troop reported, during the advance on Grytviken:

'In the area where the Brown Mountain ridge line joined the coast we saw what appeared to be men in brown balaclavas among the tussock grass. They were engaged by GPMG fire from approximately 800 metres and by naval gunfire. Captain Hamilton and I also engaged a possible enemy position on the top of Brown Mountain with Milan [anti-tank missile]. Advancing across open ground towards the ridge line we discovered that the balaclava'd enemy were in fact seven or eight elephant seals, which were now somewhat the worse for wear! The enemy position on Brown Mountain had been a piece of angle iron on which we had scored a direct hit.'

Captain Hamilton was subsequently killed at Port Howard while covering the withdrawal of his four-man patrol, an action for which he was posthumously awarded the Military Cross.

On 25 April, the SAS, together with Royal Marines, accepted the surrender of the Argentinian garrison at Grytviken. Next day the remaining enemy troops at Leith surrendered to the SAS. All this would have been relatively straightforward, had it not been for the exceptionally difficult weather. However, the SAS's major contribution to re-taking the Falklands was still to come.

On 1 May, almost exactly a month after Argentina invaded, the first surveillance patrols of G Squadron were landed by helicopter on East Falkland. For nearly three weeks they stayed close to enemy positions, observing and reporting, and so provided the vital information which enabled the Task Force to make the landings at San Carlos, the key operation leading to total victory. On 14 May, about a week

before the main landings, D Squadron, fresh from their success in South Georgia, were committed to a classic SAS-type raid on the airfield at Pebble Island. This involved a 45-minute flight by three Sea Kings from HMS *Hermes*, followed by a four-mile walk from the Landing Zone to a secure base, then on a further two and a half miles to the airstrip. Supported by naval gunfire and illuminating rounds, the raiders shot up the aircraft with smallarms and rockets, despite some enemy fire and a land mine which blew one SAS man some 10ft backwards, but without injuring him too badly. An enemy patrol was nearby during their return journey, but was quickly silenced by automatic fire. Mission completed, the raiders all flew back to *Hermes* having destroyed 11 enemy aircraft and a considerable amount of enemy ammunition and explosives.

Soon after this there was a tragic accident. During a cross-decking from *Hermes* to *Intrepid* a Sea King helicopter with 27 passengers and three crew crashed into the sea, probably caused by an albatross flying into the engine intake. Eighteen men of D and G Squadrons were lost. One survivor of the crash spoke of being trapped by his leg in the wreckage of the seats as the Sea King was sinking. Suddenly, he felt a hand grasp his ankle and a sawing motion as the webbing holding his leg was cut away. He then felt two taps on his ankle, 'like a judo wrestler submitting to a hold', and he was free to swim through the broken tail up to the surface. His benefactor perished. Yet even this tragedy did not prevent the SAS continuing with their vital duties. As SAS Group Commander, Brigadier Peter de la Billière wrote at the time: 'The Regiment has taken it well and are getting on with the fighting at present.' But he added that he would be happy when all his men were ashore, their lives in their own hands.

D Squadron still had plenty to do. They covered the main landings with diversionary attacks at Darwin and Goose Green. After the main landing had been successful, they inserted a patrol at Mount Kent and subsequently reinforced it, an action which proved of vital importance in the subsequent advance to Port Stanley. They also ambushed enemy patrols, carried out raids, gathered information about Argentinian positions and strengths, mounted operations on West Falkland, and helped in the final capture of Port Stanley with further harassing and diversionary attacks. It was all in the best SAS traditions of daring, versatility, discipline, initiative and determination in the face of setbacks and losses. It was a further demonstration of what could be gained from the imaginative, bold and skilful use of small numbers.

Meanwhile, G Squadron was just as busy on intelligence-gathering duties. One of the citations for a gallantry award for the commander of a four-man patrol gives an impression of one such mission:

'Inserted by helicopter on to East Falkland from HMS *Hermes* at a range of 120 miles, he positioned his patrol in close proximity to enemy positions, cut off from any form of rescue should he have been comprom-

Below: The upturned wreck of one of the Wessex helicopters lost in the appalling weather that dogged the SAS insertion on South Georgia. Below right and bottom: Scenes from the airstrip on Pebble Island where D Squadron executed a raid in the finest traditions of the SAS.

ised. This position he maintained for a period of 26 days. During this time he produced a clear picture of enemy activity in the Stanley area, intelligence available from no other means, which has proved vital in the planning of the final assault.'

The citation went on to explain how exemplary this patrol's reports had been. It enabled an air strike to be successfully directed against enemy helicopter concentrations, thus robbing them of their ability to redeploy troops rapidly. Moreover, the conditions under which the patrol lived were frightful – freezing rain, gale-force winds, with little or no cover either from the elements or from view, simply shallow holes

scraped in the ground with camouflaged chicken wire to help hide them. In spite of this extreme vulnerability the patrol's intelligence reports were regular and detailed. 'In this respect,' concludes the citation, 'the endurance and fortitude of all his patrol was magnificent. By his personal example he set the highest standards which his patrol both admired and responded to in the most positive way. His actions, carried out in a totally hostile environment, were in the highest traditions of his Regiment.'

Deep-penetration surveillance operations are much more difficult than one would imagine. Watching enemy positions requires the constant counting of individual soldiers in order to discover whether the position is occupied by a platoon, a company or a battalion. To be of any use, the information must be very accurate. Often the only way to get this is actually to walk in and take a look, but weighing the risk against the possible advantage is always difficult. Peering through high-powered telescopes is a very tiring business.

Long-term operations get worse as they go on because only a small ration of food can be carried

NCO, 22 SAS
Falklands conflict 1982

This Fijian NCO wears a civilian Gove-Tex weatherproof jacket for protection against the extreme weather conditions prevalent in the Falklands. He wears an unorthodox mixture of webbing, DPM trousers and carries a camouflaged 7.62mm SLR.

STRIKE ON PEBBLE ISLAND

In the days before the main British landings at San Carlos on 21 May, there was considerable concern that the newly formed beachhead would be attacked by Argentinian ground-attack aircraft based on Pebble Island, off the north coast of West Falkland. To ascertain the extent of the threat, an eight-man SAS team from 17 Troop of D Squadron was landed on West Falkland with their canoes on the night of 11 May. Rough weather kept the team on West Falkland until the night of the 13th, when they paddled across to Pebble Island and checked out the Argentinian forces there. Indeed, there was a 100-strong garrison and a substantial number of aircraft on the island. On the night of the 14th, Sea Kings from *Hermes* carried a party of 45 men from Major Cedric Delves' D Squadron to Pebble Island. They made their way from the landing site to the airstrip where they began to attack the parked enemy aircraft. Moving quickly among the planes, the SAS placed demolition charges and attacked the aircraft with smallarms fire and 66mm rockets.
Their job done, the SAS fell back off the airstrip towards the waiting Sea Kings for the extraction phase of the operation. Taking off in a Force 9 Gale they headed back to the Task Force. The raid on Pebble Island is a perfect example of how a small body of well-trained men, decisively led, can achieve a great deal – 11 enemy aircraft were destroyed and the SAS came out virtually unscathed. More than 40 years had passed since the formation of the Special Air Service but the Pebble Island raid proved that they were still masters of the art of raiding airfields – a speciality of their forebears in the Western Desert during World War II.

The opening phase of the South Atlantic campaign of 1982, the retaking of South Georgia, saw two SAS landings in the vicinity of suspected enemy positions. Despite near disaster on one occasion when two Wessex helicopters crashed in a blizzard, the SAS took part in the recapture of the island along with a mixed force of marines. During the battle for the Falklands, SAS patrols carried out forward observation duties to identify Argentinian targets. In a classic hit-and-run operation on 14 May, in advance of the main landings at San Carlos, members of D Squadron destroyed 11 enemy aircraft on Pebble Island. As British forces closed on Stanley, SAS detachments roamed behind enemy lines, noting Argentinian troop strengths and dispositions.

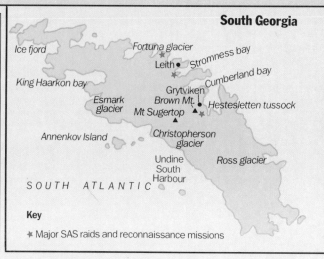

South Georgia

Ice fjord
Fortuna glacier
Leith
Stromness bay
King Haarkon bay
Cumberland bay
Grytviken
Esmark glacier
Brown Mt.
Hestesletten tussock
Mt Sugertop
Annenkov Island
Christopherson glacier
Ross glacier
Undine South Harbour
SOUTH ATLANTIC

Key
★ Major SAS raids and reconnaissance missions

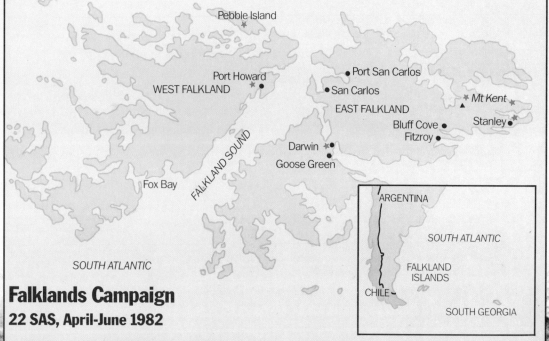

Pebble Island

Port Howard
WEST FALKLAND
Port San Carlos
San Carlos
EAST FALKLAND
Mt Kent
Bluff Cove
Stanley
Fitzroy
FALKLAND SOUND
Darwin
Goose Green
Fox Bay
SOUTH ATLANTIC

Falklands Campaign
22 SAS, April-June 1982

ARGENTINA
SOUTH ATLANTIC
FALKLAND ISLANDS
CHILE
SOUTH GEORGIA

Above: Captain John Hamilton, 22 SAS, who was killed in action on 10 June. Hamilton and his signaller were surrounded by enemy forces at Port Howard but decided to fight their way out. Hamilton ordered his signaller to go first while he supplied covering fire. The officer recommending him for a posthumous MC added, 'I consider that his actions fall little short of the ultimate award of the Victoria Cross.'

and, by the end, hunger overtakes cold, exhaustion and wetness as the main source of discomfort to the observation team.

Patrols had to move with extreme caution, spending the daylight hours surveying the ground over which they intended to move that night. Carrying heavy packs filled with supplies for long operations had to be done steadily, moving carefully and quietly over treacherous terrain. Peat bogs, knee-high tussock grass and interminable boulder runs were among the natural hazards to movement, which was invariably at night when even the most attuned eyesight could make out very little.

Carrying heavy packs on long night marches was a succession of stops and starts. Ground up ahead had to be checked out and men who had fallen and were pinned down by a bergen too heavy for one man to lift on his own, had to be assisted. Despite the cold, such heavy work causes sweating and soaks the clothing from the inside.

Cooking could only be done during the day, and then only when the patrol was certain that it was safe. Rations often had to be eaten cold – which was fine with confectionery and biscuits, but not so good with tins of bacon burger and packets of hot-chocolate drink! All the basic things in life became a problem, taking up inordinately large amounts of time. Surprisingly, water was not always easy to find, even in such a wet climate. Care had to be taken to sterilise water, but even so, many suffered from stomach ailments after the war ended.

All in all, G Squadron's surveillance operations were so successful that they were able to give a detailed picture of what the Argentinians were up to from the time they initially deployed on 1 May until final victory six weeks later. It was an exemplary illustration of living behind the enemy lines, under extremely uncomfortable and hazardous conditions, often so close to enemy positions that accurate details of their guns, defences and aircraft could be reported. Such details, of course, enabled the British Task Force to subject the Argentinian postions to naval gunfire and air strikes, all part of the relentless pressure which in the end led the Argentinian commander to give up.

In war much depends on the personality and determination of the commanders concerned, and Lieutenant-Colonel Rose, CO of 22 SAS, was convinced from the outset that the man leading 3 Commando Brigade, Brigadier Julian Thompson, would be the key figure in the land battle, particularly as many of his decisions would be influenced by the information gained by SAS patrols. It was therefore to Brigadier Thompson's headquarters that the CO of 22 SAS attached himself. The two of them agreed early on that some sort of psychological operations would be necessary, and after some false starts, Rose was able to persuade the demoralised Argentinians to consider surrender.

One of the first important steps was opening a line of communication to the Argentinian headquarters, which was done on 6 June. About a week later, Rose flew by helicopter, accompanied by Royal Marine Captain Rod Bell, who had been born in Uruguay and spoke perfect South American Spanish, to Port Stanley to see Brigadier-General Menéndez. Their Gazelle, flying slowly because of the large boulder they had slung underneath it to keep a white bed sheet flag of truce flapping prominently, was able to enter the Argentine air defences of Port Stanley safely – but not without a great deal of nail-biting by those on board.

It was soon plain that the past week of psychological persuasion had been effective. After some hours of negotiation, Menéndez agreed, and soon after that, on 14 June, General Jeremy Moore arrived to sign the official instrument of Argentinian surrender.

THE AUTHOR Major-General John Strawson served with the 4th Hussars during World War II and was Chief of Staff, United Kingdom Land Forces before retiring. He has written several books including *A History of the Special Air Service Regiment*.

Right: A member of D Squadron, armed with an Armalite and dressed against the freezing weather. Left: Members of D Squadron await the helicopter lift-out of crates containing unused weapons, mostly Milan missiles.

ASSAULTING ARMOUR

There exists a popular misconception that, with the advent of sophisticated anti-armour weapons, the days of the tank and armoured fighting vehicle are numbered. Nothing could be further from the truth. Anti-tank weapons are, above all, defensive weapons, while the tank is geared towards offensive action. Today's armour offers a combination of firepower, mobility and protection that is unrivalled on the modern battlefield, and once a massed force of tanks has broken through your defences you will find it very difficult to regain the initiative. Enemy armour, then, is an opponent to be reckoned with.

While a tank force can be halted by judicious use of such anti-armour weapons as TOW, Milan or anti-tank grenade launchers, there may be instances when anti-armour weapons are not available to you. Obviously, you will not be in a position to ward off the attack of a full squadron of tanks or armoured personnel carriers (APCs), but there does exist the possibility of taking out one, perhaps two, of the enemy vehicles by using what are called 'field expedient devices'. Before moving on to these improvised weapons, we will analyse the main vulnerabilities of enemy armour.

Today's composite armour, a well-known feature of the British Army's Challenger main battle tank and believed to be fitted to most Soviet T-72s, makes the chances of a successful direct frontal assault on the hull itself virtually non-existent. Tanks do have weak points, however, and it is against these that you must concentrate your efforts.

Your primary target should be the fuel tanks: the Soviet T-62 and T-54 have these located forward of the engine compartment, with two large jettisonable secondary fuel tanks mounted to the rear. The T-72 has a slightly different layout, with its integral fuel tanks all located behind the engine. Common to most Soviet designs is the storage of ammunition in steel sleeves that actually go into the fuel cells. Although Soviet diesel fuel has a high flashpoint, photographs

Background: Incendiary devices aimed at the tyres of such wheeled armoured vehicles as this Cadillac Gage Commando V-300 can reduce their effectiveness. Below: Karen guerrillas in Burma wait in ambush.

COMBAT SKILLS of The Elite

of burnt-out hulks of Soviet tanks, taken at war zones all over the world, have testified to their vulnerability. Make the fuel arrangement of any armoured vehicle your first objective.

Two more targets that are worth aiming for are the ammunition storage compartment, usually located to the rear of the hull, and the engine compartment. The latter is the less protected of the two and, since the engine and transmission systems of Soviet tanks are notoriously unreliable, there is a reasonable chance that you may be able to render a tank immobile. In addition, the suspension system is vulnerable to attack, but you will have to take into account the armoured skirting plates that are fitted to most tanks to protect them from HEAT warheads and fragmentation shells.

There are a few preliminaries to be carried out before launching your main attack. Use your rifle or machine gun to fire at the vision blocks or to take out any optical systems such as the laser rangefinder or passive night vision device, and make sure to douse the tank's searchlights if you are operating under the cover of darkness. Against a tank that is 'buttoned up' against attack, these measures will cause only limited damage, but they may significantly affect its ability to fight.

The first type of field expedient device is one that relies on the use of fire to blind a vehicle's crew. If the

The satchel charge
Time fuze
Fuze igniter
Satchel (sealed with string, rope or tape)
Charge (TNT or C4)

Below: Afghan guerrillas pose on a knocked-out Soviet BTR-60 APC. Anti-tank weapons supplied by Western powers now play a large role in the Mujahidins' operations against Soviet armour. Bottom: A guerrilla's eye view of a Chieftain tank.

flames spread, the men will be faced with the prospect of asphyxiation unless they abandon their charge. The crudest of all these weapons is the Molotov cocktail, a simple incendiary device that relies on the combination of a breakable container, inflammable liquid and a simple cloth fuse to create an explosion.

More sophisticated, and packing far more destructive potential, is the 'Eagle fireball'. This can be made by filling an ammunition box with a mixture of petrol and oil. A white phosphorus grenade should then be wrapped in detonating cord, one end of which is attached to a non-electric firing system. Once the grenade has been placed inside the can, with the time fuze extending out of a slit that you have cut, secure a rope to the can with bent nails or a grapnel. Choose your target carefully, light the fuze and throw the fireball. The nails or grapnel should hook the device onto the vehicle before detonation. A similar weapon can be fashioned using smoke and thermite grenades.

There are three other types of explosive device that you can deploy against armour in the absence of anti-tank missiles. The first of these is the towed charge. Construct this by linking a series of live anti-tank mines with rope or communications wire. Anchor one end of the rope on one side of the road and stretch the other end a sufficient distance from the other side for you to be able to detonate the mines without suffering injury. Then attach an electrical firing system to each of the mines and connect this to your main detonator. It is important that you then carry out a circuit check before connecting the firing wire to a blasting machine.

When a tank or APC appears along the road, wait until the last possible moment before pulling on the rope and dragging the towed charge in front of the approaching vehicle. Fire the charge when the target is directly over the explosives.

The second type of explosive device is known as a pole charge, and comprises TNT or C4 explosives, non-electric blasting caps, a time fuze, detonating cord, some form of tape or string, fuze igniters and a long pole. Once you have primed the explosives with the blasting caps, attach them to a small board and tie this board to the pole. The fuze will only need to be some six inches long, as the occupants of the target vehicle will be alerted to your intentions the moment the pole is placed in position. The areas to aim for are under the turret, over the engine compartment, in the suspension system or in the main gun barrel.

The third, and final, type of explosive is the satchel charge. Used very effectively by the Viet Cong against American armoured vehicles during the Vietnam War, the satchel charge is constructed from the same materials as the pole charge, but seal the charge in the satchel, leaving the time fuze and fuze igniter hanging out of the bag. Fire the igniter, take aim, and hurl the charge onto your target. Crude but effective.

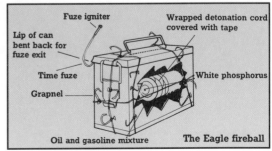

Fuze igniter
Wrapped detonation cord covered with tape
Lip of can bent back for fuze exit
Time fuze
White phosphorus
Grapnel
Oil and gasoline mixture
The Eagle fireball